ARCHITECT'S HANDBOOK OF PRACTICE MANAGEMENT

are to be ~turn~ on or before

Seventh Edition

Architect's Handbook of Practice Management
Seventh Edition

© RIBA Publications 2001
Reprinted 2005

Published by RIBA Companies Ltd, which trades under the name of
'RIBA Publications', 1-3 Dufferin Street, London, EC1Y 8NA

ISBN 1 85946 119 0

Product code: 27535

1st edition published 1965*
2nd edition published 1967*
3rd revised edition published 1973*
4th revised edition published 1980*
5th edition published 1991
6th edition published 1998
*under the title RIBA *Handbook of Architectural Practice and Management*

British Library Cataloguing in Publication Data
A catalogue record for this book is available from the British Library.

Editor: Sarah Lupton
Publisher: Mark Lane
Commissioning Editor: Matthew Thompson
Project Manager: Ramona Lamport
Project Editor: Katy Banyard
Design and typesetting by Hobbs the Printers, Hampshire
Printed and bound by Hobbs the Printers, Hampshire

Whilst every effort has been made to check the accuracy of the information
given in this book, readers should always make their own checks. Neither the
Editor or the Publisher accepts responsibility for mis-statements made in it or
misunderstandings arising from it.

Editor's notes

Editor's notes

This seventh edition of the *Architect's Handbook of Practice Management* was prepared shortly after the publication of the seventh edition of the *Architect's Job Book*, and is intended to be a complementary publication. It covers a wide spectrum of knowledge required for the successful managing of an architectural practice, including business and financial management, marketing, communication and information management.

The seventh edition has been restructured, with the eight larger sections of the sixth edition split into 13 shorter sections, and arranged in a different sequence. Any duplicated material covered by the *Job Book* has been removed, some new sections have been added, and an index has been included. As the *Handbook* is intended as a first port of call, it now includes lists of references and suggestions for further reading at the end of each section, and information on key industry bodies together with their contact details.

Considerable updating was necessary, as there has been a significant amount of new legislation since the sixth edition, for example that relating to limited liability partnerships, to employment law, and to tax. New sections were added where it was felt topics needed more coverage, for example on staff appraisals, and on IT and CAD.

Since the sixth edition of the *Handbook* the ARB has published a new code, *The Architects Code: Standards of Conduct and Practice*, and the RIBA has published a new set of regulations for the Examination in Professional Practice. The sections on the profession and registration have been updated accordingly.

The section on employment law has been revised to take account of the Employment Relations Act 1999, the Part Time Workers (Prevention of Less Favourable Treatment) Regulations 2000, and the effect of the Pensions Schemes Act 1993. There is a new section on financial management, which groups the relevant business management and financial management sections of the sixth edition, and includes new sections on book-keeping and an expanded section on VAT. There have been significant revisions to the section on insurance, with an expanded section on car insurance. The section on PII has been re-written, making reference to the new ARB requirements. The chapter on communications has been expanded to include new sections on attending meetings, on giving presentations, and on telephones, faxes and e-mails.

Many people contributed and assisted in the preparation of the seventh edition, and I am grateful to all of them for their help. In particular I would like to thank the following people who commented on various sections, and in many cases re-wrote parts of the text: Stanley Cox (architects and the construction industry), Julie Dalzell of Short Richardson & Forth (working with staff), Chris Pomeroy of Smith Williamson (financial management), Alison Hamilton of the Heath Lambert Group, Ian Salisbury and Frances Paterson (insurances and risks), Tim Jefferies (quality management), Sylvia Harris (library services) and Roland Phillips (for the new edition of the Model Safety Policy).

Sarah Lupton

1 ARCHITECTS AND THE CONSTRUCTION INDUSTRY

1.1 The construction industry today

1.2 Recent changes in the industry

1.3 Traditional practice and the new way of working

1.4 Key roles in the construction industry
1.4.1 Clients
1.4.2 Architects
1.4.3 Quantity surveyors
1.4.4 Structural engineers
1.4.5 Building services engineers
1.4.6 Contractors
1.4.7 Sub-contractors

1.5 Key representative bodies
1.5.1 Client organisations
1.5.2 Professional organisations
1.5.3 Contractor organisations
1.5.4 Industry organisations

1.1   The construction industry today

In the UK the construction industry forms a major sector of the economy, providing just under ten per cent of the gross domestic product. The industry currently includes around 19,000 construction firms, and employs around 1.4 million people. Construction professional services account for £6.7 billion, equivalent to around one per cent of the gross domestic product, and are provided by a total of 350,000 professionals, of whom around 30,000 are registered architects.

The construction industry is engaged in a wide variety of activities including not only the design and erection of building and civil engineering projects, but also in related activities, such as the design and manufacture of special components and equipment, and the maintenance of buildings and other structures. The industry is characterised by the fact that most work consists of unique physical projects which are site specific, in contrast to say 'consumer good' industries where products are manufactured en masse rather than commissioned. The products are generally one-off designs; very few sectors of the construction industry include any standardisation, with perhaps the house-building sector involving the most.

Another key characteristic is the wide range of project values from minor works – frequently either domestic projects or maintenance work – which cost a few thousand pounds or less, through to major infrastructure projects with budgets of several billions of pounds. Clearly there are enormous differences in the skills, knowledge and resources needed to execute projects of such differing size, and this is reflected in the differences in scale to be found within the industry. Most sectors comprise a small number of large companies and a very large number of small firms and sole traders; in the architectural profession there are a few practices with several hundred employees, yet around 90 per cent of practices consist of fewer than ten people.

1.2   Recent changes in the industry

The last ten years have seen a great deal of debate and significant changes in the industry. Increasing concern with health and safety, the environment and the need for sustainable development have resulted in higher standards being expected by clients and required by law. Rapid technological advances have resulted in increasing specialisation in the industry. Projects have become more sophisticated in terms of the design and construction expertise required, and processes have become more demanding in terms of information flow, coordination and programming.

Reviews such as Sir Michael Latham's report *Constructing the Team* (1994) have drawn attention to the dissatisfaction among clients with the service and products provided by the construction industry. In particular, it noted that projects were not delivered on time, ran over budget, were not of the quality expected, and that too a high a proportion of turnover was spent on disputes and claims. The report emphasised the importance of the client's role, the need for better briefing, new and less adversarial forms of procurement and contracts, improved methods of selecting the team, and more efficient ways of dealing with disputes.

The recommendations were put into action through the work of the Construction Industry Board, set up in 1995, with its principal objective 'to implement, monitor and review' the recommendations of the Latham Report. Although no longer in existence, it has had a significant impact on the industry in securing 'a culture of co-operation, teamwork and continuous improvement in the industry's performance'.

The work of the CIB was given further impetus by the report *Rethinking Construction* (1996) prepared by the Construction Task Group chaired by Sir John Egan. This report echoed the Latham Report in its references to client dissatisfaction, and made comparisons with other industries, such as the car industry, whose processes were felt to be more efficient. It pointed out the urgent need for a reduction in accidents on site, and in the defects which frequently plague finished projects. It also called for a significant improvement in efficiency through more co-operative methods of procurement involving partnering and supply chain management.

Undoubtedly the reports have had significant effect. The Latham Report was the direct cause of the Housing Grants Construction and Regeneration Act 1996, which has had profound effects on construction contract forms and dispute resolution. The reports have influenced procurement methods used both in the private sector and by the Government; for example, Government has produced guidance documentation which endorses the policy that all procurement should be on the basis of value and not lowest price. Model projects based on this new ideology have been successfully completed and wisely publicised through the Construction Best Practice Programme and in the construction industry press.

1.3   Traditional practice and the new way of working

Within this context the roles of all professionals within the industry, including that of the architect, need to evolve to meet new expectations. Traditionally, the architect has been the client's first point of contact, and design has been largely in the hands of the architect and other construction consultants. With traditional procurement the activities of design and production have been carried out by separate organisations. However, increasing specialisation has meant that a great deal of technical and design expertise has developed in what had traditionally been thought of as the 'supply side', i.e. within contractors, specialist sub-contractors and manufacturers. *Constructing the Team* and *Rethinking Construction* recognised the need to bring in both construction management expertise and specialist design input to the early stages of a project, and called for a more efficient and integrated approach to the design process and to procurement. The Government's continuing use of the Private Finance Initiative procurement method, and larger clients like BAA's adoption of a policy of 'close partnering' for key supplies, one of which is architecture and design, reflect this need for early integration.

Such so-called 'framework deals' mean that for many larger projects the architect's traditional role of lead consultant may be coming to an end. The architect is likely to be part of a much larger team in the initial stages, in fact to be considered by the client to be part of the 'supply chain'. Although the team may be led by architects, frequently this will not be case. The project may be procured through a core relationship between consultant and 'constructors', possibly through the use of design-build or construction management procurement, or through the use of traditional procurement coupled with a partnering charter, or through the use of a multi-party partnering contract. Although these arrangements will generally be confined to larger projects, and the role of the 'general practitioner' architect will undoubtedly continue, even smaller practices may find themselves asked to participate in partnering arrangements or to join consortia. It is essential that architects take a proactive role in managing their response to these new arrangements, and seize new opportunities where they arise.

1.4 Key roles in the construction industry

Although it is difficult to make generalisations in a rapidly changing context, it is still useful to distinguish key roles. Broadly, these can be defined as follows:

1.4.1 Clients

The person or organisation who commissions the project. This is often, although not necessarily, the owner of the site and the eventual owner of the building. Clients can range from individual consumers having work carried out to a dwelling, to government bodies or multinational corporations.

1.4.2 Architects

Architects form a relatively small group among the large number of qualified professionals working within the construction industry. Architects are regulated under the Architects Act 1997, although it should be noted that this legislation protects the title rather than the role – there is no requirement under the law for the designer of any building to be an architect. In practice it is normally the architect's responsibility to co-ordinate and integrate the work of designers and specialists into the overall design, and the architect has traditionally also acted as the overall lead consultant and administrator of the building contract. This is no longer the case on many large projects, where a project manager or other consultant may take this role.

1.4.3 Quantity surveyors

Traditionally the quantity surveyor's role was limited to the preparation of Bills of Quantities for tendering purposes. This expanded during the 20th century to include the preparation of valuations and final accounts. The quantity surveyor's role is now broader, and related to the financial management of the project. The quantity surveyor can assist in assessing special site and other problems such as access, topography, economic site use and working. He or she can analyse cost information on other similar projects, local levels of building costs and cost trends, etc and can judge whether the client's budget is realistic and compatible with other stated requirements. The quantity surveyor can prepare the financial appraisal for the feasibility report. They will also advise on procurement and tendering processes, on contract documentation on cash flow forecasting, financial reports and interim payments, and on the final account.

1.4.4 Structural engineers

The structural engineer advises on and prepares the structural design for the project, including the foundation design. He or she can advise the architect on local conditions relevant to the site, such as soil and geotechnical factors, roads, sewers, water supply, etc. The engineer can identify hazards and hazardous substances, arrange for site, structural and drainage surveys, advise on alternative structural solutions, prepare design criteria and calculations and advise on structural aspects of party walls, temporary structures and demolition work.

1.4.5 Building services engineers

The mechanical and electrical (M & E) engineers will advise on and prepare designs for the various service systems in the building. They will advise on climatic conditions, energy use and conservation, emission problems, etc and will consult relevant authorities as necessary. They will often liaise with a specialist sub-contractor, but this should normally be done through the lead consultant. M & E engineers can prepare feasibility studies, estimates, forecasts and maintenance cost options; prepare energy management studies; and report and prepare design criteria and calculations.

1.4.6 Contractors

The constructor of the building. Generally most actual work is sub-contracted. Contractors vary in size from small firms with only a few permanently employed staff and close links with other small firms and self-employed tradesmen, to large organisations with a head office, permanent staff and often regional and possibly international offices. Most firms practise as limited companies, with some of the larger ones being public limited companies.

1.4.7 Sub-contractors

Sub-contractors are companies to whom work is sub-let by contractors. They range from firms who provide relatively unskilled labour for general construction work, through to those who provide traditional trades such as carpentry, or are highly specialised, for example pipe laggers, to firms who provide, in addition to the workforce needed to carry out a task, highly technical expertise which contributes to the design of a project, for example cladding manufacturers. Generally the choice of sub-contractor is left to the contractor and their performance is entirely the contractor's responsibility. Sometimes, however, the client or designers determine the choice of sub-contractor, particularly where specialist design input is needed.

1.5   Key representative bodies

1.5.1 Client organisations

British Property Federation (BPF)

Trade association of the property industry, representing owners and investors in commercial and residential property. Aims to assist members in sustaining and developing their businesses. Property assets of members total over £100 billion. Membership includes property developers, housing associations, banks and insurers, and professionals, including architects. Member of JCT Ltd.

www.bpf.propertymall.com

Local Government Association (LGA)

Established in 1997. Membership comprises 100 per cent of all Local Authorities (nearly 500 in total, representing over 50 million people). Member of JCT Ltd.

www.lga.gov.uk

Confederation of Construction Clients (CCC, Formerly the Construction Clients' Forum)

Launched in December 2000, it aims to encourage clients 'to achieve value for money through best practice'. Its members include BAA, McDonald's restaurants, London Borough of Tower Hamlets and the University of Surrey. It publishes surveys of client satisfaction.

www.clientsuccess.org

1.5.2 Professional organisations

Architecture and Surveying Institute (ASI)

A multi-discipline professional body including over 15 different disciplines in its membership. Its services include QA certification, dispute resolution, technical advice and PI insurance. Maintains registers, e.g. of Party Wall specialists and adjudicators. Member of the CIC.

www.asi.org.uk

Architects' Council of Europe (ACE)

Architect representatives from the professional institutions of Member States in the European Union. Aims include promoting achitecture and architects in Europe. Task groups review topics such as 'Education and Research', 'Competition and the EU Legal Framework', and 'Trade in Services'.

www.ace-cae.org

Association of Building Engineers (ABE)

Founded in 1925, its membership includes a variety of construction professionals specialising in the technology of building. Runs seminars and publishes a journal. Member of the CIC.

www.abe.org.uk

Association of Consultant Architects (ACA)

Members with a particular involvement in private consultancy. Founded in 1973. Publishes its own building contracts, including the innovative partnering contract PCC2000. Publishes a directory and carries out research. Member of the CIC.

www.acarchitects.co.uk

Association of Consulting Engineers (ACE)

Over 650 member firms, including engineering, technical ad management consultancies. Members abide by a Code of Conduct. Services offered to potential clients and to members, including technical and legal advice. Runs seminars and CPD workshops Member of JCT Ltd.

www.acenet.co.uk

Association of Planning Supervisors (APS)

Publishes a Directory of Practice and a Register of Members. Members abide by a Code of Conduct. Aims to set out best practice in fulfilling CDM regulations requirements. Publishes guidance and model procedures. Gives legal and practice advice to members. Member of the CIC.

www.aps.org.uk

Association of Project Managers (APM)

Over 8,000 individual members. Offers a Professional Project Management Qualification and members may also apply for recognition as Certified Project Managers. Publishes Guidance and Model Procedures, and organises seminars and CPD events. Member of the CIC.

www.apm.org.uk

Commonwealth Association of Architects (CAA)

An association of national architectural institutes covering nearly all Commonwealth countries. Founded in 1965, now with 38 member institutes representing over 37,000 members. Runs the Architectural Exchange web page, which publishes information about events, awards and competitions.

Institute of Clerks of Works of Great Britain (ICW)

Founded in 1882. Runs examinations for clerks of works. Publishes guidance including a Manual for Clerks of Works. Member of the CIC.

www.icwgb.sagehost.co.uk

Institute of Civil Engineers (ICE)

Founded in 1818, now with over 80,000 members. Activities include a library, awards and competitions, conferences, CPD and publishing (through Thomas Telford Ltd), including standard contract forms such as the ICE forms and the ECC. Member of the CIC.

www.ice.org.uk

Institute of Electrical Engineers (IEE)

Founded in 1871, the IEE is the largest professional engineering society in Europe and has a membership of just under 140,000. Provides a very wide variety of services to its members, including accrediting degree courses and CPD events, maintaining a library and INSPEC, a large computerised database on physics and electrical engineering.

www.iee.org.uk

Institute of Mechanical Engineers (IMechE)

Around 83,000 members. Organises conferences and CDP events. Publishes a number of journals and books through Professional Engineering Publishing.

www.imeche.org.uk

Institute of Structural Engineers (IStructE)

Founded in 1908, it now has over 20,000 members. It maintains a library, and publishes a journal (also on-line) and technical reports prepared by its engineering practice committee, examining matters such as building legislation and structural design codes. Member of the CIC.

www.istructe.org.uk

International Union of Architects (IUA)

An international non-governmental body, founded in Lausanne in 1948. Represents all the major architectural societies in the world, amounting to 92 national associations representing over one million architects. It provides a voice for architecture on bodies such as UNESCO, WHO, ILO, etc.

www.uia-architectes.org

Landscape Institute (LI)

Around 4,500 members, 50 per cent of whom work in the public sector and 50 per cent in private practice. Maintains a library and a register of practices. Publishes guidance information, standard terms of engagement and standard contract documentation for landscape works. Member of the CIC.

www.l-i.org.uk

Royal Town Planning Institute (RTPI)

Founded in 1914, publishes a Code of Conduct, maintains a library (also on-line). Publishes good practice guides, surveys and commissioned studies. Funds and undertakes research. Member of the CIC.

www.rtpi.org.uk

Royal Institution of Chartered Surveyors (RICS)

110,000 members and 18 faculties, including diverse fields such as antiques and fine art, facilities management, mineral and waste management and project management. Activities include a library, awards and competitions, conferences, CPD and publishing. Member of the CIC and of JCT Ltd.

www.rics.org.uk

Royal Institute of British Architects (RIBA) (see section 2)

Over 32,000 members. Offers a variety of services including Client Services, Specialist Advisor Panels, professional indemnity insurance and dispute resolution. Owns RIBA Companies including National Building Specification, RIBA Publications, RIBA Information Services, etc. Member of the CIC and of JCT Ltd.

www.architecture.com

Royal Incorporation of Architects in Scotland (RIAS)

www.rias.org.uk

Royal Society of Ulster Architects (RSUA)

www.rsua.org.uk

Royal Institute of Architects in Ireland (RIAI)

www.riai.ie

Royal Institute of Architects in Wales (RSAWI)

www.architecture-wales.com

1.5.3 Contractor organisations

Construction Confederation (CC)

Founded in 1997. Over 5,000 member companies responsible for over 75 per cent of construction in Great Britain. Membership comprises seven construction organisations including the Civil Engineering Contractors Association, the National Federation of Builders and the National Contractors Federation. Member of JCT Ltd.

www.constructionconfederation.co.uk

1.5.4 Industry organisations

British Board of Agrément (BBA)

This organisation works in conjunction with the European Organisation for Technical Approvals, and is responsible for assessing new building products and issuing related certificates, including European Technical Approvals and Agreement Certificates.

www.bbacerts.co.uk

British Standards Institute (BSI)

The authority responsible for the preparation and review of national standards covering a wide range of matters such as definitions, dimensions, preferred testing methods, performance, and for the preparation of codes of practice. Many of these standards and codes apply to the construction industry. The organisation must also publish British versions of European Standards, and withdraw any conflicting national standards.

www.bsi-global.com

Building Research Establishment (BRE)

Undertakes research and publishes reports on building materials and various aspects of construction technology. Provides consultancy, testing and information services. Member of the CIC.

www.bre.co.uk

Building Services Research and Information Association (BSRIA)

Undertakes research and publishes reports on various aspects of building services. Provides consultancy, testing, information and market research services. Runs on-line bookshop. Member of the CIC.

www.bsria.co.uk

Building Cost Information Service (BCIS)

Publishes and distributes up-to-date cost information including indices, trends and market conditions.

www.bcis.org.uk

Construction Industry Council (CIC)

Established by the Government in 1988, it is the largest pan-industry forum representing all aspects of the built environment, including most of the professional bodies, most research organisations and many of the specialist trade associations. Carries out quarterly surveys of construction industry activities. The RIBA is represented on several of its committees and working parties.

www.cic.org.uk

Construction Industry Board (CIB)

Set up by the Government in 1995 following the report *Constructing the Team* by Sir Michael Latham to improve the performance of the UK construction industry. It was mainly concerned with the implementation of the recommendations in the Latham Report and the Egan Report. It ceased to exist in June 2001, but many of its initiatives continue, mostly run now by the Government through the CIC.

www.ciboard.org.uk

Construction Industry Research and Information Association (CIRIA)

Funds and co-ordinates research activities, although it has no laboratories or testing facilities of its own. It is funded by government grants and research contracts from industry. It publishes a newsletter and reports, disseminating the research it has funded.

www.ciria.org.uk

Construction Industry Training Board (CITB)

This was established under the Industrial Training Act 1964, with its remit to improve training so that there would be an adequate supply of suitably qualified people to work at all level of the construction industry. It runs courses at its training centres, co-operates with Colleges of Technology, and gives grants to employers who undertake its courses.

www.citb.org.uk

Joint Contracts Tribunal Ltd (JCT)

The organisation which publishes and keeps under review the standard forms of building contract and sub-contract generally used throughout the building industry. It also publishes guidance related to these forms as Practice Notes, and funds and publishes research. The RIBA is represented on the JCT Board through its membership of the Consultants' College.

National House Building Council (NHBC)

Independent regulating body for the UK house-building industry. Maintains register of 18,000 house buiders who construct 85 per cent of new houses in the UK. Sets technical standards for construction of new homes, with the aim of reducing defects. Offers warranty and insurance services that house builders can pass on to home buyers. Member of the CIC.

www.nhbc.co.uk

Timber Research and Development Association (TRADA)

International centre for specification and use of timber and wood products. Undertakes research and publishes reports, books and other guidance information. Runs an on-line bookshop. Member of the CIC.

www.trada.co.uk

References and further reading

Chappell, D. and Willis, A. (2000) *The Architect in Practice,* Oxford, Blackwell Science.

DETR (1996) *Rethinking Construction.*

Latham, M. (1994) *Constructing the Team,* London, HMSO.

Martin, I. (1999) *Small Practice Networks,* London, RIBA Publications.

Powell, C. G. (1996) *The British Building Industry since 1800: an economic history*, London, E&FN Spon.

Zogolovitch, R. (1999) *Meeting the Challenge,* London, RIBA Publications.

2 PROFESSIONALISM

2.1 Practising as an architect

2.2 Statutory regulation

2.3 Role of the ARB

2.4 ARB Code

2.5 ARB disciplinary procedures

2.6 RIBA – the organisation

2.7 RIBA – the purpose

2.8 Control over entry to the RIBA
2.8.1   Entry requirements
2.8.2   Schools of Architecture
2.8.3   Professional experience
2.8.4   The Examination in Professional Practice and Management
2.8.5   The completed PEDR

2.9 Control over the professional conduct of Members
2.9.1   The RIBA Code of Professional Conduct and Standard of Professional Performance

2.10 Control over the performance of Members

2.11 CPD

2.1   Practising as an architect

In order to use the description 'architect' in the UK in the course of business or practice, you must be registered with the Architects Registration Board (ARB). In addition to becoming registered, most architects also join a professional body. The largest, and the only one with exclusively architect membership, is the Royal Institute of British Architects (RIBA). There are a number of other bodies directly relevant to the practice of architecture, some of which can properly be described as representative professional institutes. These include the Association of Consultant Architects and the Architecture and Surveying Institute.

Both the ARB and the RIBA publish Codes of Conduct and implement disciplinary procedures. The RIBA's primary role is the promotion of architecture, as discussed under section 2.7, whereas the role of the ARB is restricted to that defined by statute, which is principally aimed at consumer protection. Both organisations take an active role in education, jointly validating courses which lead to qualification. The ARB has a statutory duty to oversee the education and training of architects to ensure they have a required level of professional competence before being admitted to the Register. Although the RIBA's role has traditionally been more proactive in this area, including the development of criteria for validation and regulations for the examination in professional practice, the ARB has recently been taking an increasingly active role.

2.2   Statutory regulation

The Architects Registration Board is a government funded organisation. Its role is to protect the consumer and safeguard the reputation of architects, in other words to ensure that those practising under the title 'architect' are competent to do so.

The Register of Architects was set up in 1932 under an Act of Parliament which restricted use of the title 'Registered Architect', and in 1938 this was followed by measures to give statutory protection to the business use of the title 'Architect'. Some of the intentions behind such legislation might have been questionable at the time, but undeniably it brought a measure of consumer protection because the public were now able to distinguish between those properly qualified persons admitted to the Register of Architects and other persons who were no longer legally entitled to call themselves architects.

In 1997 the statutory Architects Registration Council of the United Kingdom was succeeded by the Architects Registration Board, which has greater powers to act in dealing with allegations of misconduct or incompetence. Registered persons found guilty of unacceptable professional conduct or serious professional incompetence can be disciplined, and issues of competence can relate to the way in which business is carried out as well as the service provided. Moreover, the ultimate control in reaching such decisions now rests with non-architects, as they have a voting majority of one on the Registration Board and the Professional Conduct Committee.

2.3   Role of the ARB

The ARB consists of seven elected members (elected by ballot from among registered persons but not necessarily RIBA Members) and eight appointed members (appointed by the Privy Council but not registered persons). The members elect their own chairman. Duties of the ARB include the following:

- to appoint the Registrar of Architects;
- to establish a Professional Conduct Committee and other committees as may be necessary;
- to discipline architects who are found guilty of unacceptable professional conduct;
- to issue a Code of Practice;
- to publish an annual *Register of Architects*;
- to prosecute people using the title 'architect' who are not on the Register;
- to rule on various matters concerning registration;
- to set the educational and professional practice standards to qualify for admission to the Register.

The Registrar of Architects is appointed by the Board, and its duties include:

- maintaining the *Register of Architects*;
- carrying out various prescribed functions concerned with registration;
- maintaining a list of visiting EEA architects (i.e. from European Economic Area States).

The Professional Conduct Committee consists of four elected members of the Board (i.e. all architects, including at least one Scottish representative), three appointed members of the Board, and in addition two persons nominated by the Law Society. A voting majority on both the Board and the Professional Conduct Committee therefore lies with non-registered persons (i.e. outside the architectural profession).

The ARB recognises three main routes of registration as an architect in the UK:

UK qualifications

- completion in the UK of the examinations leading to the award of Part 1 and Part 2 qualifications in architecture recognised for registration purposes; and
- completion of a period of practical training experience in architecture and the award of a recognised Part 3 qualification in professional practice.

Other European qualifications

- certification by the Competent Authority of a Member State of the European Union or the European Free Trade Association that a national of that state holds a qualification listed in the Directive for the purposes of mutual recognition within Europe; and
- certification of completion of two-year period of post graduate practical training experience, subject to certain conditions.

Other overseas qualifications

- qualifications in architecture awarded outside Europe which are deemed by ARB, after assessment, to be equivalent to recognised UK qualifications; and

- completion of a period of practical training experience in architecture in the UK and a Part 3 examination in professional practice recognised by ARB.

Note that the 'Directive' refers to the Architects Directive relating to mutual recognition of qualifications in the EU. Anyone wishing to apply for registration should contact the ARB for details of the relevant procedures.

Only persons who are registered may practise or carry on business using the name, style or title containing the word 'architect'. Any contravention will be an offence leading to a fine on summary conviction. Where a company is being registered whose title includes the word 'architect' or 'architectural', the application may be referred to the ARB. The normal pattern is for a certificate of non-objection to be issued where the company's articles of association include a form of words indicating that the control of the architectural work will remain in the hands of a person or persons on the ARB *Register of Architects* so long as the title subsists.

To remain registered, a person must:

- pay the annual retention fee at the appropriate time;

- notify the ARB of any change of business address;

- not be found guilty of unacceptable professional conduct (i.e. conduct that falls short of the standard required) or serious professional incompetence;

- not be subject to a 'disciplinary order' which amounts to suspension or erasure.

If an architect is off the Register for more than two years, he or she may have to satisfy the ARB regarding competence in order to be re-admitted. This is to prevent architects who have not practised for many years having an automatic right to be reinstated on the Register as 'qualified', as after such a length of time they may be out of touch with current practice.

2.4   ARB Code

The ARB Code, which was revised and re-published in 1999 under the title of *Architect's Code: Standards of Conduct and Practice*, consists of an introduction and standards which are intended to be read together. It should be noted that the full title includes the words *conduct* and *practice*, understandable in view of the emphasis given in the Act to rejecting both unacceptable professional conduct and serious professional incompetence. As with the RIBA Code, it is stated that technical non-compliance will not necessarily result in proceedings, but that the spirit of the Code must be observed at all times.

The Code applies to all architects whatever the form of practice or business they choose to adopt. Employer architects and employee architects are equally bound to respect and observe the Code obligations. UK registered architects are still subject to the ARB Code when they practise abroad, and only if it can be shown that compliance would be inconsistent with local law and customs will any relaxation be possible. The standards which are incorporated in the ARB *Code of Professional Conduct and Practice* are shown in Figure 1.

Figure 1: The ARB Standards

Section 1: Conduct and Competence

Standard 1: Architects should at all times act with integrity and avoid any action or situations which are inconsistent with their professional obligations.

1.1 Architects should not make, support or collaborate in any statement, written or otherwise, which is contrary to their professional opinion, or which they know to be misleading, or unfair to others, or otherwise discreditable to the profession.

1.2 Architects should disclose in writing to any prospective client or employer any financial or personal business interests of which, if not so declared, would or might be likely to raise a conflict of interest and doubts about their integrity.

1.3 Architects should, when finding that their personal or professional interests conflict with those of their client or of other relevant parties (thereby risking a breach of this Standard), either withdraw from the situation, or remove the source of conflict or obtain the agreement of the parties concerned to the continuance of the engagement.

1.4 Architects should not (in an architectural practice) be a partner, co-director or take up employment with an unsuitable person. Examples of unsuitable persons are:

• A person whose name has been removed from the Register of Architects by virtue of disciplinary measures;

• A person disqualified from membership of a recognised professional body.

1.5 Whenever an Architect offers, or takes part in offering, a service which combines consultancy services with contracting services, the Architect should make it clear to all parties in writing that their services will not incorporate the independent functions of an Architect.

Standard 2: Architects should only undertake professional work for which they are able to provide adequate professional, financial and technical competence and resources.

2.1 The duty under this Standard arises when a contract is entered into, and continues throughout the term of contract. The duty does not extend to architects taking part in competitions or otherwise engaging in speculative work.

2.2 Where professional work is carried out on behalf of an Architect by an employee or by anyone else acting under an Architect's direct control the Architect is responsible for ensuring that such person is competent to perform the task and, if necessary, is adequately supervised.

Standard 2 continued

2.3 A sole practitioner should have adequate arrangements for the conduct of their business in the event of their death, incapacity or other absence from work.

Standard 3: Architects should only promote their professional services in a truthful and responsible manner.

3.1 In advertising his services or otherwise drawing them to the attention of a potential client, Architects should not make untruthful or misleading statements.

3.2 Advertisements should conform, as appropriate, to the British Code of Advertising Practice and the ITC and Radio Code of Advertising Standards and Practice.

3.3 The business style of a practice should not be misleading.

3.4 Architects should ensure that the work of their office or any branch office insofar as it relates to architecture is under the control and management of an architect and that the identity of that architect is apparent to clients and potential clients.

Standard 4: Architects should carry out their professional work faithfully and conscientiously and with due regard to relevant technical and professional standards.

4.1 Architects, when acting between parties and giving advice, should exercise impartial and independent professional judgement to the best of their ability and understanding.

4.2 Architects should perform their work with due skill, care and diligence.

Standard 5: In carrying out or agreeing to carry out professional work, Architects should pay due regard to the interests of anyone who may reasonably be expected to use or enjoy the products of their own work.

5.1 Whilst Architects' primary responsibility is to their clients, they should nevertheless have due regard to their wider responsibility to conserve and enhance the quality of the environment and its natural resources.

Standard 6: Architects should maintain their professional service and competence in areas relevant to their professional work, and discharge the requirements of any engagement with commensurate knowledge and attention.

6.1 The fact that an Architect has not maintained their professional competence may count against them in the event of their competence being investigated.

Standard 7: Architects should preserve the security of monies entrusted to their care in the course of their practice or business.

7.1 When Architects hold monies belonging to a client or third party they should arrange for its receipt to be carefully recorded and for it to be kept (wherever possible) in an interest-bearing account in a bank or similar institution separate from any personal or business account.

7.2 Such an account should be designated a 'client account' and the bank or similar institution should be given written instructions that all money held in it is held as clients' money and that the bank or similar institution is not entitled to combine the account with any other account or to exercise any right of set-off or counterclaim against it.

7.3 Money may only be withdrawn from a client account to make a payment:

   a to or on behalf of a client; or

   b on the client's specific written instructions (for example, in order to defray the Architect's fees).

7.4 Unless otherwise agreed by the client, any interest (or other benefit) accruing to a client account should be paid to the client.

Standard 8: Architects should not undertake professional work without adequate and appropriate professional indemnity insurance cover.

8.1 The need for cover extends to professional work undertaken outside an Architect's main professional practice or employment and to work undertaken by employees of an Architect.

8.2 Employed Architects, should as far as possible ensure that professional indemnity insurance cover or other appropriate cover is provided by their employer.

8.3 Without limiting an Architect's duty to maintain professional indemnity cover which is adequate and appropriate for the work the Architect is undertaking, Architects must maintain, in any event, minimum cover in accordance with the Board's guidelines on professional indemnity insurance issued from time to time and provide such evidence in such form as the Board may require demonstrating compliance with this standard.

Standard 9: Architects should ensure that their personal and professional finances are managed prudently.

9.1 The following are examples of acts which may be examined in order to ascertain whether they disclose a wilful disregard by an Architect of their responsibilities or a lack of integrity, namely:

   • an order of bankruptcy;

Standard 9 continued

- the placing into liquidation of a company of which they are a director; (other than for amalgamation or reconstruction purposes);

- an accommodation with creditors (including a voluntary arrangement);

- failure to pay a judgment debt.

Standard 10: Architects should promote the Standards set out in this Code.

10.1 Architects should conduct their professional working accordance with this Code and, subject to any restriction imposed by law or the courts, report to the Registrar any serious breach of this Code which may come to their notice.

10.2 Architects need not report matters widely reported in the press and should not make unreasonable or vexatious reports, bearing in mind the provisions of Standard 1.

10.3 When an Architect is an arbitrator, adjudicator, mediator, conciliator or expert witness and is in receipt of privileged information the Board accepts that their duty in this role may take precedence over any requirement to report breaches of this Code to the Registrar.

10.4 An Architect should not (except in the circumstances described in 10.3 above) enter into a contract other than the settlement of a dispute, the terms of which would prevent any party from reporting any apparent breach of the Code by another architect to the Registrar.

10.5 An architect should report to the Registrar within 28 days if they:

- are convicted of an indictable offence or sentenced to imprisonment in respect to any offence; or

- are made the subject of an order of court disqualifying them from acting as a company director; or

- are made the subject of a bankruptcy order; or

- are a director of a company which is wound up (other than for amalgamation or reconstruction purposes).

10.6 Failure to make prompt report may count against an Architect in the event of disciplinary proceedings.

10.7 An Architect is required to co-operate with an Investigator appointed under the Architects Act 1997.

10.8 Failure by an Architect to co-operate promptly and fully with inquiries by such an Investigator will count against them in the event of disciplinary proceedings and related matters before the Professional Conduct Committee. Failure to co-operate may also in itself constitute grounds for disciplinary proceedings.

10.9 Any threat by an Architect to bring defamation proceedings in an attempt to frustrate the investigation of a complaint by the Registrar, Investigator or the Board's Solicitor, may be regarded as unacceptable conduct in itself and treated accordingly.

Section 2

Client Service and Complaints

Standard 11: Architects should organise and manage their professional work responsibly and with regard to the interests of their clients.

11.1 Architects should not undertake professional work unless the terms of the contract have been recorded in writing as to:

- the scope of the work;
- the fee or method of calculating it;
- the allocation of responsibilities;
- any limitation of responsibilities;
- the provisions for termination;
- any special provisions for dispute resolution;

and they have informed the client that Architects are subject to the disciplinary sanction of the Board in relation to complaints of unacceptable professional conduct or serious professional incompetence.

11.2 At the end of a contract (if requested) or otherwise on demand an Architect should promptly return to a client any papers, plans or other property to which the client is legally entitled.

11.3 Architects should ensure that their firm has:

- appropriate and effective internal procedures, including monitoring and review procedures; and
- sufficient suitably qualified and supervised staff;

such as to enable it to deliver an efficient and effective client service.

11.4 Architects should carry out their professional work without undue delay and, so far as is reasonably practicable, in accordance with any timescale and cost limits agreed with the client.

11.5 Architects should keep their client informed of the progress of work undertaken on their behalf and of any issue which may significantly affect its quality or cost.

11.6 Architects should observe the confidentiality of their client's affairs and should not disclose confidential information without the prior consent of the client or other lawful authority, for example, when disclosure is required by order of a court.

Standard 12: Architects should deal with disputes or complaints concerning their professional work or that of their practice or business promptly and appropriately.

12.1

a In the case of a firm or company comprising four or more partners or directors, a senior staff member should be designated as being responsible for dealing with complaints instance and the client advised accordingly.

Standard 12 continued

b Where the designated person is unable to resolve a complaint to the satisfaction of the complainant, they should refer it promptly to the senior partner or managing director.

c If, after reviewing the complaint, the senior partner or managing director is unable to resolve the complaint to the satisfaction of the complainant, they should advise the complainant that the matter can be referred to the Architects Registration Board if there are alleged breaches of the Code involved.

12.2 In the case of a sole practitioner or a firm of three or fewer partners or directors complaints should be referred directly to the sole practitioner, senior partner or managing director, who should deal with them as in sub paragraph (c) of the previous paragraph.

12.3 If appropriate, alternative methods of dispute resolution, such as arbitration or conciliation, should be encouraged.

12.4 Complaints should at every stage be handled courteously, sympathetically and where possible in accordance with the following time scale:

- an acknowledgement should be sent within 10 working days from the receipt of a complaint; and

- a response addressing the issues raised in the initial letter of complaint should be sent within 30 working days from its receipt.

All correspondence from the Architects Registration Board concerning complaints and/or compliance with the Code will, where possible, be handled within the same time limits as shown above, unless otherwise instructed by the Board.

Some essential points of a practical nature should be noted. All registered persons are required to:

- bring adequate professional, financial and technical competence or resources to all work undertaken, and maintain that level of competence; [cf Standards 2 and 6 with RIBA Code Undertaking 1.3]

- promote their work only in a truthful and responsible manner, without the risk of misleading or confusing clients; [cf Standard 3 with RIBA Code Undertaking 2.3]

- perform to the standard of skill and care expected of a professional – and with diligence, particularly concerning time-scales and cost limits agreed with clients; [cf Standard 4 with RIBA Standard Undertaking 1]

- see that the terms of an appointment are clearly defined and agreed in writing; [cf Standard 4.1 with RIBA Code Undertaking 1.2]

- be alert for any conflict of interests when accepting work, or which might arise during a commission, and take appropriate action; [cf Standard 1 with RIBA Code Undertaking 2.1]

- pay due regard to the interests of anyone who may reasonably be expected to use or enjoy his or her work [cf Standard 5 with RIBA Code Principle One]. This could have far-reaching implications, including giving proper consideration to environmental matters;

- treat client monies responsibly, and place them in a separate identifiable account. Architects must also manage their own personal and professional finances prudently; [cf Standard 7 with RIBA Code Undertaking 2.11 and 'Members' Rules for Clients' Accounts']

- have adequate professional indemnity insurance cover for all professional work undertaken. [cf Standard 8 with the less demanding RIBA Code Undertaking 1.2]

Standard 2 of the Code includes some sensible obligations relating to the management of professional work. For example, architects are required to:

- ensure that sufficient suitably qualified staff are available, and that they are properly supervised; [Standard 2.2]

- ensure, in the case of sole practitioners undertaking a project, that there are contingency plans in the event of enforced absence. [Standard 2.3]

Architects are under a duty to report to the Registrar information concerning convictions or disqualification orders imposed on them by the courts. However, personal observance of the Code with the standards might not always be sufficient. Architects also have a duty to promote the standards, to the extent that if they are aware of serious shortcomings on the part of other architects, then these must be reported to the Registrar. [Standard 10]

For all registered persons, who are also RIBA Members, the current Codes will need to be taken in conjunction. They have moved far beyond earlier notions of ethical behaviour. Matters of competence, performance and sound business practice have now been established as obligations. The Codes are as much concerned with the interests of those who commission the services of architects as with the protection of the profession and its members.

2.5   ARB disciplinary procedures

When a complaint is made the Board will consider it in detail through its Investigation Committee, and may appoint an investigator (from a panel of experienced registered architects) to advise on whether there is a case to answer. The architect in question is always contacted, given full details of the complaint made, and invited to respond. If the Board decides there is a case to answer, the complaint is referred to the Professional Conduct Committee (PCC) for a public hearing and decision. (Full details of the procedure can be found in the Investigation Rules and the Professional Conduct Committee Rules which are set out on the ARB web site.) The ARB's decisions are final but are subject to appeal to the High Court in England and Wales and the Court of Session in Scotland.

Complaints must fall under the two disciplinary headings in the Architects Act 1997: serious professional incompetence or unacceptable professional conduct.

Serious professional incompetence is defined in the Code as 'a service, which falls short of the standards required of a registered person'. This could be interpreted as a failure to demonstrate the care and skill of a competent architect in carrying out the services undertaken, for example in giving advice, preparing designs and technical information, and in managing a project or administering a contract. The failure would need to be significant to rank as 'serious', and could comprise one major error or a series of less major errors, the cumulative effect of which causes considerable problems to the client or third parties.

Unacceptable professional conduct is defined in the Code as 'conduct which falls short of the standard required of a registered person'. This is normally understood as relating to matters of ethics. It therefore goes further than the making of errors or the demonstration of poor judgement. It should involve a moral or ethical element, such as deception of any sort, misappropriation of the client's funds, failure to deal openly with the client, and breach of any of the detailed parts of the Code which relate to such matters. This could include such matters as conflicts of interest, not having the appropriate PI insurance cover, and breaching client confidentiality.

At the time of writing it is understood that the ARB is giving consideration to publishing guidance on the definitions of these two disciplinary headings.

Following the hearing, the Professional Conduct Committee is empowered to make a disciplinary order which can be:

- a reprimand;

- a penalty order (this means paying a specified sum based on the standard scale of fines for summary offences). In the event of non-payment, a name can be removed from the Register;

- a suspension order (this means removal of a person's name from the Register, with re-entry when the suspension period, not exceeding two years, is over);

- an erasure order (this means removal of a person's name from the Register). It will not be re-entered unless the ARB so directs.

If the Investigation Committee does not consider the complaint serious enough to warrant a PCC hearing, but nevertheless has concerns about the conduct of the architect, it may issue the architect with a 'warning' letter as to his or her future conduct.

2.6   RIBA – the organisation

The RIBA was founded in 1834 (see appendix A) and at the time of writing has around 32,000 members. The headquarters of the RIBA is 66 Portland Place, London W1N 4AD. Here a Chief Executive heads staff who are charged with administering Institute policy. The Chief Executive is supported by full time officials who in turn head departments, each of which consists of a directorate backed by specialist units as appropriate. These units are also responsible for servicing the various boards or advisory groups on which sit invited, nominated or elected members of the Institute who have particular expertise and interests.

At present the departments have allocated responsibilities for education and professional development; practice; finance and administration; library; membership and international affairs; public affairs. The Chief Executive's office deals with matters relating to arbitration, discipline and professional conduct.

The RIBA Council, a body of some 60 members elected by ballot to ensure national and regional representation, is chaired by the President. This is an honorary office, and the Charter allows for 'such other Honorary Officers to be elected as the Bylaws prescribe'. At present these include Vice Presidents, an Honorary Secretary, and an Honorary Treasurer.

The RIBA is an Institute which functions internationally but with a UK focus. It is a considerable global force, particularly in those countries which are members of the Commonwealth Association of Architects (CAA). For RIBA members, contact with the Institute is likely to be through specific activities, Regional Offices and Branches. All RIBA members are allocated to membership of a Branch, of which there are about 80. Most members belong to the Branch in which they live or work, but the choice of Branch is the prerogative of the individual. Each Region has its own office with a Director and staff. This is the vital grass roots part of the network, responsible for organising seminars, courses, lectures and visits. This is where local practice contacts and support can flourish, and problems can be tackled at a personal level. The network also provides members with an opportunity to exercise considerable influence over RIBA affairs.

The traditional organisational framework of the Institute is both geographic and knowledge-based. The network of local offices is overlaid with a pattern of committees concerned with broad issues such as practice, education or marketing. The *Strategic Study of the Profession* took an in-depth client-centred look at architecture. It found a client group who sought to be able to distinguish one architectural practice from another on the basis of demonstrable specialist skills. New communication mechanisms have allowed the development of a locally accessible knowledge-based network superimposed on the old geographic structure. The new networks know no geographic or national boundary, and help the Institute both to meet clients' needs and to exploit its international potential. Activity such as the establishment of RIBA client forums, or professionally-led 'specialist interest groups', are evidence of this trend, as is the Institute's development of its own electronic network, Ribanet, and internet site, architecture.com.

2.7   RIBA – the purpose

The RIBA Supplemental Charter 1971, in paragraph 2.1, states that 'the objects of the Royal Institute are the advancement of Architecture and the promotion of the acquirement of the knowledge of the Arts and Sciences connected therewith'. Ever since the original Charter, primacy has been given to the advancement of architecture, not to the advancement of architects.

Currently RIBA efforts to advance the cause of architecture are expressed in many ways:

- by raising environmental and ecological concerns and seeking to influence government and public opinion;

- by facing the challenges to architectural quality in times of changing building procurement and technology;
- by providing support services for practitioners;
- by striving to improve the status and competence of architects through continuing professional education and research;
- by engaging in consultation on legal, technical and financial controls and constraints within which architecture is now practised;
- by maintaining the architect's professed concept of providing a unique design service.

From a list of support services now offered by the RIBA to members, the following are likely to be of particular interest to practitioners:

- Practice Register (details of all registered practices, published annually);
- Practice Database (computer-aided matching of suitable practices with client enquiries by the Clients Advisory Services team);
- Members' Information Centre (professional library help service responding to most kinds of architectural queries);
- Specialist Practice Consultants (telephone advice on practice matters, including legal and contractual matters);
- Archives Collection (photographs, drawings, record documents);
- Register of Planning Supervisors (of accredited architects undertaking CDM work);
- Conciliation Service (for resolving disputes between architects and clients);
- Members' Business Centre (rooms and facilities for hire at 66 Portland Place);
- Insurance Agency (RIBA approved policies for professional indemnity cover).

In addition, through RIBA Companies, the following services are offered:

- Appointments Bureau (for members looking for work or seeking to recruit staff);
- Office Library Service (helping practices to manage trade and technical information);
- National Building Specification (standard clauses and guidance kept up to date on a subscription basis);
- RIBA Information Services;
- RIBA Publications (books and documents of relevance to architects, and bookshops, including an on-line shop).

As befits a learned society, the RIBA also demonstrates through its Journal, sessional programmes, education policy, library and drawings collections, its right to be seen as a centre of knowledge upon which the practice of architecture is based. Through its Code of Professional Conduct and Standards of Professional Performance, its admission standards, appointing documents, and range of other publications, the Institute is able to assure the public of the standards of integrity and competence of its members. The RIBA is affiliated to, and represented on, various associations of direct relevance to architects, including the ACA, the

SCALA, Architects in Industry and Commerce, Architects in Agriculture and the Countryside, the CAA, the ACE, and the UIA.

Of particular concern to members in practice, the RIBA has direct representation on many bodies which, although outside the immediate profession, are prominent in the construction industry including the JCT (through the Consultants' College), the CIC, the CIB and the NHBC.

The RIBA is also actively represented on various bodies which are principally concerned with environmental matters, including urban and building conservation.

2.8   Control over entry to the RIBA

Most professional institutions lay down minimum standards for entry, and exert discipline on members through codes of professional conduct. The RIBA takes a keen interest in the way that architecture is handled in school curricula, and closely monitors the way that architecture is taught in higher education. It reviews courses and examinations in schools of architecture on a quinquennial basis jointly with Visiting Board representatives from the Architects Registration Board. Continued recognition depends on standards being maintained.

Many young aspirants glimpse their first possibility of a career in architecture through short periods of work experience in an architect's office. This is often initiated by the school careers teacher, who will be keen to establish and maintain a link with sympathetic practices. Such an arrangement can bring mutual benefits.

Practitioners may sometimes be asked about suitable courses and requirements for young people interested in pursuing a career in architecture. Information is available in the RIBA booklet, *A Career in Architecture*, on the RIBA website, and through enquiries to the RIBA Education Department.

2.8.1 Entry requirements

The RIBA offers the recognised schools of architecture the following guidance on minimum entry requirements, but schools are at liberty to require higher standards, perhaps in specific subjects, and competition for places is keen.

The General Certificate of Education and the General Certificate of Secondary Education (England, Wales, Northern Ireland)

Candidates should have passes in two subjects at the Advanced level or one subject at A level with two AS levels of the GCE together with passes in three other subjects in the GCSE. Both the GCE A level subjects and at least two GCSE subjects should be drawn from the academic fields of study. The following are important: (1) English (2) Mathematics or a science subject. Botany, Zoology, Biology or Geology are acceptable GCSE subjects where accompanied by Mathematics at either level. These subjects may be taken at either GCE A level or in the GCSE.

The traditional craft subjects are not sufficient in themselves for a career in architecture, but many schools will accept one of the newer courses which have a strong element of design and problem-solving rigorously taught and assessed within an academic framework.

The Scottish Certificate of Education

Requirements for the Scottish Certificate of Education are similar, except that at least three of the subjects should be passed at the Higher grade, but the other two subjects may be passed at the Ordinary grade. Passes in any two of the additional Mathematics subjects (Elementary Analysis, Geometry, and Dynamics) will count as one Higher grade for this purpose. All three Higher grade subjects and one Ordinary grade subject should be drawn from the field of study specified above.

BTEC Certificate

Under certain circumstances it is possible for students with a high standard of pass in the Business and Technician Education Council (BTEC) Certificate in Building Studies, supplemented by a pass in English in the GCSE syllabus, to be accepted by some schools, but others might also require three additional subjects to include Mathematics. Candidates should apply to the school of architecture concerned for its specific views on entry requirements.

2.8.2 Schools of Architecture

There are currently 36 schools of architecture in the UK, with full-time courses and examinations recognised by the RIBA as giving exemption from its own examinations. The schools are inspected by the Joint RIBA/ARB Validation Panel at least every five years.

Full-time courses traditionally require the equivalent of five academic years of full time in residence academic study supplemented by at least two years' professional experience. A few schools offer alternatives to this pattern, for example with part of the 'in residence' course replaced with periods of distance learning in supervised placements. The RIBA publishes a booklet, *Schools of Architecture,* which gives information about each school, the type and length of courses offered, and details of entry requirements.

As an employee in an architect's office it is also possible to study architecture as an external candidate with a view to qualifying by taking the RIBA's own examinations. This external route is the only practical option for some students, but it is somewhat arduous. At the time of writing arrangements have been made by the RIBA to 'franchise' the external examinations to Oxford Brookes University, which will also offer the enrolled candidates support in the form of tutorials and workshops. Anyone seeking to qualify in this way must be practice-based and have had the equivalent of at least six years' practical experience, and must satisfy the minimum entry requirements set by the RIBA. The external examinations currently comprise 'The Examination in Architecture for Office Based Candidates' (Parts 1 and 2), to be followed by 'The Examination in Professional Practice' (the so-called 'Part 3'). Information about the syllabus, regulations and submission requirements may be obtained from the Examinations Office, RIBA Education Department or from Oxford Brookes University.

Part-time courses, which may be modular, are offered at some colleges. In-company training programmes (which may recognise some work undertaken in the office) are another way of obtaining additional academic qualifications at the same time as professional development. Enquiries about such opportunities should be made directly to the academic institutions concerned.

Most schools of architecture also operate Higher Degree Schemes. These may entail a full-time commitment of between a few months (a taught course which might lead to a supplementary Master's degree at the end of Part 2) and three years (a research programme which might lead to a Master's degree or Doctorate). Many such courses are modular. A list of post-graduate courses is available from the RIBA Education Department, but the field is fast-moving and prospective candidates are advised to contact institutions directly.

2.8.3 Professional experience

Professional experience is regarded by the RIBA as an integral part of an architect's education, and it forms an essential component of the RIBA Part 3 Examination in Professional Practice (see below). Full details of the RIBA requirements for professional experience are set out in the RIBA on-line *Professional Experience Development Record (PEDR)* which can be viewed at *www.pedr.co.uk.* What follows below is a brief summary, and the *PEDR* should be consulted for all details. Students should also consult the ARB website for the ARB professional experience requirements.

Under the RIBA rules the first period of up to one year usually comes at the end of the first three years of the academic course (at a point equivalent to Part 1 of the RIBA Examination). The second period starts on completion of a further two years' academic study (at a point equivalent to Part 2 of the RIBA Examination). However, there are some variations to this pattern.

As far as employers are concerned, there are four undertakings which should be regarded as setting a minimum standard. These are:

- To give a student reasonable opportunities to gain an adequate breadth and depth of experience from the range described in the *PEDR*.

- To nominate an experienced architect (or other professional in non-architectural settings) who will be personally responsible for directing the student's work and supervising and guiding the student's professional experience so that the range, quality and depth of the activities undertaken shall be such as to satisfy the objectives of professional experience. This person is known as the employment mentor.

- To allow up to ten paid working days per annum for professional activities, which have the educational objective of broadening the student's professional training.

- To sign, date and comment on the student's *PEDR* in a fair, accurate and timely manner at the end of each three-month period of professional experience.

Each school of architecture which offers a Part 3 programme is responsible for appointing a professional studies advisor (PSA) who can cooperate with employers in a joint effort to secure the best training possible for students. Advisors welcome details of any likely vacancies for students and as much information as possible about the office and its work. During professional experience, the status of a professional trainee is that of an employee first and a student second, and a PSA is normally well qualified to comment on such matters as salary levels and student capabilities. Most PSAs have other responsibilities in their schools, but they will try to visit the office at least once during the first year of professional experience. The PSA normally talks first with the student and then discusses progress separately with the employment mentor. Advice given to students by a PSA is impartial.

The usual pattern is for professional trainees to attend seminars of practice and management back at the school. The employer may expect confirmation by the school's PSA that any proposed activity requiring formal leave of absence is of educational importance. The office should also arrange a programme of complementary activities such as visiting sites, attending client and contractor meetings, listening to planning enquiries, observing specialists' operations, and accompanying clerks of works, planning supervisors or quantity surveyors on their inspections.

Employment mentor

The student should ensure that one person is nominated as the employment mentor, who will be responsible for overseeing the educational and professional development of the student in the workplace. In addition, the employment mentor's responsibilities include:

- Establishing an organisational framework which will facilitate the provision of high quality professional experience.
- Ensuring the student is not overburdened by responsibilities inappropriate to his or her experience.
- Discussing work objectives and learning opportunities with the student at the start of each three-month period of experience.
- Signing, dating and commenting in the *PEDR* on the student's achievements for each three-month period of experience.

2.8.4 The Examination in Professional Practice and Management

Both the RIBA examination and equivalent recognised courses at schools of architecture contain a strong professional studies element. The examination in professional practice is the final mechanism for controlling standards of entry to the profession and has the following components:

A documentary submission, which will contain some or all of the following:

- a professional cv;
- a professional training experience evaluation prepared by the candidate;
- a folio of professional case work;
- written examination papers and course work.

2.8.5 The completed PEDR

A professional interview, at which the candidate's knowledge and experience generally will be probed.

This qualifying examination is intended to establish a high baseline of competence for entry to membership of the RIBA and registration, and with potential for continuing professional development. The range and quality of experience that candidates will be expected to demonstrate is unlikely to be acquired in less than three years and many candidates have four or five years' experience. The regulations for this examination have recently been revised by the RIBA and are set out in the Descriptions, Regulations & Outline Syllabus, agreed by the

RIBA education committee on 19 September 2001. These regulations are effective from September 2002.

2.9 Control over the professional conduct of members

Issue 11 of the RIBA *Code of Professional Conduct* was published in 1997 and included the Standard of Professional Performance for the first time. The booklet is available from RIBA Publications.

The object of the Code is to promote the standard of professional conduct, or self-discipline, required of members of the RIBA in the interests of the public. All members, including Student members, are required to uphold this standard, and their conduct is governed by the Code.

The Code comprises three principles which are of universal application, dealing with competence, integrity, the interests of members generally and the public who commission the services of an architect (see Figure 2). This means keeping in mind the interests of all who use or might be affected by the work of an architect, and also having regard for environmental matters, such as use of natural resources, the cultural heritage, etc.

The three principles are supported by undertakings which are essentially advisory and intended to illustrate the application of the principles. The wording used in the principles is pre-eminent, but it should be noted that members must at all times be guided by the spirit of the Code and not just the words. This could prove to be a very wide obligation to satisfy.

Members are governed by the RIBA *Charter, Byelaws and Regulations* in addition to the Code. Disciplinary measures are provided for under the byelaws. The RIBA can hold a member personally accountable when acting through a corporate or unincorporated body, and members will not be able to evade this by pleading a higher obligation.

Revisions to the Code, and relevant practice notes, may appear in the RIBA *Journal* from time to time. Members will be expected to be familiar with any new provisions right from the date of their introduction, and to comply with them. Ignorance will be no defence.

2.9.1 The RIBA Code of Professional Conduct and Standard of Professional Performance

Principle One

A Member shall faithfully carry out his duties applying his knowledge and experience with efficiency and loyalty towards his client or employer, and being mindful of the interests of those who may be expected to use or enjoy the product of his work.

To uphold this Principle a Member undertakes:

1.1 When acting between parties or giving advice, to exercise his independent professional judgement impartially to the best of his ability and understanding.

1.2 When making any engagement, whether by an agreement for professional services, by a contract of employment or by a contract for the supply of services and goods, to state whether or not professional indemnity insurance is held, and to have defined beyond reasonable doubt and recorded the terms of the engagement and the scope of the service, responsibilities and any limitation of liability, the method of calculation of remuneration and the provision for termination and adjudication.

1.3 Before accepting or continuing with any work to establish that his competence and resources are adequate to provide a service which meets the RIBA Standard of Professional Performance and, if engaged as a full-time employee, give prior notice to both parties before accepting the engagement elsewhere.

1.4 To arrange that the work of his office and any branch office, insofar as it relates to architecture, is under the control of an architect.

1.5 Not to transfer his responsibilities, or reduce the scope of his services by sub-contracting, without the prior consent of his client or without defining the changes in the responsibilities of those concerned.

1.6 Not to evade his obligations by abandoning a commission.

Comments

Principle One applies to all professional relationships, whether between an employer member and a salaried staff member, or between a member and a client.

• Note that these undertakings require that the scope and precise terms of agreements between architect and client must be defined and recorded beyond reasonable doubt.

• Members are required to disclose whether or not professional indemnity insurance is held. As yet holding such insurance is not an RIBA requirement, but it is required under the ARB Code.

• It is essential to establish that both competence and resources are adequate for the commission to be undertaken.

• There is a requirement that work cannot be sub-contracted without the consent of the client, and that members cannot simply walk away from an undertaking once entered into.

Principle Two

A Member shall, at all times, avoid any action or situation which is inconsistent with his professional obligations or which is likely to raise doubts about his integrity.

2.1 To declare in writing to any prospective client or employer any business interest the existence of which, if not so declared, would or might be likely to raise a conflict of interests and doubts about his integrity by reason of an actual or apparent connection with or effect upon his engagement. If the prospective client or employer does not in writing accept these circumstances, the Member must withdraw from the situation.

2.2 When finding that in circumstances not specifically covered elsewhere in this Code his personal or professional interests conflict so as to risk a breach of this Principle, either to withdraw from the situation, or remove the source of conflict, or declare it and obtain the agreement of the parties concerned to the continuance of the engagement.

2.3 Not to make, support or acquiesce in any statement, written or otherwise, which is contrary to his own knowledge or bona fide professional opinion, or which he knows to be misleading, or unfair to others or otherwise discreditable to the profession.

2.4 Not to practise as or purport to be an independent consulting architect and simultaneously be a principal, partner, director or co-director in a firm which engages in the business of: trading in land or buildings; or as property developers, auctioneers, or house agents; or as contractors, subcontractors, manufacturers or suppliers in or to the building industry unless that firm is distinct from the architectural practice and clearly identified as such.

2.5 Not to carry out or purport to carry out the independent functions of an architect or any similar independent functions in relation to a contract in which he or his employer is the contractor, or where the architectural practice and the contractor's firm are under substantially the same management or control.

2.6 Not to disclose, or use to the benefit of himself or others, confidential information acquired in the course of his work without the prior written consent of the parties concerned.

2.7 Not to give or accept any commissions or gifts or other inducement to show favour to any person or body, or allow his name to be used in advertising any service or product associated with the construction industry.

2.8 Not to have or take as a partner or co-director in his firm any person who is disqualified for registration by reason of the fact that his name has been removed from the Register under Section 7 of the Architects (Registration) Act 1931, as amended by the Housing Grants, Construction and Regeneration Act 1996; any person disqualified for membership of the Royal Institute by reason of expulsion under Byelaw 5.1; any person disqualified for membership of another professional institution by reason of expulsion under the relevant disciplinary regulations, unless the Royal Institute otherwise allows.

2.9 Irrespective of the form of this practice, and notwithstanding the provisions of the Companies Acts, to conduct his business in a manner consistent with this Principle.

2.10 On becoming personally or professionally insolvent or being disqualified under the Company Directors Disqualification Act 1986, to notify the Royal Institute's principal executive officer of the facts.

2.11 To conform with the Members' Rules for Clients' Accounts. Principle Two is relevant to all other business or personal interests which a Member might have which impinges in any way on a commission. The Member must then disclose this fact to the client. Preferably this will be before accepting the commission, but if a potential conflict of interests arises only after accepting the commission, then the Member must either withdraw or see to it that any cause of conflict is removed, or continue only with the express agreement of all parties concerned.

Comments

Note that :

• Members must not make supportive statements, written or otherwise, including advertising material, which could bring discredit to the profession.

• Members must not act as independent consultants whilst also being part of a firm of estate agents, developers or contractors, unless the architectural practice is clearly separate.

• Members must not purport to act as independent contract administrators for a building contract where the architectural practice and the contracting organisation are under substantially the same management or control.

• Members must not disclose confidential information which has been acquired during a commission, without written consent from the parties concerned.

• Members must conform to the *Rules for Clients' Accounts*. These are printed in full in the current edition of the Code.

• Reference to registration legislation in Undertaking 2.8 should be read in conjunction with the Architects Act 1997, which has repealed the legislation cited.

Principle Three

A Member shall in every circumstance conduct himself in a manner which respects the legitimate rights and interests of others.

To uphold this Principle a Member undertakes:

3.1 Not to offer discounts, commissions, gifts or other inducements for the introduction of clients.

3.2 When offering services as an independent consultant, not to quote a fee without receiving an invitation to do so and sufficient information on the nature and scope of the project to enable a quotation to be prepared which clearly indicates the service covered by the fee.

3.3 When offering services as an independent consulting architect, not to revise a fee quotation to take account of the fee quoted by another architect for the same service.

3.4 Not to attempt to oust another architect from an engagement.

3.5 Not to enter any architectural competition which the Royal Institute has declared to be unacceptable.

3.6 Not when appointed as a competition assessor subsequently to act in any other capacity for the work.

3.7 Not maliciously or unfairly to criticise or attempt to discredit another Member or his work.

3.8 On being approached to undertake work upon which he knows or can ascertain by reasonable enquiry that another architect has an engagement with the same client, to notify the fact to such architect.

3.9 When engaged to give an opinion on the work of another architect, to notify the fact to that architect unless it can be shown to be prejudicial to prospective or actual litigation to do so.

3.10 Appropriately to acknowledge the contribution made to his work by others.

Comments

Principle Three applies to all professional dealings, not just between members but also with persons outside the profession in respect of legitimate (i.e. legal and moral) interests.

Note that:

• Members must acknowledge appropriately the contribution made to their work by others – and this presumably includes contributions from team colleagues who are not members and may be from other professions.

• Members must, when employing other architects, make sure that their authority, responsibility and liability are clearly established.

• Members must ensure that full time staff have the benefit of subrogation waivers from the practice's indemnity insurers.

• Members must report to the RIBA any known alleged breaches of this Code, unless the law or the courts have imposed a restriction.

• Members must report to the RIBA any conviction for a criminal offence, including any disqualification from being a company director.

2.10 Control over the performance of members

Alongside the Code, the RIBA publishes a *Standard of Professional Performance* with the object of defining a level of competence with which all members must comply.

THE STANDARD OF PROFESSIONAL PERFORMANCE

Members are required to maintain in their work and that of their practices a standard of performance which is consistent with membership of the Royal Institute of British Architects and with a proper regard for the interests both of those who commission and those who may be expected to use or enjoy the product of their work.

Members and their practices will meet the requirements of their engagements with commensurate knowledge and attention so that the quality of the professional services provided does not fall below that which could reasonably be expected of Members of the Royal Institute in good standing in the normal conduct of their business.

To uphold this Standard, the Member, and where appropriate the practice, undertakes:

1 To comply with all reasonable instructions, to carry out and complete the work entrusted to him honestly, competently, diligently and expeditiously in accordance with the timescale and any cost limits previously agreed so far as reasonably possible.

2 To fulfil CPD obligations and when employing other Members on a full-time basis to allow them reasonable time to do likewise.

3 To operate where appropriate an internal complaints procedure which should ensure that clients are informed whom to approach in the event of any problems with the professional service provided, and establish procedures which will ensure that complaints are properly and promptly attended to.

4 To make arrangements with an appropriately qualified person for the running of their offices and administration of contracts during a period of absence and inform clients of those arrangements.

5 To seek appropriate advice when faced with a situation which they recognise as being outside their own experience or knowledge.

6 When in practice as a sole practitioner or sole principal to make reasonable attempts to establish professional contact with other Members which could provide opportunities for the mutual exchange of experience and knowledge.

7 As a partner or co-director of an architectural practice to have proper regard to the experience and capability of staff when delegating responsibility.

8 Not to lay claim to expertise which they do not have, or accept commissions which they know are beyond their skill and experience, without arranging for appropriate assistance and advice which will enable them to satisfy the Standard of Professional Performance in the discharge of their professional duties.

Comments

In upholding the standard, the undertakings are both personal upon members and upon practices. All members undertake to engage in CPD activities, and to see that employees who are members are also allowed reasonable time for this.

2.11   CPD

The term 'continuing professional development' (CPD) is used by the profession to describe those activities that constitute part of the learning process which should continue throughout an architect's professional career. CPD is a matter both for individuals and collectively for offices and departments. It implies the need to formulate a positive plan of action rather than perfunctory attendance at a given number of random events. The RIBA has a national CPD Service, with convenors or managers at regional level.

The RIBA has had rules in place regarding CPD since 1999, the sanction for non-compliance being that the practice may be dropped from the register of practices. All corporate members of the RIBA who are not fully retired are required to do the following every year:

- 35 hours CPD, in tandem with 100 points CPD;
- record activity on a CPD record sheet for the current year;
- maintain a CPD plan for the following year;
- wherever possible, obtain half the CPD in a formal course-based activity.

Formal courses should have been assessed by a third party and might include:

- RIBA regional or branch events;
- RIBA CPD Providers Network events or material;
- allied construction institution events;

- CPD clubs;
- courses, seminars, workshops, events;
- in-house lectures or workshops;
- certificates or diplomas in relevant subjects;
- second degrees in relevant subjects;
- NVQs/SVQs;
- MSCs;
- postgraduate courses at schools of architecture;
- RIBA Distance Learning Library.

Other activities might include:

- serving the profession in the branch or regional structure through work on various committees or ad hoc groups, and learning at the same time;
- a programme of self-directed learning activities;
- teaching;
- research and writing;
- practice (for those in teaching posts);
- service on BBA or BSI committees.

References and further reading

ARB *Advice for Clients*.

ARB *Architects Code. Standards of Conduct and Practice*.

ARB *Facing a Complaint*.

ARB *Investigation Rules and Professional Conduct Committee Rules. PI Insurance Guidelines*.

ARB *Making a Complaint to ARB. Understanding the Process*.

ARB *Retirement from practice and resigning from the register*.

ARB *Section 20. Guidance Note*.

RIBA *Code of Professional Conduct and Standard of Professional Performance*

RIBA *Professional Experience Development Record* www.pedr.co.uk

RIBA (1999) *Royal Institute of British Architects Continuing Professional Development Requirements and Guidance Notes*.

RIBA (1999) Schools of Architecture with courses recognised by the RIBA.

Smith, Sir C. (1999) *Architecture Education for the 21st Century*, London, RIBA.

3 THE LAW

3.1 Legal considerations

3.2 Claims in contract

3.3 Claims in tort

3.4 Legislation

3.5 Some key statutes
3.5.1   Human Rights Act 1998
3.5.2   Supply of Goods and Services Act 1982
3.5.3   Defective Premises Act 1972
3.5.4   Unfair Contract Terms Act 1977
3.5.5   Unfair Terms in Consumer Contracts Regulations 1994
3.5.6. The Housing Grants, Construction and Regeneration Act 1996
3.5.7   Contracts (Rights of Third Parties) Act 1999
3.5.8   Late Payment of Commercial Debts (Interest) Act 1998

3.6 Sources of information
3.6.1   Relevant texts and sources of information

3.1 Legal considerations

Whatever their mode of practice, and regardless of their status within an organisation, all architects as professional people have some legal obligations for which they may be held personally or jointly accountable. These are most likely to arise in connection with:

- occupying premises for business purposes;
- running the business;
- employing staff;
- providing professional services under architect-client agreements;
- carrying out projects.

Some of these obligations will be subject to common law, where actions which result in injury to others could result in claims for damages. Other obligations will arise from legislation where non-compliance could be a breach of statutory duty giving grounds for prosecution.

Architecture can be a high risk business and all persons involved in formulating briefs, writing specifications, reporting on the state or potential of land or buildings, designing, inspecting work and administering building contracts, etc could at some time or other be faced with a reference to adjudication, arbitration, or litigation. Sometimes the architect may be forced into the position of claimant, or become caught up as a witness of fact, or be joined as co-defendant in proceedings, or have to face allegations of breach of contract or negligence.

3.2   Claims in contract

Claims against professionals may arise in contract or in tort, sometimes under both heads. There are important differences.

A contract is an agreement enforceable at law, or for a breach of which the law will provide a remedy – usually monetary compensation or damages. Contractual obligations can arise from express or implied terms, the latter usually because of trade custom, or because they are necessary to make the contract workable, or most likely because they are implied by statute and cannot readily be excluded. Only the parties to a contract are bound by its terms, and the obligations which it gives rise to are therefore relatively controllable. By and large, the parties are free to agree whatever bargain they wish, and the courts will not be concerned about its fairness, only that it is workable and not contrary to public morality and the law.

Where a contract obligation is not met, an action for breach of contract may be brought and damages claimed in respect of all the losses suffered. An architect liable for breach of contract will often be in breach of an express or implied term to exercise that degree of skill and care expected of an ordinary, competent architect. However, if the contractual duty is a strict liability one, i.e. to achieve a particular result, as for example with a 'fitness for purpose' warranty, then it will not be necessary to rely on a lack of skill and care. The fact of failure will, of itself, be sufficient to establish breach of contract. Contract law puts no restrictions on the kind of losses that are recoverable in damages, and economic losses are freely recoverable so long as they arise directly from the breach and it may be supposed that they could reasonably have been within the contemplation of the parties at the time they entered into the contract.

It is therefore important to consider carefully the terms of any contractual arrangement. It is essential that contracts for professional services are put into writing, and that the obligations of the parties are set down in clear and precise terms. Such contracts will usually be 'construction contracts', and subject to the terms of the Housing Grants, Construction and Regeneration Act 1996.

Under the Limitation Act 1980, the time for bringing an action for breach of contract will be six years from the date of the breach in the case of simple contracts, or twelve years in the case of a contract entered into as a deed.

3.3   Claims in tort

Tort is a civil wrong outside of contract, although a tortious duty may exist in parallel with a contractual one. Many kinds of tort are relevant to the practise of architecture (for example, trespass, libel, nuisance), but actions in tort against architects are usually for alleged negligence.

We are all personally liable for any torts which we commit, whether these are the result of actions or a failure to act in particular circumstances. In general, anyone can sue or be sued in respect of injury so caused, provided it is not too remote. Normally it is the actual wrongdoer who will be liable, but the law imposes a responsibility also on persons who are vicariously liable for the actions of others under their control, for example their employers.

There are three essentials for a claim in tort to be established:

* There must be a duty of care owed to the plaintiff by the defendant. For a professional person this will usually be a duty to use reasonable care and skill to the standard of the ordinary skilled man or woman exercising and professing to have that special professional skill. The standard of care expected of a reasonably competent person is likely to be judged in the light of the technical knowledge and standards prevailing at the time, i.e. the 'state of the art'. This is why it is important that architects retain all technical information and manufacturers' trade literature relating to specific projects.

* The duty of care must have been breached by carelessness, to an extent which in law amounts to negligence.

* Damage must have resulted from that breach.

Often the plaintiff will have no contract with the defendant, and therefore of necessity any claim has to be founded in tort. However, even where there is a contract, the courts may nevertheless find that a duty in tort also exists. There can be advantages for a plaintiff in bringing a tort action because:

* the time limits before an action becomes statute barred due to the Limitation Act 1980, could be greater in tort than in contract. This could be particularly important in the case

of design defects where time will start to run from the date that damage first occurred, and of course this could be much later than the date of the breach of contract;

- differences in the basis for calculating damages as between tort and contract could also be advantageous to a plaintiff, even though it is usually easier to establish breach of contract than to prove negligence in tort.

Against this it should be remembered that recovery of damages for pure economic loss, unrelated to physical damage or personal injury, seems much less likely to succeed in tort than in contract with the law as it is at present. As a result, it is generally considered better for actions to recover economic loss to be framed in contract. Third parties such as funders, lessees, subsequent purchasers, etc who were not involved with the original contract and who would otherwise have to rely mainly on tort, usually try to establish contractual relationships by seeking collateral agreements or warranties. These should never be entered into if the terms are more onerous than the original contracts, but even so the additional contractual relationships can only increase liability.

The limitation period applicable for an action in tort is six years after the damage was first sustained, regardless of whether or not it was discovered. This is often likely to be far more favourable for a plaintiff than the period for breach of contract, and even this longer period can be further increased by the provisions of the Latent Damage Act 1986. This amends the Limitation Act 1980 in certain respects concerning tort actions. It introduces a three-year discoverability period, but also imposes a 15-year absolute time bar except where there has been deliberate concealment.

3.4   Legislation

Legislation imposes conditions on the practising architect's work, and is increasingly used to reformulate areas of law which have become unwieldy. It is also used to introduce new areas of law, some of which are the result of complying with European Directives.

Legislation is made in Parliament, and only Parliament can introduce, amend or repeal it. Its interpretation, however, is solely a matter for the courts. Acts which have application nationwide form the bulk of legislation passed in each parliamentary session. Nonetheless a considerable number of local Acts are in force, particularly concerning matters of building and the environment, which should not be overlooked.

When a Parliamentary Bill has reached its final reading, it receives the Royal Assent and becomes an Act with a Chapter number for that year, a long title with a date, and is headed by a short title. It may or may not come into force immediately even though it will be on the Statute Book. If there is nothing to the contrary in the Act, it comes into force on the morning of the day on which it receives Royal Assent. More commonly these days, a commencement date some time in the future is given, or it may be indicated that a Secretary of State has the power to designate 'an appointed day'. Sections of an Act may fall into any of these categories, and it may be necessary to establish whether all or only part of the Act is in force. All Acts not immediately enforceable may be brought into force by a Statutory Instrument, or more than one if different dates are needed for various sections. It is therefore not always easy to establish whether certain provisions in Acts are actually in force.

An Act remains in force until it is repealed by another Act. A part or sections of an Act may be repealed, leaving the remainder unchanged; there is often a Repeal section or schedule in an Act. An Act may be amended by subsequent legislation – the wording may be altered and the effect of the Statute may be altered. The law, once in force, must be observed; ignorance of it is no defence. It will also be no excuse that printed copies were not available, as has happened in the past when supplies were interrupted by industrial action.

As well as the Acts themselves, there is an enormous amount of delegated legislation which can come out of provisions contained in an Act enabling a Secretary of State to move rapidly on matters of detail. Much of this delegated legislation is likely to be of considerable interest to the architect in practice, and may be in the form of:

- Orders in Council, where rule-making powers are vested in the Privy Council (these are generally used in emergencies);
- Statutory Instruments, commonly used when a Secretary of State makes regulations by virtue of delegated powers;
- By-laws, usually enforced by local authorities or public bodies and made under powers granted by Parliament.

It should be remembered that delegated legislation has the full weight of law and can be implemented without much warning, although in practice there tends to be a reasonable period for consultation.

Circulars or guidance notes are often published to accompany pieces of legislation. They are written in plain English and are an invaluable aid to a better understanding of legislation, sometimes giving a clear indication of what Parliament intended. However, they are not part of the law, unlike Approved Documents or Approved Codes of Practice, which often have legal standing to the extent that they describe minimum acceptable standards.

European law has been a major influence on English legislation for some time. Both the Council of Ministers and the European Commission can make 'Regulations'. These are directly applicable in all Member States and are published in the *Official Journal of the European Community*. In other cases they may issue 'Directives' or 'Decisions', which are usually also published in the *Official Journal*. Directives, usually the most relevant for architects, are binding in substance on Member States, but the UK Parliament must then implement them in whatever form it chooses. Decisions are binding in their entirety on those to whom they are directed, and are enforceable in national courts. Mere recommendations and opinions have no binding force.

3.5   Some key statutes

Acts of Parliament likely to be most relevant in connection with the practise of architecture are shown in the table of statutes given as Figure 2, and an outline of the some of the more important Acts is given below. Note that Figure 2 includes only Acts, and not the many Statutory Instruments which flow as delegated legislation, and which usually carry the detail so often important for the practitioner. Local legislation is not included either. Although the legislation included in the table was correct at the time of writing, it is always liable to change, and readers should check its currency and effectiveness for themselves.

Figure 2: Relevant legislation

Business premises
Occupier's Liability Acts 1957-84
Offices Shops and Railway Premises
   Act 1963

Running the business
Business Names Act 1985
Civil Liability (Contribution) Act 1978
Companies Acts 1985-89
Copyright Designs and Patents
   Act 1988
Data Protection Act 1998
Employer's Liability (Compulsory
   Insurance) Act 1969
Health and Safety at Work, etc Act 1974
Insolvency Act 1986
Limitation Act 1980
Limited Partnership Act 1907
Limited Liability Partnership Act 2000
Partnership Act 1890

Employing staff
Disability Discrimination Act 1995
Employment Protection (Consolidation)
   Act 1978
Employment Acts 1980-88
Employment Rights Act 1996
Employment Relations Act 1999
Equal Pay Act 1970
National Minimum Wage Act 1998
Pensions Schemes Act 1993
Race Relations Act 1976
Sex Discrimination Acts 1975-86

Professional services
Architects Act 1997
Arbitration Act 1996
Consumer Protection Act 1987
Housing Grants, Construction and
   Regeneration Act 1996

Supply of Goods and Services Act 1982
Trade Descriptions Acts 1968-72
Unfair Contract Terms Act 1977
Contracts (Rights of Third Parties)
   Act 1999

Projects
Ancient Monuments and Archaeological
   Areas Act 1979
Building Act 1984
Control of Pollution Act 1974
Control of Pollution (Amendment)
   Act 1989
Countryside and Rights of Way Act 2000
Defective Premises Act 1972
Environmental Protection Act 1990
Environment Act 1995
Factories Act 1961
Fire Precautions Act 1971
Highways Act 1980
Historic Building and Ancient Monuments
   Act 1953
Housing Acts 1974-96
Latent Damage Act 1986
Law of Property Acts 1925-69
Licensing Acts 1964-88
Museums and Galleries Act 1992
Noise and Statutory Nuisance Act 1993
Party Wall, etc Act 1996
Planning and Compensation Act 1991
Planning (Listed Buildings and
Conservation Areas) Act 1990
Prescription Act 1832
Rights of Light Act 1959
Safety of Sports Grounds Act 1975
Sale and Supply of Goods Act 1994
Town and Country Planning Act 1990
Wildlife and Countryside Act 1981

3.5.1 Human Rights Act 1998

This Act, which came into effect on 2nd October 2000, introduced the European Convention on Human Rights into British law, and means that anyone wishing to pursue an action where they believe their rights under the Convention have been violated may do so in the British courts rather than the European Court of Human Rights. The Act also requires public bodies to act in a way which is compatible with the Convention. The Convention includes such rights as the right to life, to freedom from torture and slavery, and the right to a fair and public trial. If a court believes that an Act of Parliament is a breach of human rights, it may require the government to reconsider the Act. If it believes a piece of secondary legislation breaches rights, it may set it to one side. The court may award damages against a public body who has violated a person's rights. This Act is of particular relevance to issues such as Planning Application procedures and dispute resolution.

3.5.2 Supply of Goods and Services Act 1982

This statute covers contracts for work and materials, contracts for the hire of goods, and contracts for services. Most construction contracts come under the category of 'work and materials'. For these contracts the Act implies terms regarding care and skill, time of performance and consideration. For example, section 14 implies a term that where the supplier is acting in the course of business, the supplier will carry out the services within a reasonable time, provided of course the parties have not agreed terms regarding time themselves.

3.5.3 Defective Premises Act 1972

This Act applies where work is carried out in connection with a dwelling, including design work. It states that 'a person taking on work in connection with the provision of a dwelling owes a duty to see that the work which he takes on is done in a workmanlike or, as the case may be, professional manner, with proper materials and so that as regards that work the dwelling will be fit for habitation when completed' (section 1(1)). This appears to be a strict liability, and is owed to anyone acquiring an interest in the dwelling.

3.5.4 Unfair Contract Terms Act 1977

This has the effect of rendering various exclusion clauses void including: any clauses excluding liability for death or personal injury resulting from negligence; any clauses attempting to exclude liability for Sale of Goods Act 1979 section 12 obligations (and the equivalent under the Supply of Goods and Services Act); any clauses attempting to exclude liability for Sale of Goods Act 1979 sections 13, 14 or 15 obligations (and the equivalent under the Supply of Goods and Services Act) where they are operating against any person dealing as consumer. It also renders certain other exclusion clauses void insofar as they fail to satisfy a test of reasonableness, e.g. liability for negligence other than liability for death or personal injury, and liability for breach of sections 13, 14 and 15 obligations in contracts which do not involve a consumer.

3.5.5 Unfair Terms In Consumer Contracts Regulations 1994

These only apply to terms in contracts between a seller of goods or supplier of goods and services and a consumer, and where the terms have not been individually negotiated (this would generally include all standard forms). A consumer is defined as a person who in making a contract, is acting 'for purposes which are outside his business' (section 2). An 'unfair term' is any term which causes a significant imbalance in the parties' rights to the detriment of the consumer, and the regulations state that any such term will not be binding on the consumer. An indicative list of terms is given in schedule 3 and includes, for example 'any term excluding or hindering the consumer's right to take legal action ... particularly by requiring the consumer to take the dispute to arbitration...' It is important, therefore, that if the arbitration option is selected, or if any other amendments are made which could be seen as limiting the employer's rights, that these have been explained and discussed, in order that they can be considered to have been individually negotiated.

3.5.6 The Housing Grants, Construction and Regeneration Act 1996

This requires that all construction contracts falling within the definition of the Act contain certain provisions including the right to stage payments, the right to notice of the amount to be paid, the right to suspend work for non-payment, and the right to take any dispute arising out of the contract to adjudication. If the parties fail to include these provisions in their contract, the Act will imply terms to provide these rights (section 114) by means of The Scheme for Construction Contracts (England and Wales) Regulations 1998. The Act's definition of 'construction contract' includes the appointment of a professional. The Act is of broad application, but with one important exception in the context of minor works – it does not apply to a 'construction contract' with a residential occupier. This means an appointment relating to operations on a dwelling which the client occupies or intends to occupy (section 106). However, work on other residential properties, for example for landlords, Local Authorities or Housing Associations, will usually be covered by the Act.

3.5.7 Contracts (Rights of Third Parties) Act 1999

This Act provides that where a term of contract expressly confers, or purports to confer, a right on a person who is not a party to that contract, the party has the right to enforce that term. It is possible to exclude this right, and all standard forms of appointment published by the RIBA contain an exclusion clause, to prevent third parties bringing claims against the architect. Architects should ensure that an exclusion clause is included in any non standard terms to which they agree.

3.5.8 Late Payment of Commercial Debts (Interest) Act 1998

This Act implies a term into any contract to which the Act applies that any qualifying debt created by the contract carries simple interest in accordance with the Act. The contract may avoid the provisions of the Act being implied if it includes terms which give a 'substantial remedy' of interest on any late payment of an amount due. The contracts to which the act applies would include most forms of construction contract or professional appointment. A debt could be created by the obligation to pay a certified amount or fee, and interest will start to run the day after the debt becomes due. The Secretary of State has the power to set the rate of interest due.

3.6 Sources of information

Architects need an awareness of the legislation that applies to particular situations and a working knowledge of the consequences of its application. In a High Court case in recent years, the judge commented that where the client pays for independent and skilled advice he is entitled to just that, and the architect should not simply have accepted without question the view or opinions of a planning officer of a local authority, operating a policy which was wrong in law. He said that architects are not expected to have an expert knowledge of the legislation, but they need to know what is required in terms of compliance, and what procedures need to be adopted.

3.6.1 Relevant texts and sources of information

Architects should have acquired a basic understanding of those areas of law generally relevant to the practice of architecture in order to satisfy the requirements for registration. As a refresher to this knowledge, easy to read books such as *Learning the Law* by the late Professor Glanville Williams might be found helpful.

For a more detailed knowledge of law relevant to specific areas or for situations which arise in practice, architects are advised as follows:

- Refer to texts (preferably those written by lawyers with architect readers in mind). The RIBA *List of Recommended Books* is published annually and includes selected titles on practice and legal matters, e.g. procurement, design liability, building contracts, contract administration, arbitration, etc. A law dictionary such as Osborn's *Concise Law Dictionary* will also be useful.

- Subscribe to, or make arrangements to access, case law reports and other authoritative texts, e.g. *Building Law Reports*, *Construction Law Reports*, *Construction Law Digest*, *Construction Industry Law Letter*, etc. These will often be available for reference at libraries in universities with architecture or law departments.

- Refer to authoritative and up-to-date annotated legislation such as will be found in *Halsbury's Statutes*, *Current Law Statutes*, or *Statutes in Force*. Such reference works will usually be available at university law libraries.

- Data bases such as Lexis-Nexis, which holds all reported recent case law, may also be available, but a charge will normally be made for this kind of service.

- Use the RIBA Members' Information Centre for specific queries, or seek advice by telephone from the RIBA Specialist Practice Consultants through the members' subscription line.

- Keep up to date on developments in the law relevant to practice by reading the technical press and perhaps compiling a file of articles from, for example, the RIBA *Journal*, *Architects' Journal*, and the legal sections from *Building*. Attend CPD events and seminars which feature practice issues and often include legal topics.

Some architects may wish to develop their expertise further and perform associated roles such as:

- Adjudicator: the RIBA is an appointing body for qualified persons to act under the adjudication provisions of section 108 of the Housing Grants, Construction and Regeneration Act 1996.
- Arbitrator: the RIBA President is an appointor in cases of disputes to be determined by an arbitrator.
- Conciliator: the RIBA administers a Conciliation Scheme in collaboration with its Regional Directors, where disputes arise over architect-client agreements.
- Expert: where the architect acts as an expert to determine disputes (although not as an arbitrator), or acts as an expert witness, a quite different role.

Such persons might also wish to join like-minded architects in membership of one or more of the specialist professional groups. Among these are:

Architects' Law Forum (ALF)

A law society for architects involved with or interested in construction law, under the aegis of the RIBA. It holds regular meetings at Portland Place and facilitates the dissemination and sharing of knowledge. It seeks to promote the cause and appointment of architects in arbitration, alternative dispute resolution, as expert witnesses, etc. Further information may be obtained from the Honorary Secretary, Architects' Law Forum, c/o 66 Portland Place, London W1N 4AD.

Society of Construction Law (SCL)

Formed in 1983 to enable those interested in construction law to meet and discuss matters of common interest. It provides a forum for lawyers and non-lawyers alike, and meets on a regular basis, usually at King's College, London. Further information may be obtained from The Society of Construction Law, The Old Watch House, King's College, London WC2R 2LS.

Chartered Institute of Arbitrators (CIArb)

Founded in 1915 and a multi-disciplinary organisation with worldwide membership, its primary object is to promote and facilitate the determination of disputes by arbitration, but it is also active in promoting other means of dispute resolution. Publishes a quarterly journal, *Arbitration*, and organises a wide range of activities nationally, internationally, and locally through its branch network. Further information may be obtained from The Secretary General, Chartered Institute of Arbitrators, International Arbitration Centre, 12 Bloomsbury Square, London WC1A 2LP.

Architects with a sufficient grasp of legal considerations should be able to recognise possible hazards, legal or otherwise, and the likely consequences if the right kind of professional advice is not sought at the appropriate time. Architects should take care to avoid making unwarranted assumptions or sweeping generalisations when faced with reports of case law and interpretations of legislation. They should be able to recognise the nature of the legal problems entailed, and seek appropriate legal advice.

Many architects enjoy long and mutually beneficial association with solicitors; sound legal advice can save a great deal of money and worry in the long term. Information on suitable firms of solicitors currently in practice, together with particulars of their expertise, may be obtained from The Law Society, or by referring to a recent edition of *Waterlow's Solicitors' and Barristers' Directory*, or similar.

References and further reading

Burns, A. (1994) *The Legal Obligations of the Architect*, London, Butterworths.

Lavers, A. and Chappell, D. (2000) *A Legal Guide to the Professional Liability of Architects*, London, Chappell-Marshall.

Speight, A. and Stone, G. (2000) *Architect's Legal Handbook*, London, Butterworth-Heinemann.

Waterlow's Solicitors' and Barristers' Directory, London, Waterlow.

Williams, G. (1982) *Learning the Law*, London, Stevens and Sons.

4 SETTING UP A PRACTICE

4.1 Forms of practice
4.1.1   The sole principal
4.1.2   The partnership
4.1.3   The unlimited liability company
4.1.4   The limited liability company (Ltd)
4.1.5   Considering incorporation
4.1.6   The public limited liability company (Plc)
4.1.7   The limited partnership
4.1.8   The limited liability partnership (Llp)
4.1.9   Cooperative and collaborative arrangements
4.1.10 Other formal and informal arrangements

4.2 Developing a business strategy
4.2.1   SWOT analysis

4.3 Business advisors
4.3.1   Accountants
4.3.2   Legal advisors
4.3.3   Clearing banks
4.3.4   Insurance brokers

4.4 Business premises
4.4.1   Suitability
4.4.2   Location
4.4.3   Requirements
4.4.4   Acquiring premises
4.4.5   Managing the premises

4.1 Forms of practice

There are no legal restrictions on the form of practice architects might decide to adopt for the operation of their businesses.

4.1.1 The sole principal

An architect may practise as a sole principal either entirely alone, or with a few or several employed staff to assist. Many architects choose this form of practice as they are attracted by the freedom of carrying on a business on their own account, in tune with their own talents, over which they have absolute control. Although the portfolio of work of sole principals is sometimes limited to very small projects, this is not necessarily the case, and sole practitioners can often handle a limited number of medium range projects, particularly if they have efficient IT systems in place and employ or sub-contract some assistance. However, this is one of the hardest forms of practice in that sole principals can sometimes feel isolated from their fellow professionals. Whilst they are entitled to all the profits from the business, they also have to manage it single-handed and face the risks alone. Sole principals are responsible for debts and any damages awarded against them for breach of contract or tort, and are liable to the full extent of their personal and business assets. They can be made bankrupt.

4.1.2 The partnership

The Partnership Act 1890, defines partnership as 'the relationship which exists between two or more persons carrying on business in common with a view to profit'. Although there is no legal requirement for a written agreement, it is usual for a partnership to be established by a formal deed of partnership which set out the rights and responsibilities of the partners. These should be discussed and agreed before they are written into the deed, which should ultimately be drawn up by a solicitor. Compatibility of objectives, skills and personalities is of crucial importance in a partnership, and the executive responsibilities of each partner must be clearly identified. Matters such as the name of the practice, the apportioning of profits and losses, payment of interest on capital, and banking arrangements and authority should be agreed and recorded in the partnership deed. Other matters it should clarify are pension provision, retirement, and the admission of new partners. It is usual to include an arbitration clause to cover dispute resolution.

In a partnership the equity is owned by the partners; they share both the profits and the risks, and have the right to participate in the daily management of the business. Partnership offers many advantages, and it is a popular form of practice. It is generally more efficient for several principals to combine staff, facilities, accommodation, etc, although this could be done without forming a partnership (see below). The key advantages lie in the profit sharing, the greater potential for new work through the pooling of client contacts, the security a partnership offers to a client and, of course, the benefits of sharing and developing design ideas. However, partnership carries with it a high level of individual responsibility and risk.

Each partner is liable jointly with the others for all debts and obligations incurred while a partner, and should he or she die, this liability falls upon the estate. The partnership is liable for all negligent acts committed by any one of its partners, even though the others might have taken no part in such negligent action. The same applies to people who were partners at the time, but who have subsequently retired from the practice. A partner's liability extends to all his or her business and personal assets. Someone bringing action for damages against a partnership may bring it against one or several partners, or against the partnership as a whole, or any combination of these. If brought against one person, that partner may recover the damages from the others but initially may have to bear the loss alone.

To join an existing partnership, a new partner will in some cases have to 'buy in' to the partnership. This will involve contributing a capital sum which is calculated on the basis of the share of the annual profits which the partners will receive. As it is often difficult for a young partner to raise this sum, it is usually paid in stages over several years. These days it is increasingly common to offer a share in the partnership without any capital sum requirement, but in return the partner agrees to leave a proportion of earnings in the partnership as working capital. In some cases, the partnership agreement provides for a salary to be paid to one or more of the partners in addition to a share in the profits. Such partners are referred to as 'salaried partners'. This is often a difficult position to be in, as the share of the profits is often very small, yet the liability is no less than that of the other partners.

New partners are sometimes drawn from outside the practice, but as a great deal of mutual knowledge and understanding is needed to make a partnership work successfully, they are frequently appointed internally. In many practices promising staff and potential partners are offered 'associate-ships'. An associate does not normally share in the profits or risk, although they are often placed on a bonus scheme, and may be offered other advantages such as a health care package.

When a partner retires or leaves the partnership this does not remove liability, and similarly liability is not removed if the partnership dissolves. It is usual for partnerships to retain professional indemnity cover for any retired members.

4.1.3 The unlimited liability company

Very few practices are in the form of unlimited liability companies. The main advantage is that, unlike a partnership, a director's liability ceases 12 months after he or she leaves the company. There is also no requirement for filing reports with the Registrar of Companies. However, members of an unlimited liability company can be required to contribute personally if the company's assets are not sufficient to pay its debts.

4.1.4 The limited liability company (Ltd)

The limited liability company is a legal entity separate from its members (i.e. shareholders), where the liability of each shareholder is limited to the nominal value of his or her shareholding.

It is governed by the Companies Acts 1985 and 1989 and must register with the Registrar of Companies. There is no limit to the number of members, although if it falls to lower than two for a period of over six months that member can incur personal liability. Companies must have a company secretary and at least one director. Annual audited accounts must be filed with the Registrar where they are available for public inspection.

A company has a clearly identified management structure administered by a board of directors, who are all paid a salary. The senior level of management might include equity and non-equity directors (i.e. directors who are not shareholders). Under this structure, young architects of calibre are not deterred from reaching the top of a firm by the prospect of having to buy themselves in, as they might have to with a partnership, as they can be appointed directors on a salary. Non-architectural staff of calibre, such as finance, computer or office managers, are also able to enhance their status and progress their careers as well-rewarded directors. In both cases remuneration could be increased if share options are available.

Under English law, directors and other employees, as agents of the company they serve, generally enjoy immunity from personal liability for the company's debts and its obligations towards third parties. However, all employees of a company owe a duty of care to the company itself.

Numerous architectural practices sought incorporation in the 1980s and early 1990s, and while a notable few have prospered, many have not. With the benefit of hindsight, general reasons for such failures would appear to be over-optimism about economic prospects for the construction industry, and a mistaken belief that trading as a company would provide total protection of personal assets for directors. However, a more obvious cause of failure in many instances was that firms did not seek the best available legal and financial advice.

A partnership considering incorporation may at first glance identify many attractive operational advantages:

- The directors are not normally personally liable for the debts of the company.
- It is easier for a company than a partnership to raise outside finance, as security can more readily be created over the assets of a company.
- The taxation position is relatively simple and overall taxation is likely to be lower than for a partnership.
- All employees, including directors, are subject to PAYE, which they may prefer as it avoids sudden large tax demands later.
- All salaries, including directors', are deductible before calculation of profit for corporation tax purposes.
- An interest in a company may be given more readily than in a partnership, by making architects and non-architects with useful expertise directors on a salary or shareholders.
- It is easier to remove an unsatisfactory director than an unsatisfactory partner.
- The company does not dissolve when a director leaves or shares change hands, and there are no complex legal procedures involved.
- Companies are internationally recognised, therefore it may be easier in many cases to develop business relations overseas than it would be with a partnership.

However, other issues may not be quite so straightforward and should be given careful consideration:

Management

An apparent advantage of incorporation is that the separation of ownership from the management should lead to improvements in operational efficiency and cost-effectiveness. However, in the company situation there is always a danger that ownership may pass outside the original architectural proprietor, whose professional control and influence may thereby be diminished.

Companies have to comply with the formalities laid down by the Companies Act, which relate to all aspects of the company's formation and operation. Management is therefore less flexible than with a partnership and there is a considerable additional administrative and financial burden. Companies whose turnover exceeds a certain limit are required to have their audited accounts published, whereas a partnership is able to keep its financial affairs confidential. Companies also have a duty to provide their shareholders with appropriate information, and this can be a significant extra cost.

Liability

The personal assets of a director of a company are not as safe as many think them to be, especially if the directors conduct their business without regard to the detailed legislation governing the management of companies. Trading through an incorporated business does, in theory, limit the liability of shareholders to the extent of the funds that they contribute as share capital, but this advantage tends to be eroded because shareholders and directors are often required to give personal guarantees to the company's bankers. However, there remains some protection for shareholders and directors where trade creditors are concerned.

Pension provision

The pension benefits that can be provided for directors and employees of a limited company tend to be more beneficial than those that can be provided via retirement annuity and personal pension schemes entered into by an individual.

The benefits that a company pension scheme can provide are, in the main, flexible and generous, depending on the type of scheme adopted. The company's contributions into the pension scheme are generally deductible in calculating the company's taxable profits. This should be compared with the fairly rigid limits that apply to the tax relief available on contributions into retirement annuity and personal pension schemes.

Professional indemnity insurance

In terms of exposure to indemnity claims, a change from partnership to limited company does not materially change the risk from the insurer's point of view. However, the insured will now be the company, a separate legal identity from its directors. The policy must therefore be extended to indemnify the individual directors and employees as well as the company. It is vital that any change, whether to a new partnership or to a company, does not leave the practice unprotected vis-à-vis its continuing liability for claims. It may be best to incorporate this cover in the new policy, but legal advice should be taken.

Tax and National Insurance

The implications of incorporation for tax and National Insurance can be significant because, at the time of writing, there are different rules for employees/directors of a company and self-employed persons/partners. However, a potential tax advantage for companies is the ability to defer tax liabilities by retaining profits within the company, rather than paying them out as remuneration or dividends.

Passing on the business

The proprietors of the business should always consider their future intentions as regards disposing of or passing on a family business. Trading through a limited company has the advantage that shares in the company can be gifted to other members of the family as potentially exempt transfers for inheritance tax purposes. Therefore such gifts can be made without there necessarily being any effect on the running of the business.

A fundamental disadvantage of trading via the medium of a company is the potential double tax charge that can arise on winding up the firm. The company pays corporation tax on retained profits and also on any gains that it makes, and individual shareholders will also pay capital gains tax on the disposal of their shares. This only becomes a problem where assets or the business of the company are sold. If the business is expected to run for many years and pass to future generations, this point may not be of concern to the proprietors.

4.1.5 Considering incorporation

The practicalities of incorporating a business do tend to be underestimated, and it is important to consider all taxes and their impact on the parties involved. It should also be borne in mind that it is difficult to dis-incorporate a business once it has been incorporated, so it is not a decision to be taken lightly.

Clients should be advised of any change in the composition or form of a practice, and the firm's advisors should be asked about the legal implications and how clients may best be notified. Some clients would prefer to trade with partnerships as they consider the formation of a company to be unprofessional. They may see it as an attempt to avoid personal responsibility for work undertaken, as in extreme circumstances a company can be wound up, whereas partners remain liable even after the partnership dissolves. This notion of 'unprofessionalism' is often a key factor in practices deciding to remain as partnerships.

4.1.6 The public limited liability company (Plc)

The difference between the Ltd company and the Plc is that members of the public may buy and sell shares of the latter. The Plc also requires a higher level of share capital and has to operate under stricter rules. A company that intends to offer its shares for sale to the public must register as a public company, include the letters 'Plc' after its name, and have a subscribed share capital of not less than £50,000. It cannot obtain a certificate from the Registrar of Companies to allow it to start trading until the stipulated sum has been subscribed. It should be noted that a practice which becomes a public limited company will not be able to continue to describe itself as 'architects', as it will fall foul of the ARB requirement that such a practice should be controlled by architects.

4.1.7 The limited partnership

A limited partnership must be registered under the Limited Partnership Act 1907. In this form of practice one or more of the partners must agree to be responsible for all the liabilities of the practice. It is possible to have other partners who contribute capital to the partnership, but their liability is limited to the proportion of capital they contribute. It is very little used, its only advantage being to enable the taking on of partners who would otherwise be unwilling to contribute due to the liability position.

4.1.8 The limited liability partnership (Llp)

This is a new form of practice, governed by the Limited Liability Partnership Act 2000, which combines some of the characteristics of both partnerships and limited liability companies. It is a separate legal entity distinct from its members. It is treated as a partnership for the purpose of UK income tax and capital gains tax. It must register with the Registrar of Companies and must send annual audited accounts to the Registrar. The members are not jointly and severally liable in the normal course of their business, and their liability is limited to their stakehold in the partnership. There is no requirement to appoint directors.

Internally the Llp may be run very much like a partnership, in that it has complete freedom of internal organisation, except that two people must be designated to perform duties similar to that of a company secretary and director. Externally, however, they are accountable in a similar way to companies.

4.1.9 Cooperative and collaborative arrangements

The terms cooperative and collaborative are used to describe various forms of practice. There are a number of registered architects' cooperatives and these are in effect workers' cooperatives. Those who work in the enterprise both own and control it.

A cooperative may be owned collectively, in which case nobody has an individual shareholding beyond a nominal £1, and it is a common ownership cooperative. This is the type most frequently found in architecture, often for ideological reasons.

There is also a co-ownership cooperative in which dividend-earning shares are held by the members. In some schemes the shares remain at a fixed value, whilst in others they increase or decrease according to the value of the business. Control is dependent on votes (one per person) and is independent of shares. Where an established partnership is converting to a cooperative, this model might be more appropriate, as long-standing partners can hold personal shares commensurate with the value of the assets they have built up.

Both types of cooperative can be legally established either by registering as a cooperative with the Register of Friendly Societies under the Industrial and Provident Societies Acts 1965-87, or with the Registrar of Companies as a company limited by guarantee of £1 per member. Both kinds of organisation carry limited liability.

4.1.10 Other formal and informal arrangements

Two or more firms may arrange to assist each other with varying degrees of commitment on individual projects, or a range of specialisations, or other market activities. This is likely to be short-term cooperation on an informal basis. Other firms might wish to engage in a continuing association, either for mutual help or the sharing of facilities, but stopping short of carrying out projects jointly. On a more formal basis, firms may wish to join in partnership for a particular project, exercising a joint venture method of working. This would need to be a legally constituted arrangement with joint and several liability.

Firms of different disciplines may elect to collaborate by establishing a consortium arrangement which could offer the benefits of an integrated approach. Such an arrangement could simply be a continuing informal association, or one which carried out projects jointly. The identity of each firm in the consortium could still be retained for other concurrent projects handled separately.

Whenever formal collaborative arrangements are contemplated, appropriate legal advice should be sought, and professional indemnity insurance arranged to cover the particular situation.

The opportunities for practice in the European Union are likely to increase as British architects explore the potential of the wider market. The forging of links between British and overseas practices provides informal means of promoting joint architectural opportunities. More formal associations and collaborative working can be expected to develop as business relationships are actively encouraged by Chambers of Commerce in the respective countries. In some cases British-based firms have opened branches or subsidiaries abroad, whilst others have elected to collaborate with local practices in carrying out projects. Legal systems and insurance obligations in particular differ throughout Europe, and any arrangements for collaborative working should be subject to appropriate legal advice.

4.2   Developing a business strategy

At any point in its life, a practice should be operating in the context of a described strategy: it should know where it is going and how it is going to get there. It is important to set goals and work to them, both as a means of quantifying achievement and as an expression of purposeful leadership which unites the efforts of all those who work for the practice, and focuses them on worthwhile objectives.

Every new practice should formulate a business strategy. Its existence allows the principals to evaluate their decision-making against a described position, and the plan itself will constitute the basis of the practice's Business Plan when it needs to seek funds or financial backing. It should cover a period of between three and five years – the fluctuating nature of architectural work makes it difficult to make more distant assumptions and predictions. Short-term targets will be set in the firm's annual budget. Formulating the strategy will take much time and thought, and an honest and objective attitude will be needed.

An existing practice will need, first, to evaluate the current position of the business; second, to decide where the principals would like the business to be in, say, five years' time; and third, to devise an operational plan for moving the business from its current position towards achieving its defined objectives. An example schedule of goals is given as Figure 3.

Figure 3: Example schedule of goals and targets

Goals	Targets
1 To achieve steady and significant growth in the existing design practice.	1 Set a target % growth rate over the next five years.
2 To expand the geographic base of the practice by opening new offices.	2 Establish a London office and an EU link-up by a given date.
3 To set up a separate section or wholly owned subsidiaries to exploit related fields, e.g: • energy surveys and audits; • interior design and total furnishing contracts; • facilities management.	3 Set up at least two sections or subsidiaries providing positive contributions within the next five years.
4 To establish improved management throughout the practice.	4 Evaluate the current management structure and the effectiveness of staff training and career development.
5 To achieve a high reputation for design and quality of service.	5 Draw up an appropriate CPD programme immediately. Institute a quality management system and auditing procedures.
6 To achieve financial security for the practice as a whole.	6 Reassess the financial gearing of the firm. Aim to reduce debt capital by a specified amount.

The practice's current position could be assessed under the following headings:

- A review of its development and achievements.
- An evaluation of its position in the market-place.
- An assessment of its design philosophy and standards.
- A review of its staffing levels and organisation.
- An analysis of its financial performance over the last three years.
- A summary of its Strengths and Weaknesses, what its Opportunities are, and where it faces Threats (SWOT).

4.2.1 SWOT analysis

Self-analysis can make a valuable contribution to the practice's assessment of where it is and where it wants to go. Various techniques have been developed and the SWOT method is well-tried.

A SWOT analysis will enable managers at all levels to describe their current positions and think about the way the practice should be going in the future. They are invited to schedule their perception of the strengths and weaknesses of the organisation (i.e. internal issues) and what they see as its opportunities and threats (i.e. external influences). The results are reviewed and analysed by various working groups to identify priorities; the findings are then summarised and presented. An example SWOT exercise is included as Figure 4. An alternative would be to hold structured discussions or a 'brainstorming' session at senior management level, which could work to an agenda of set questions on the same lines as the SWOT method.

Evaluating the implications

Once objectives have been defined, their implications will need to be evaluated, described and quantified. For example, if a principal objective is to increase turnover by a stated percentage, the implications might include:

- an increase in marketing effort;
- the prediction of future levels of income, expenditure and profit to support the growth targeted;
- an increase in staff resources by recruitment or retraining;
- increased logistical support, such as new information technology;
- the cost implications overall.

Most of these issues will require investigation in their own right and could be made the responsibility of various members of senior management.

The business strategy must be flexible enough to be able to respond to market forces and not to collapse if circumstances change. If its predictions fail to materialise it may have to be revised, and it is important to consider how this might affect the practice's staff, workload and finances.

Staff consultation

Principals are often reluctant to discuss strategic and financial matters with staff, but when anything as fundamental as the rationale and direction of the practice is under review, it is in the interests of the practice as a whole to allow as wide a consultation as possible, since the operational matters arising are of immediate interest and importance to staff. They will be more prepared to identify with new thinking or a change in pace or direction if they have been involved in the decision-making leading up to it.

Figure 4: Example of a SWOT exercise

1 EVALUATION

Strengths:
- Confident leadership.
- Staff with good mix of skills.
- Good commercial awareness.
- Strong client base.
- High quality professional service.
- Plenty of repeat work.

Weaknesses:
- Senior management personality-dominated, youngest is over fifty.
- Over-confidence about job-getting; some clients are known to be high risk.
- Management decisions often intuitive; rule of thumb job costing.
- Long-term viability of firm may be threatened when top management retires.
- Staff loyalty taken for granted, some acknowledged salary anomalies.
- Old-fashioned administrative set-up.

Opportunities:
- Regional work opportunities materialising; could open a branch office.
- Upturn in conservation work; could import specialist staff to exploit situation.
- Demonstrable track record in green buildings; could tap into current public awareness.
- Invitation to write one of a series of practice articles in technical press; could get some useful publicity.

Threats:
- Two new design practices recently opened in head office area.
- Economic climate uncertain.
- General election within the next 24 months may reverse funding policies.
- Certain key staff have been approached by competitors.
- Two former and one existing client have gone out of business.

2 ASSESSMENT

What kind of picture emerges so far?

Here is an apparently thriving practice, well liked in the local business community, with strong leadership, competent staff and a reputation for providing a good professional service. It admits it has some weaknesses and fully intends to get round to dealing with them – one day. It is doubtful about moving further into uncertain territory such as new construction or information technology. It is well aware that it might be advantageous commercially to seek QA certification, but feels that the practice is not suited to a procedures-dominated style of operation and dislikes the necessary disturbance that such changes will bring. It considers marketing to be unnecessary and slightly undignified.

Its attitudes might be expressed like this:
- 'You have to admit we're doing pretty well.'
- 'The trouble with change is it brings hassle and problems with staff – and clients might not like new procedures.'
- 'Everyone has problems: of course we'll deal with them – if they become serious.'
- 'Competitors? Good luck to them: our clients will stay loyal.'
- 'It's too soon to upgrade our computer system – and all that retraining.'
- 'Marketing is a bit pushy for a practice like ours. We don't really need it.'
- 'We're thinking about quality management, but clients may think our fees will go up. And to go the whole hog and seek certification takes years and years . . .'

It may be that as long as the status quo continues, all will be well. Unfortunately the status quo is vulnerable to a great many influences that are outside a practice's control, and as soon as there is some significant change the whole management rationale may be overturned. One alternative is to leave well alone and hope for the best; the other is to recognise the potential dangers and take immediate and positive action.

3 ACTION

- Revise the management structure so that younger staff are given more responsibility and influence.
- Review technical, financial and administrative procedures. Then consider, with experts if necessary, whether the practice would benefit from instituting a quality management system and/or installing an up-to-date computer system.
- Fend off competition by instituting a marketing initiative directed at new and existing clients.
- Deal promptly with any salary anomalies; this is the sort of aggravation that tempts staff to move on – particularly if there is competition close at hand.
- Take steps to consolidate the financial basis of the firm: reassess gearing, consider whether a different form of practice could bring benefits and greater security.

4.3   Business advisors

The support of good advisors is essential for successful business management: the accountant and the solicitor are the two key long-term professional consultants that all practices need sooner or later. It is wise to look for firms who have other architect clients and will know the kind of special needs that architectural work generates. A fellow practitioner may be able to recommend someone suitable, but otherwise the practice must either make its own enquiries or approach the relevant professional institute. It is important to consider a firm's reputation and prosperity, whether the range of services offered will meet its current and future needs, and whether its offices are conveniently placed. It is also wise to consider whether the attitude and philosophy of the firm is in tune with that of the practice – whether, that is, the professional chemistry is right.

Other advice that will be needed on setting up a practice will be from the bank (often to arrange a start-up loan), and from insurance brokers to arrange professional indemnity and, if appropriate, premises insurance.

4.3.1 Accountants

An accountant is a professional keeper and inspector of accounts. J. Smith ACA would be a chartered accountant, i.e. an associate member of the Institute of Chartered Accountants in England and Wales. Accountancy firms vary in size from the small office that offers mainly auditing and tax advice, to the large prestigious firm with an international network of offices offering a wide range of financial and management services.

The standard services that an architectural practice might engage an accountant to provide are:

- preparation of the firm's annual audit;
- advice on tax matters;
- advice on book-keeping procedures;
- advice about the practice's financial state of affairs.

Many accountancy firms also provide management consultancy services, and some offer services connected with corporate recovery and insolvency, and corporate finance and investigations.

Under the Companies Act every company above a certain size is required to submit audited accounts to Companies House where they can be inspected by interested parties. Accounts also have to be submitted to the Inland Revenue. The auditors' duty is to review the accounts and the systems from which they are derived and give a professional opinion as to whether they give 'a true and fair view' of the company's results.

The question of fees should be clarified at the outset of the consultancy and it is important, particularly when any extensive piece of work is commissioned, to set a budget for it and to stipulate that this is not to be exceeded without express permission. It is desirable to build up a good working relationship with the accountant; not only can he or she save the practice money in the short term, but may be able to warn it of troubles ahead.

4.3.2 Legal advisors

Legal services are provided by solicitors and barristers. Lawyers qualified in other jurisdictions are available if such special advice is needed, and lawyers employed by banks and accountants will often offer an advisory service to third parties. Since 1990 it has been possible for architects to instruct barristers directly without having to use a solicitor as an intermediary.

The legal services that an architectural practice might require are various. Its first needs might relate to the form of practice to be adopted and the conveyancing of practice premises, followed by a continuing general consultancy as the practice finds its feet. It may need specialist legal advice about building contract conditions and claims, professional indemnity, construction litigation, planning legislation, copyright of drawings and so on.

Fees are likely to be on a retainer basis to cover routine and day-to-day advice, and time-charged for major consultancies. As with architects' work, there are various hourly rates, and the procedures for charging expenses and disbursements and for billing will need to be agreed. Solicitors have to be meticulous in their work, and it may come as a surprise to the architect client to be charged for amounts as small as the price of a first-class postage stamp. There are lessons to be learned from the way the legal profession renders its accounts.C

4.3.3 Clearing banks

It is in the interests of banks to support local business initiatives, and they are usually ready to lend money if they consider that a firm's approach is businesslike and its prospects are good. Banks make money from the interest they charge on loans and are usually prepared to allow a running overdraft provided they are confident that the architect will be in a position to pay the interest. Similarly they will be pleased to see sensible intentions for business expansion – which may mean an increased need for borrowing.

Although banking has become an intensively competitive business, banks are aware that the best way to keep their customers is to give them support and advice, and this can be invaluable, particularly to a new architectural practice.

A wide range of banking services is available, some of which may help a practice to streamline its financial administration. For example, payment of creditors' accounts can be made through BACS (Bank Automated Clearing Service) as an alternative to making payments by cheque, although this is probably only worthwhile where more than 100 or so cheques a month are prepared. Arrangements can also be made whereby surplus funds in current accounts are automatically transferred into an interest-earning account as soon as they reach an agreed level. New electronic services are coming on stream all the time, and it is always worth seeking the bank's advice about ways of making the most of the practice's finances.

4.3.4 Insurance brokers

A broker is an intermediary between two parties – in the case of insurance, between an insurer and the person buying the insurance. Until the 1977 Insurance Brokers (Registration) Act, anyone could call themselves an insurance broker; now only registered brokers can do this, although anyone can operate as a broker under any other name or description.

The insurance broker's remuneration is the commission he or she receives from the insurer.

It is important to remember that insurance brokers are therefore not obliged to place the interests of the client first: they are commission-driven, and the service they offer should not be compared with that provided by, say, the accounting or legal profession. Insurance claims are evaluated and met (or not, as the case may be) by the insurer, not the insurance broker.

Insurance brokers are well placed to give advice about the best deals going among the insurance companies, their promptness or otherwise in meeting claims, and which companies specialise in the particular insurance cover required. Firms of insurance brokers tend to specialise in certain types of insurance cover, and as soon as the first job comes in an architect will need to look for one who specialises in professional indemnity insurance. Risk management, including trade credit risks, is another specialism of interest, and so is claims handling.

4.4 Business premises

After salaries, premises are usually the most significant outlay in any organisation, often taking up to 20 per cent of a firm's revenue. The adequacy and suitability of premises should therefore be a policy matter which is kept under regular review.

Organisations constantly change and develop, and as a result there may be a need to increase accommodation or use space more efficiently. Furniture and equipment rapidly becomes obsolete, and the effectiveness of environmental control may need improving. It is essential to make one person in the practice responsible for the review and management of all matters relating to premises.

4.4.1 Suitability

A number of interrelated factors need to be considered when evaluating the suitability of premises as follows:

- The size of the practice (e.g. the number of permanent and temporary staff both at present and in the foreseeable future); whether the office is headquarters or a branch office; whether the office is a self-contained unit, multi-disciplinary or part of a consortium; whether IT-related work arrangements such as outsourcing, hot desking or telecommuting should be catered for; whether all work stations are planned to be occupied all the time.

- The form and nature of the practice (e.g. sole principal, partnership, company or collaborative); the range of activities and equipment to be accommodated; and the support spaces likely to be needed.

- The organisation and structure of the practice (e.g. hierarchical, functional or egalitarian). This might influence the space planning and standards to be followed; it might determine the appropriate ratio of open plan to cellular layout.

- 'Fit' and 'feel good' factors. What is the preferred shape of the premises relative to the optimum space requirements of the practice; the ratio of dead or unusable space to usable area (at least 85 per cent of the area available should be usable); whether a layout will be compromised by the position of structural members, existing services and other elements; and whether there is likely to be flexibility for sub-division of areas with minimal reorganisation.

- The amount of adjustment needed to bring premises into line with modern standards and current legislative requirements, e.g. the Workplace (Health Safety and Welfare) Regulations 1992 and the Disability Discrimination Act 1996. This will particularly apply to circulation routes, minimum room dimensions, planning of work stations, workers' access to windows, opening and safe cleaning, washing and sanitary conveniences ventilation, lighting, etc. It may be that an access audit will need to be carried out to establish whether major modifications will be needed.

4.4.2 Location

Modern working methods and communications in the electronic age of the lap-top, mobile phone, fax machine, e-mail and networking, in one sense make the location of the office less critical. Working from home might be a satisfactory initial or permanent arrangement given efficient electronic backup and accessibility, but it requires a disciplined attitude and a methodical approach to ensure that all business is conducted in an environment free from domestic interruption. This is more likely where the office can be located in a dedicated area (e.g. converted outbuildings or a purpose-built studio) with a separate entrance for visitors and all necessary support services separate and self-contained.

Otherwise the location of a practice should be a prime consideration, not only in terms of image and identity but also for the sake of accessibility and convenience for staff and visitors. Ideally, there should be good public transport links with shops, restaurants and other amenities.

Where a suite of offices is located within a building, it is important for access to be direct and obvious, the entrance well signed and close to car parking for delivery services and also for visitors. Any staircase or lift to the particular floor should enhance the approach and not be perceived as a barrier. The front door – the point where the design philosophy of the practice becomes clear – should open to the main point of contact, i.e. the reception area and desk. First impressions are all important.

4.4.3 Requirements

Any schedule of office accommodation will include the usual requirements for cellular offices, work stations layouts, conference and interview areas, etc. Other matters for consideration might be:

- Adjustments to the physical features of the premises, if this is a duty of the employer under Section 6 of the Disability Discrimination Act 1995.

- Library, information and research area. Even with electronic and microfiche systems, hard copy is still needed. This could be invaluable when seeking to establish the 'state of the art' on some future occasion.

- Archive arrangements, whether completely or partly in-house. These should be conveniently placed to allow for the orderly deposit and retrieval of key material. Access might be needed for up to 20 years, and lawyers prefer original documents.

- Appropriate amenity areas for staff, e.g. hot and cold drinks machines, kitchen facilities, rest and first-aid area, changing rooms and showers, parking for cycles, etc.

- Smoking areas. If premises are designated as non-smoking, facilities for smokers are best planned to be unobtrusive as well as convenient. The sight of desperate smokers loitering outside a main entrance does not give a businesslike impression.

- Adequate storage for equipment, including survey and site visit gear, materials samples, office supplies and stationery, etc. Difficult to quantify, but often underestimated.

- Requirements relating to premises which arise from legislation include the following:

Occupiers Liability Act 1957

The long title of this Act refers to 'the state of the property or to things done or omitted to be done there', and Section 2 requires that the premises be 'reasonably safe'. This is a provision which could apply to landlords and their tenants.

Fire Precautions Act 1971

A fire certificate might be necessary depending on the number of staff employed, and where they are placed within the building.

The Workplace (Health Safety and Welfare) Regulations 1992

These deal with space allocation, environmental conditions, circulation and sanitary provisions. Note in particular:

Reg 6   Suitable and effective ventilation, natural or mechanical;

Reg 7   Reasonable temperature during working hours, normally at least 16°C;

Reg 8   Suitable and sufficient lighting, natural or artificial. Also refers to fittings, switches, etc;

Reg 10   Sufficient floor area, height and free space at work stations. Allow volume of at least 11 cubic metres per person;

Reg 15   Position and operation of opening windows and roof lights, so as not to endanger occupants;

Reg 17   Organisation of traffic routes, both for people on foot and travelling in vehicles;

Reg 20   Number of sanitary conveniences, accessibility, lighting and ventilation;

Reg 21   Number and suitability of washing facilities;

Reg 22   Provision of 'wholesome' drinking water;

Reg 25   Suitable rest facilities, including where relevant, suitable places to eat meals.

Requirements relating to furniture and fittings arise from the Health and Safety (Display Screen Equipment) Regulations 1992. These concern the use and position of VDU screens and minimum requirements (including environmental) for work stations. (Note that there are regulations governing equipment – see 6.9.)

Fixtures and fittings are usually a major item of office expenditure. At the time of writing, the cost can be set against capital tax allowance, with 25 per cent recoverable in the first year and 25 per cent of the balance recoverable at each subsequent year. As with all tax or revenue matters, it is essential to check the current situation with the firm's accountants. This concession applies only to mobile items or systems, including screens and partitions. If anything is permanently fixed, then recovery will not be possible. In this respect, work stations will usually be mobile, either as assembly or stand-alone items or units in an integrated system. While the latter has attractions, the choice often brings a measure of inflexibility and commits the user to continued use of the same system.

If consideration is being given to taking on a lease on existing premises, requirements should include ensuring that accurate records and plans of the area are available and that there is evidence (e.g. copies of inspection reports) that:

- passenger lifts have been properly maintained at regular intervals;
- electrical equipment and installations have been properly maintained, comply with legislation, and have sufficient capacity for intended loads;
- water systems and water heating installations have been properly maintained.

In addition, it would be advisable to check whether a current Fire Certificate is held (if relevant), and whether a Health and Safety File is deposited in respect of any recent work.

It can sometimes be a good move to bring in an outside firm of architects where a practice needs to remodel premises for its own occupation. An outside firm is likely to take a more objective view and be well removed from any of the influences and constraints often generated by internal politics. The outcome may be both more effective and more economic overall.

4.4.4 Acquiring premises

The acquisition of premises will have a considerable impact on practice finances. The main considerations are the type of tenure and any associated terms of availability or restrictions on the use of the building; the cost of acquisition; the condition of the building and the extent of liability for its maintenance and repair; and costs in use. The basis for rating buildings used for business purposes varies according to the local authority involved. The amount to be paid may be considerable, and it is wise to discover at the outset what it is likely to be.

Whatever method of acquisition is considered, legal and financial advice should always be sought.

Leasing

The most common method of acquiring premises is to lease them for a short, medium or long term. Normally, leasing payments are met out of income, but some capital outlay may be needed if a premium is required or if fixtures and fittings have to be purchased or provided. These costs can sometimes be recovered upon relinquishing the tenancy. There may also be opportunities to sub-let at a profitable rental or to assign a lease for a lump sum consideration.

Occupiers of business premises are given some protection in law, but nevertheless a landlord has the right under certain circumstances to obtain repossession. Leases should be carefully drafted, and a solicitor's advice should always be sought.

Restrictions on use of premises are often introduced in a lease. These should be looked at carefully in the light of future development, because even a change of legal persona or a consortium could be prohibited. Such restrictions could make it difficult to dispose of the lease in mid term.

Also, the conditions under which a lease may be disposed of before its term has run may be limited by the lease itself. The longer the lease the more important it is to have the ability to dispose of it with reasonable freedom. The principal ways in which this may be done, some or all of which may be permitted, are as follows:

- Assignment, i.e. getting another party to take over the unexpired portion of the lease. It may be possible to take a premium. The right to assign may be subject to certain restrictions and may be prohibited entirely. It is certainly likely to be difficult to find a taker for a leasehold interest with less than five years to run.

- Sub-letting, i.e. retaining an interest in the lease but finding a tenant to occupy all or part of the premises and pay a rent. The holder of the lease is still responsible to the landlord. Sub-letting may be specifically prohibited or may be subject to restrictions. In any event, the landlord's consent will usually be required.

- Break clauses. Certain leases permit one or both parties to determine the lease at certain fixed points during the term. The effect of this is that the lease, instead of running for its full period, ends at the earlier date. It is important to be aware whether the landlord has this right. If he has, it is useful to regard the lease as being for the shorter term with the possibility of extension.

Restrictions on hours of access may be introduced in the lease, particularly where circulation includes common areas where the one building is divided between several lessees.

Leases of more than six years usually have a rent review clause, under which rent is to be renegotiated at certain points. New rents are usually adjusted in line with market values, but in some leases the chance of a downward shift is specifically excluded.

Leases should state clearly and precisely the obligations on the lessee concerning repair, maintenance, and insurance. Full repairing terms in a lease should be regarded with caution, and never entered into without an agreed schedule of condition.

Buying or building

Instead of renting or leasing, premises can be bought. If capital is available, the property can be purchased outright. Alternatively, funds may be borrowed. However, it is not always wise to tie up capital in such a way, and buildings are not necessarily a good investment. Professional advice should always be sought on the merits of a particular course of action at a particular time.

Building brings the obvious attraction of accommodation customised to the needs of a practice. It might also be possible to secure income by letting part of the premises, perhaps to another construction professional.

Sale and lease-back

Having purchased or built new accommodation, the asset may then be sold subject to the granting back of a lease. This permits the release of invested capital and may also offer a capital gain. The vendor may try to incorporate terms in the lease favourable to himself or herself; if so, the sale price may have to be lowered.

Sale and lease-back is sometimes attempted purely for an initial profit, but it may also be a useful method of raising capital.

4.4.5 Managing the premises

Efficient management of the premises can make an important contribution to the economic as well as the smooth day-to-day operation of a practice, and it must be the responsibility of a nominated person in the practice. It is essential for someone to have an overview of the operation of the building as a whole.

The operating cost of premises is the total cost of running and maintaining fabric and services. The key cost elements are:

- energy consumption;
- security;
- cleaning;
- insurance;
- maintenance;
- renewal.

Offices in urban areas also often incur heavy service charges, which will add significantly to running costs. With these in mind, attention should be paid to each of the above elements.

Energy consumption

This should be monitored. Devices can be introduced to reduce wasteful consumption of energy, and staff should be informed of the levels appropriate to particular tasks and circumstances and be encouraged to observe them. Demands on installations change over time, and obsolete or worn fittings can often reduce efficient consumption. It is sensible to establish a policy for regular checking and replacement.

Security

The cost of providing and maintaining a special security system, which might be a priority in some urban areas, will be a significant one-off cost commitment and special financial provision should be made for it. It is advisable to seek advice on security from a specialist firm, or from the local police. Insurers may ask for information about the arrangements made.

Staff must be clear about procedures for locking up at the end of the day, for setting alarms and systems, and for entering the premises outside normal working hours. It is important to make staff security-conscious; many practices have a signing-in book and require all visitors to provide identification and wear a lapel badge.

As well as the building and access to it, various items on the office premises need to be kept secure. These include:

- equipment;
- personal belongings;
- project drawings and documentation, some of which may be commercially sensitive;
- accounting and personnel records.

Computer equipment is likely to be particularly at risk and items should always be security marked.

Cleaning

Responsibility for cleaning arrangements can be a testing task for the office manager. Reliability on the part of the operatives is essential. The alternatives are to contract a professional cleaning service, which can be costly, or rely on a more informal service. The essential consideration is the trustworthiness of the personnel involved, since the office manager must be sure that people coming into the premises outside normal working hours are not a security risk.

Insurance

There should be adequate insurance cover against risks. The advice of an insurance broker should be sought (see section 8). The practice's policies should be scheduled and reviewed regularly to make sure they remain relevant and adequate, that the level of cover is sufficient, and that any requirements by insurers for security procedures and fireproof storage are being met.

Programmed maintenance

The cost of ad hoc repairs to the fabric should be distinguished from routine maintenance costs. If the condition of the building is causing excessive expenditure, a major rethink about the viability of the premises might be indicated, whereas increasing operational costs within the office are often connected with staff requirements, and might be reduced by better space planning or by replacing obsolete equipment.

References and further reading

A Guide to Starting a Practice (1999) London, RIBA Publications, Small Practices series.

5 MANAGING PEOPLE

5.1 Managing people

5.2 Leadership

5.3 Staff surveys

5.4 Delegation

5.5 Motivation

5.6 Stress

5.1 Managing people

Management is the process by which a particular group of people are brought together in order to achieve organisational goals. Plan, organise, direct and control are key words in that process. In a project-orientated group, the skills needed are a mix of technical knowledge and experience, together with the ability to understand and cope with complex situations – an essential attribute for senior managers. Strategic as well as operational foresight is required.

In architectural practice the business has to be managed, the projects have to be managed, and the practice's resources have to be managed. The primary resource of an architectural practice is the skill and talent of its architects and other employees, and this has to be harnessed and organised for the mutual benefit of all the members of the practice. A key to the success of the practice is therefore the skilful management of its human resources.

The management of people is never a cut-and-dried operation where people and roles can be firmly identified and established. It is a complex and variable process. Some roles may be only gradually defined whereas others have to be adopted quickly, at a personal as well as organisational level. In real life, the roles and personae often intermingle in various permutations. Partners and associates are often team managers, and so are job architects, but any one of them may be a member of a team under someone else. Team members may be architects on various grades, students or technicians. Any one of them may be appointed, or may emerge, as the leader of a team or group associated with projects, technical matters, practice organisation, or in-house activities of a creative or supportive nature.

Section 4 looked at the identification of practice objectives and the development of a business strategy. To manage people it is necessary to understand the forces that drive them to function well as individuals and within a group, and what will persuade them to identify with the practice's goals. A practice will operate most effectively where its members understand and sympathise with the practice's key objectives, and where their personal objectives correspond with, or at least are not at odds with, those of the practice.

5.2 Leadership

As soon as people come together as a group, whether spontaneously or as the result of some direction, a group identity is born.

Within an architectural practice, there may be many different staff performing the role of leader at any given time. The practice goals and strategy will probably be developed by the partners or directors, who form the leaders of the practice, but individual groups working on a specific project or task will also have a leader. The key functions of any leader are to develop goals and strategies for achieving them, and to ensure that they are followed effectively. There are a wide variety of different styles of leadership, but it is increasingly common for managers to adopt a 'leading from behind' approach, rather than a more authoritative and dictatorial method of 'leading from the front'. In the former, sometimes referred to as a 'trickle up' management approach, the leader or leaders take care to include all members of the team in the development of goals, and to listen and have regard to their views on key issues. In the latter, the leader will tend to dictate how things should be and be less concerned with the group's view.

In either role the leader is the group's natural focus and representative, final decision-maker, trouble-shooter and negotiator. He or she will be responsible for keeping it informed so that it can function effectively, for obtaining the resources and staff it needs, and for seeing that everyone is adequately rewarded and their careers properly developed.

In any group of people, and particularly creative people, conflicts of attitude, style and personality can arise, and handling these is a test of managerial skill. Architectural education and training place great emphasis on developing an individualistic approach towards design. Whilst this is clearly in tune with architects' creative aspirations and fundamental to their work philosophy, to some extent it conflicts with the practicalities of project work, where the architect is required to work as a member of a team as a first objective, and strongly held personal convictions have to be put aside in the general interest. As a result, tensions may build up and, unless identified in good time, can quickly develop into confrontation.

The style of a practice can sometimes lead to conflict. Some practices establish an identifiable style, a reflection perhaps of the personality of a founding partner. To architects outside the practice a unique corporate persona may be attractive – and can certainly play a useful part in staff recruitment. However, preserving a distinct 'style' means that attitudes and approaches are expected to conform to it, and new staff may find that the freedom of operation they previously took for granted is suddenly out of order.

The introduction of change into the practice can generate conflict if it is not handled with great care. A strongly led practice, confident that it 'knows best', may not be sensitive to the hostility that can quickly build up if changes are imposed in a heavy-handed way. On the other hand, a practice that takes its managers into its confidence and leads by encouraging participation may be better able to retain the trust and cooperation of its staff.

Conversely, practice principals sometimes have pressure put on them by staff to introduce changes in organisation or procedures, or to change the way they run the practice. There may be a very good reason for this dissatisfaction with the status quo, and it is sensible for principals to stand back and take an objective view of the way the practice is operating. A staff survey (*see* 5.3) can be a useful management tool in this respect.

The essence of good management is working with people, whether or not they are senior or junior in the posts they hold and the powers they exercise. It is a matter of taking the time and trouble to find out the patterns and approaches that will get things done. People usually respond better to decisions that affect them if they have been involved in the decision-making process that led to them.

5.3   Staff surveys

It is essential to analyse at regular intervals the effectiveness or otherwise of the flow of information within the office. Are messages reaching the right destination? Are project staff being properly informed about technical matters? Are all staff aware of the practice's long- and short-term goals, its policies and philosophy? Are principals aware of any groundswells of discontent over salaries and working conditions?

Figure 5: Example of a staff survey exercise

Areas of enquiry

1 Business strategy
Do staff perceive that there is one?

2 Organisation and structure
Is it always clear who is in charge?
Are responsibilities properly defined? Does
everyone know to whom he or she is accountable?

3 Management style
Is the style adopted effective and appropriate?
Does it succeed in motivating staff?

4 Staff development and training
Are staff aware of the need for training? Are they
interested?

5 Communications
Are formal lines clearly recognised? Is there a
general exchange of information at all staff
levels?

6 Excellence of service
Are staff proud of the service they provide,
corporately and individually? Does quality matter
to them?

7 Innovation
Do staff feel able to express new ideas and
formulate different approaches?

	Agree ✓	Disagree ✗
Questionnaire A (upbeat approach)		
1 It's quite clear which way this practice wants to go – on and up.	_____	_____
2 We all know who's in charge and what our own responsibilities are.	_____	_____
3 There's a good atmosphere here: we are allowed to get on with our work, but senior people are always around to help sort out problems.	_____	_____
4 Everyone should maintain their professional competence and develop their potential, even if it means making time for it.	_____	_____
5 One of the good things about this practice is that everyone talks to one another.	_____	_____
6 We like to be seen as a high quality outfit. Our clients come back for more.	_____	_____
7 If we pool ideas and come up with something new it usually gets a good hearing.	_____	_____
Questionnaire B (downbeat approach)		
1 We seem to be doing all right – what's the point of worrying about the future?	_____	_____
2 I sometimes wonder where the buck stops – not with me, I hope.	_____	_____
3 If your face fits, it's fine. I don't believe in sticking my neck out anyway – it's not _my_ practice.	_____	_____
4 CPD is fine in theory, but most of us simply don't have the time.	_____	_____
5 Everyone seems too busy to talk much; I get the feeling that no one want to listen anyway.	_____	_____
6 We all do our best, but clients thank you one day and see you in court the next. So what's the point?	_____	_____
7 I'd quite like to try out some new ideas but no one here seems interested. Better to be safe than sorry, I suppose.	_____	_____

One way to find the answers is to survey staff opinion. Surveys can be used to explore attitudes towards a particular issue or as occasional probes to check the well-being of practice morale; they are a useful 'neutral' mechanism and their results can be surprising as well as revealing. To encourage staff to participate effectively and honestly it is important to make sure that confidentiality is maintained and is seen to be maintained.

The example given as Figure 5 shows the key areas of inquiry and the underlying questions to which managers are interested in finding answers. The exercise is primarily an exploration of motivation and attitudes, and these can more easily be triggered into expression if the questions or propositions are formulated in an attitudinal way that will provoke a reaction – positive or negative. Which approach to use will be a matter for the practice to decide. Reactions can be registered on a 1-10 scale, or by marking a bar, or by ticking headings such as 'Agree/Disagree', depending of course on what is appropriate.

5.4   Delegation

An important attribute of a leader is the ability to delegate. Many architects find this difficult, particularly where design is concerned, which is usually a very personal matter. Delegation is often regarded as a loss of face or a sign of weakness, whereas it more truly indicates managerial competence and strength. In some situations it is essential – where, for instance, the task is simply too great for one pair of hands. In others it is eminently desirable – where, for instance, staff need to be given an opportunity to demonstrate their ability and potential for leadership in situations that will test them.

Before delegating, it is important to be satisfied that:

- the task and person are compatible;
- the degree of responsibility being delegated is appropriate;
- the person has been properly briefed and understands what is expected.

Staff with delegated tasks and responsibilities should not be left to sink or swim regardless; maintaining a 'hands-off' approach does not mean abrogating duties and responsibilities that properly belong to those who are more senior. Every situation should be closely monitored, and staff should feel confident that while there is no question of interference from the top, help and support will be readily given if they get into difficulties.

It is clearly in the interests of the practice as a whole to bring on its younger or junior staff. To confine all authority and responsibility to a thin top slice of management will lead eventually to a weakened practice with its continuity at risk.

5.5   Motivation

Motivation means 'moving' people (in the sense of persuading them) in identified directions towards identified goals. Most people will respond to motivation, but it should not be assumed that what moves one will move all. Needs and responses differ according to individual cultural and social environments and as age, health and family circumstances change.

People can be motivated by negative or positive forces. Negative forces are usually needs or demands which, if they are not met, will leave a person dissatisfied. They may concern:

- practice policy and administration;
- supervision;
- working conditions;
- salary and benefits;
- working relationships;
- status;
- job security.

Positive forces are needs which, if they are well handled, can be used to motivate people to realise their potential. They may be associated with:

- achievement;
- recognition;
- the nature of the work;
- responsibility;
- advancement;
- personal development.

It can be argued that staff will be broadly content if their pay and conditions are satisfactory, but this does not necessarily mean that they have been motivated to give their best. To achieve that, it is important to offer a worthwhile task, the possibility of growth with the job, recognition, and the opportunity to contribute constructively to the aims of the practice as a whole.

5.6 Stress

Motivation can be described as bringing a controlled amount of pressure to bear upon people to enable them to maximise their potential for their own benefit and that of the practice. Where such pressure is too great or is applied thoughtlessly, the result can be harmful stress.

Although most architects enjoy being 'stretched' and having to cope with the problems and challenges that arise in professional practice, some may suffer stress as they strive to match their own and the practice's expectations, and to achieve the goals set them. This may mean that they have to try to be something which is contrary to their natures. A practice that sets out to motivate people to achieve more always runs the risk of putting them under stress as a result. In extreme cases this can lead to physiological or psychological failures which are tragic in personal terms and can be costly to the practice.

Staff partners need to be alert to the signs of stress in all levels of staff, and should not forget to look out for such signs in themselves. Obvious danger signals are:

- excessive working hours;
- a drink problem;

- heavy smoking;
- unexplained absences;
- frequent errors;
- deteriorating work relationships;
- problems left unresolved;
- departures from normal behaviour.

Stress sufferers are often considered by the more robust to be inadequate in some way, but they are more often the victims of situations generated by others.

Some individuals take on too much work, or tasks which are beyond their ability, and are afraid or too proud to admit it; they may accept programmes and deadlines which they know are too tight. Others worry that they have too little to do and may be accused of being idle or of coasting along. They fear that they will be in the front line if redundancy threatens.

A job that is inadequately specified may cause stress because of the uncertainty of the situation. The incumbent does not know exactly what is expected and may be faced with having to make decisions which risk criticism as being beyond his or her remit on the one hand, or as not going far enough on the other. Stress may have been built into a job by, for example, a demand for high quality within too tight a programme. It may be impossible to meet both objectives.

Partners may cause stress by failing to support or trust their job architects and by not allowing them sufficient authority to carry out their responsibilities. They may pay lip service to 'participation', yet at the same time demand that staff 'get the work out regardless'.

A team that has been thoughtlessly constructed may have a potential for internal conflict that is far beyond the management capability of the job architect. It may be impossible to reconcile differences and motivate the team to pull together.

A practice which prefers to tell its job architects what to do rather than consult them can cause stress to staff who are not inclined to answer back. On the other hand, a practice which is so loosely organised that its managers have no framework in which to operate will make staff feel insecure.

Unhappiness about career prospects can also cause stress; some members of staff may be afraid of change or of being overtaken by the younger or abler. Others, on reaching a career ceiling, may feel that they have failed to fulfil earlier ambitions and promise.

Not everyone is stressed in the same way: some event or factor may be a source of stress at one moment in a person's life but not at another. When a person is stressed but just coping, one small addition can be the last straw. It is essential to be aware of the dangers of stress, know what signs to look for, and be prepared to respond appropriately. Regular medical checks for staff and managers alike are a sensible precaution.

5.6.1 Conflicts of responsibility

Generally speaking, architects are people of moral and ethical integrity; they will usually only work for a practice whose methods and philosophies they respect. However, there may be occasions when they will feel unable to work on a particular project. Where this kind of conflict occurs, the practice will want to know the reasons for it. If they are sound, and the person concerned is a respected member of the organisation, then a quiet reassignment to another project may be the best solution.

Conflicts of responsibility may also occur for other reasons, often arising from commitments outside the office. The practice should maintain an open-minded policy towards private work or individuals who are studying to obtain higher professional qualifications. Such activities may be time-consuming, and any serious conflicts should be averted if possible before problems arise.

Some staff believe that their only chance of promotion is by demonstrating a level of commitment well beyond the call of duty. It is true that there are times when an exceptional project demands nothing less than an all-out effort by all concerned. However, a practice that expects a blind allegiance at all times and total commitment regardless of private and family responsibilities is inhumane as well as unrealistic. Attitudes such as these may achieve short-term results, but they are likely to be self-defeating in the long term.

Self-induced pressures are also a problem. Some staff are so proud of their dedication to their work that they do not allow themselves sufficient time to relax and recharge the batteries. Inevitably they end up mentally stale and physically exhausted, and may become a burden to their families and a liability to the practice. It is important to watch out for the workaholic, and to make sure that all staff take their full holiday entitlement.

5.6.2 Counselling

People who have a problem need to talk, and often need help in identifying the cause of the problem and the possible courses of action open to them. However, there may not be anyone suitable or available, the problem may be difficult to explain, or it may be about something that arises from some conflict of personality. Family problems can be so acute that they affect a person's performance at work and yet are too personal to discuss with friends and colleagues. Problems at work are often difficult to talk about with colleagues or senior staff because they themselves may be part of the problem.

Staff with problems need to know to whom they can turn for help. Larger practices may have a staff partner or personnel officer with a counselling role, but this is rarely the case with smaller practices. People will tend to look for someone at their own level in the practice who is likely to be sympathetic. Team managers may find themselves taking on the role of counsellor simply because they are the first to notice if someone shows signs of not being able to cope.

However, it is more a matter of luck whether a practice has someone prepared to help others in this way, and designating someone as the practice's 'counsellor' might be considered. Whatever his or her title, staff would have the reassurance that there was someone in the practice with the time and will to listen to their problems.

A practice with an authoritarian approach may see counselling as a soft option which allows staff to avoid reality. However, people who seek counselling are essentially asking for help; telling them off or prescribing solutions is a waste of time. It is better to allow them to explore and explain their problems and feelings while the counsellor steers them in the direction most likely to lead to some acceptable solution.

Further reading and references

Birchall, K. 'Staff Appraisals', *RIBA Journal*, August 2000, p. 77, and September 2000, p. 94, with subsequent articles in the series such as time management (October 2000, p. 94).

6 WORKING WITH STAFF

6.1 Employment legislation

6.2 Contract of employment

6.3 Leave
6.3.1   Annual leave
6.3.2   Leave for public duties
6.3.3   Sick leave
6.3.4   Maternity leave
6.3.5   Other leave (non-statutory)

6.4 Disciplinary and grievance procedures

6.5 Termination and redundancy

6.6 Other statutory rights
6.6.1   Sex discrimination
6.6.2   Race discrimination
6.6.3   Disabled persons
6.6.4   Trade union membership
6.6.5   Rights for part-time workers

6.7 Duties of employer and employee

6.8 Self-employment

6.1 Employment legislation

Salaried architects are employed under a contract of service. Formerly the terms of this contract were left entirely to negotiation between the parties, but in recent years there has been a substantial increase in employment rights created by Acts of Parliament, and these mainly benefit employees. Employees may have a statutory right to the following:

- a written statement giving the terms of their appointment;
- an itemised pay statement;
- a minimum period of notice;
- not to be dismissed unfairly or made redundant without compensation;
- to be given reasons for dismissal;
- maternity leave or maternity pay;
- not to be discriminated against;
- to join or not join a trade union.

Employment legislation was contained principally in the Employment Protection (Consolidation) Act 1978 as amended by the Employment Acts 1980, 1982 and 1988. The Employment Rights Act 1996 consolidated individual employment legislation. Also relevant are the:

Disability Discrimination Act 1995;

Employment Relations Act 1999;

Equal Pay Act 1970;

National Minimum Wage Act 1998;

Part Time Workers (Prevention of less favourable treatment) Regulations 2000;

Pensions Schemes Act 1993;

Sex Discrimination Act 1975;

Race Relations Act 1976;

Working Time Regulations 1998; and

Trade Union and Labour Relations (Consolidation) Act 1992.

6.2 Contract of employment

A contract of service or employment arises from the time that an offer has been made and accepted. Acceptance may be oral or written, and even though an oral contract is valid and binding, it is good practice and increasingly common for the contract to be set out in writing. If an oral offer is made it is wise to confirm the acceptance in writing.

The terms of the contract will include those stated at an interview or set out in a letter, and any written contract should fully reflect these agreed terms. The terms should be fully and accurately presented, because additional and amended terms cannot be introduced once the contract is made, without the agreement of the other party.

A contract of employment may be of the normal open-ended variety or for a fixed term. An open-ended contract will continue until the employee resigns or is dismissed or made redundant.

The length of any probationary period required to confirm suitability must be stated in the contract of employment. When it has been satisfactorily completed, the employee should be notified in writing that the employment is now confirmed. For the purpose of calculating annual leave allowance, bonus, pension and other entitlements, employment will be deemed to have commenced at the beginning of the probationary period.

The law requires that details of certain terms and conditions of employment must be given to most employees within two months of the employment starting. This is called a statutory statement of particulars of employment. It is not the same as a contract of employment. The only employees who are excluded from the right to receive a statutory statement are:

- employees whose employment lasts for less than one month;
- those engaged in overseas employment (but special provision is made for employees seconded to work overseas);
- merchant seamen;
- fishermen.

The difference between the 'contract' and the 'statement' is that:

- the contract contains all the terms of the agreement reached between the employer and employee;
- the written statement is a document setting out certain terms and conditions that are required by statute to be given to employees. It does not necessarily contain the full terms and conditions of employment.

Clearly, any employee should check that the statement does not conflict with the contract, whether oral or written. Any discrepancies should be pointed out immediately.

The employer may, in the written statement or the contract of employment, refer the employee to another document for certain detailed provisions, stating where it can be inspected. The practice's office manual could contain the information required by statute and any additional policy statements. It must be readily accessible, properly incorporated by reference, and always kept up to date.

If the contract of employment contains all the information required by law, then a written statement is not required as well. However, it may be good practice to attach a summary sheet to the written contract, listing the ways in which the statutory obligations are met.

A written statement of terms must include the following information:

- the name and address of the employer;
- the name of the employee and the address of the site of employment;

- the date employment starts and the date on which the employee's period of continuous employment began;

- the title of the job;

- rates of pay and the intervals at which payment will take place;

- normal hours of work (days of the week, starting and finishing times, overtime arrangements, lunch break allowance);

- entitlement to paid holidays (including bank/public), and how such entitlement is calculated;

- details of paid leave for sickness or injury;

- details of disciplinary procedures, or an indication of where these can readily be found, and the name and job title of the person whom an employee can approach if dissatisfied with a disciplinary decision;

- an explanation of the employer's grievances procedure or an indication of where this can be found, and the name of the person with whom the employee can raise a grievance;

- details of any pension scheme provided and whether the employment is contracted out for the purposes of the Pension Schemes Act 1993 (note that from April 2001 all employers of over four people must provide a pension scheme for their employees);

- details of any period of notice binding on both parties if the employee's contract is terminated by either party;

- any collective agreement which directly affects the terms and conditions of employment including, where the employer is not a party, the persons by whom they were made.

An employee who has not received a statement may complain to an Employment Tribunal. A complaint may also be made if a statement received is incomplete. The Tribunal has the power to determine the particulars as the parties agreed them either expressly or implicitly, including any particulars that ought to have been included but were not. Tribunals have no power to enforce their decisions by making any monetary award.

6.3 Leave

6.3.1 Annual leave

There is a statutory obligation for the leave granted by an employer to be included in the employee's written statement. The statutory minimum is four weeks' paid annual leave which can include all the public or bank holidays. The majority of private practice employees will receive public and bank holidays in addition to the statutory minimum.

The leave year usually runs from January to December or follows the financial year, April to March. It is reasonable to expect employees to take all of their leave allowance within the stipulated year and unless the written statement or contract agrees otherwise, employees will lose their entitlement to annual leave unless it is taken in the relevant leave year. It is not good management practice to agree that carried-over days can be paid for instead of taken; employees (particularly those with managerial responsibilities) should be encouraged to take their full leave allowance. This is in the interests of the practice as well as the employee.

The employee's written statement or contract should state that the final salary cheque on leaving the practice will include, as appropriate, the financial equivalent of any annual leave not taken by the termination date, or a deduction for any excess annual leave taken prior to it.

The holiday commitments of new employees should be honoured where possible, and it is sensible to ask if there are any at the initial interview. Leave arrangements should in any case be discussed as early as possible to make sure that there is no conflict between employees' proposed holidays and their work commitments.

6.3.2 Leave for public duties

The Employment Rights Act 1996 refers to employees who are:

- Justices of the Peace;
- members of a local authority;
- members of any statutory tribunal;
- members of a Regional or District Health Authority in England and Wales or, in Scotland, a Health Board;
- members of the managing or governing body of an educational establishment maintained by a local education authority in England or Wales or, in Scotland, a school or college council or college of education;
- members of a water authority in England and Wales or, in Scotland, a river purification board;
- trade union officials and members.

Under this legislation an employer is required to permit reasonable time off during the employee's working hours for any of the duties of a Justice of the Peace, or duties deriving from membership of any of the bodies listed above, viz:

- attending meetings of the body or any of its committees or sub-committees;
- performing duties approved by the body necessary to discharge its functions or those of its committees or sub-committees.

Except in the case of trade union officials, statute does not require employees to be paid while carrying out their official duties.

Under the Juries Act 1974 all eligible persons summoned for jury service are obliged to attend any jury to which they are allocated. Jurors may claim from the Court travel, subsistence and other costs, as well as loss of social benefits. There is no obligation under the Act to reimburse loss of earnings in full, although a practice may consider including an undertaking in the employee's written statement or contract to continue to pay his or her salary to compensate for any shortfall.

6.3.3 Sick leave

Employers are responsible for paying Statutory Sick Pay (SSP) to their employees for up to 28 weeks of sickness in a tax year. SSP will be treated like wages in that it will be subject to PAYE income tax and to National Insurance (NI) contributions, although periods of entitlement no longer relate to the tax year. Employers are able to reclaim the NI contribution which they pay for an employee in respect of SSP. It is a statutory requirement that all periods of absence (including holidays) are recorded, and those relating to sickness identified.

Many employers supplement SSP to bring it up to employees' normal salary level. For example, the SSP of established employees could be fully supplemented for the first three months of absence, followed by three months at half salary.

Unless the employment contract states otherwise, there is nothing to prevent an employer terminating the employment of an individual if he or she is absent due to illness for a prolonged period and the employer's business cannot manage without the employee. Sometimes the contract will set out the circumstances in which this may be done, and may include a requirement for an independent medical examination should absence extend beyond a specified period. Employers are required to comply with the provisions of the Employment Rights Act 1996 and, if applicable, the Disability Discrimination legislation before terminating the employment of an individual for reasons of ill-health or poor attendance.

6.3.4 Maternity leave

Employers are required by statute to pay Statutory Maternity Pay (SMP), recouping this by deducting the amount from NI contributions.

To qualify for SMP, employees must have been continuously employed for at least 26 weeks, by the fifteenth week before the expected date of confinement. Their average weekly earnings during the last eight weeks of the qualifying period must not have averaged less than the lower earnings limit for payment of NI contributions.

A woman is entitled to 18 weeks of ordinary maternity leave. SMP is payable for a maximum of 18 weeks. It is paid at the earliest from the eleventh week before the expected week of confinement. There are two rates. Higher rate SMP is 90 per cent of the employee's normal weekly earnings and is payable for the first six weeks of maternity leave. Lower rate SMP is a set rate payable for the remainder of the maternity leave period. The current rate is £62.20 per week. From April 2002 it will be £75 per week and from April 2003 it will be £100 per week.

Maternity pay must be paid in the same way as salary (i.e. weekly, monthly, etc) in accordance with the employee's contract. The employee is entitled to SMP whether or not she intends to return to work.

Employees with at least one year's continuous service at the start of the eleventh week before the expected week of confinement are also entitled to an additional period of unpaid maternity leave. This means that an employee can return to work at any time between the end of her ordinary maternity leave period and 29 weeks after the start of the week in which her child is actually born.

Employees do not need to give any prior notice of return at the end of the ordinary maternity leave period, but returning any earlier than 18 weeks is only possible on 21 days' notice to the employer. Employees are not required to give any notice of their return from additional maternity leave unless returning early or a notice of their intention to return has been requested of them by the employer.

Employees returning from ordinary maternity leave have the right to return to their old job. Employees returning from additional maternity leave have the right to return to their old job, or if that is not reasonably practicable, to another job which is both suitable for them and appropriate for them to undertake in the circumstances.

Childcare provision

In Britain, about 40 per cent of women with dependent children do not work. An Equal Opportunities Commission report has concluded that about half a million mothers would return to work if current demands for childcare were met. It is often deplored that women architects are a small proportion of the practising profession, and it is clear that more practical initiatives are needed to help young women architects cope with the often conflicting demands of family and profession.

Architectural practices are unlikely to have the resources to provide childcare facilities in-house, but they might consider other kinds of support, such as agreeing flexible working hours or making a contribution if employees want to pay others to look after their babies so that they can return to work.

This kind of help should be offered to non-technical as well as technical staff; the administrative and secretarial staff are often the backbone of a practice, and should not be forgotten.

Employers must properly consider any request for part-time work or jobsharing from any employee returning to work from either ordinary or additional maternity leave.

6.3.5 Other leave (non-statutory)

Compassionate leave

There is no statutory requirement to give paid leave for compassionate grounds, but most practices readily grant compassionate leave in cases of urgent domestic distress or upheaval. It is a matter for the discretion of the employer, and guidelines are often laid down in the contract of employment. Each case should be judged on its merits, fairly and sympathetically.

Leave for continuing professional development (CPD)

In upholding the Standard of Professional Performance, RIBA members undertake to 'fulfil CPD obligations and when employing other members on a full-time basis to allow them reasonable time to do likewise'.

It is in the interests of architecture that architects participate in activities which relate to the profession, such as serving on RIBA committees. There should be a practice policy in place about allowing leave for these pursuits, whether it is to be paid leave, and whether a certain number of days per year should be specified for it.

Extra leave for long service

Some practices grant extra leave for long service. It could be calculated as (x) number of additional leave days each year for each additional year served (over and above a certain period of service).

Unpaid leave

Employees with one year's continuous service are entitled to 13 weeks unpaid parental leave under the Employment Relations Act 1999. This Act also gives all employees the right to take 'reasonable' time off for critical or urgent family business, although the term 'reasonable' is not defined and there is as yet little case law on the subject. Other than that, there is no statutory right to unpaid leave. Some practices do not allow any additional unpaid leave to be taken at all; some deal with it on a discretionary basis; others specify the amount that may be applied for. The best course is to have a policy about this and make it known to employees.

6.4   Disciplinary and grievance procedures

The Employment Rights Act 1996 requires that an employee's written statement should include details of the disciplinary and grievance procedures available.

An office operates more smoothly and effectively if importance is placed on maintaining an atmosphere of trust, confidence and mutual responsibility between employer and employee. However, even in the best-managed offices differences may arise which, if fundamental, may need to be handled more formally. Grievance and disciplinary procedures should be regarded primarily as a means of avoiding unnecessary damage to the employer-employee relationship rather than as a last resort when all else has failed.

A disciplinary code is needed to maintain standards and to ensure fair treatment of the individual, but it is also a means of indicating acceptable patterns of behaviour. ACAS has produced codes of practice which firms may adopt. The code should be in writing, and should specify:

- to whom it applies;
- procedures for dealing with the matter quickly;
- that the employee should be informed of the complaint;
- that the employee is entitled to representation;
- what disciplinary actions may be taken and by whom;
- that except in the case of gross misconduct, a first offence should not incur dismissal:
- that except in cases of serious misconduct there should be a warning procedure including at least one oral and one written warning followed by a sanction less than dismissal before dismissal actually takes place;
- a right of appeal, and to whom the appeal may be made.

The written statement should indicate the person whom an employee with a grievance can approach. This may be their immediate superior, or someone with responsibility for personnel.

Employees who consider that they have not received a satisfactory response should have the right to appeal to a practice principal.

6.5   Termination and redundancy

The contract of employment should state the arrangements for the giving of notice by either party. Under the Employment Rights Act 1996, after one month of continuous employment an employee must give a period of notice of not less than one week, although the contract may specify a longer period. The employer must give not less than one week's notice for each year of continuous employment, up to a maximum of 12 weeks' notice. If the contract states periods less than these, then the statutory rates will apply.

'Wrongful dismissal' occurs when there is a breach of the related contract terms, i.e. when an incorrect period of notice is given. 'Unfair dismissal' refers to a situation where procedures are followed incorrectly or not at all, or where the reason for dismissal is one which would be considered to be unfair by statute. An employee with one year's continuous service has a statutory right not to be dismissed unfairly and has the right to request written reasons for dismissal. An employee with two years' continuous service has the right to a statutory redundancy payment if their job becomes redundant.

An employer has the right to dismiss an employee without notice on the grounds of gross misconduct. Examples might include extreme cases of indiscipline, drunkenness, dishonesty, or fundamental breaches of the contract of employment.

The legislation governing redundancy is contained in the Employment Rights Act 1996. Redundancy payments are due if:

- the employee has been continuously employed for at least two years at the date of termination of contract;
- the employee has not unreasonably turned down an offer of alternative employment;
- the employee has not reached company retirement age, where applicable, or statutory retirement age;
- if the employee is over 64 the level of redundant payment is reduced by one-twelfth for every month beyond the 64th birthday.

6.6   Other statutory rights

6.6.1 Sex discrimination

Under the Sex Discrimination Act 1975, discrimination on grounds of sex or marital status is unlawful. Discrimination may occur in recruiting staff, selecting them for training, or assessing their promotion prospects.

Discrimination is direct or indirect. Direct discrimination occurs where, given similar circumstances, a person is treated less favourably than another on the grounds of sex. Indirect discrimination would occur if, say, a requirement were imposed on all employees which effectively excluded considerably more women than men or vice versa.

The requirements of this Act also apply to job advertisements. As with the Equal Pay Act 1970, employees have rights under this Act however short a period they have worked for an employer.

6.6.2 Race discrimination

The Race Relations Act 1976 makes it unlawful to discriminate against a person, directly or indirectly, in the field of employment on grounds of race, colour or nationality.

Direct discrimination is treating a person less favourably than others are or would be treated in the same or similar circumstances. For example, segregating a person from others on racial grounds would constitute less favourable treatment.

Indirect discrimination consists of applying in any circumstances covered by the Act a requirement or condition which, although applied equally to persons of all racial groups, is such that a considerably smaller proportion of a particular racial group can comply with it, and it cannot be shown to be justifiable on any other level other than racial grounds. Possible examples are:

- having a rule about clothing or uniforms which disproportionately disadvantages a racial group and cannot be justified;
- a requirement for a higher standard of language than that needed for the safe and effective performance of a job.

The requirements of this Act also apply to advertisements for job vacancies. As with the Equal Pay and Sex Discrimination Acts, employees have rights under this Act, however short a period they have worked for an employer.

6.6.3 Disabled persons

Employers' obligations towards the disabled arise out of the Disabled Persons (Employment) Acts 1944 and 1958 and the Disability Discrimination Act 1995. The legislation applies to firms of 15 or more employees. It is unlawful to discriminate against disabled persons in employment situations. Disabled is defined as including both physical and mental disability.

6.6.4 Trade union membership

Under the Employment Rights Act 1996, employees have a statutory right to belong to a trade union and to take time off to participate in its activities. Agreement has to be reached between the employer and the union representative that the latter represents the employees at that place of work.

6.6.5 Rights for part-time workers

From the 1 July 2000 there has been a statutory right to pro-rata treatment for part timers under the Part Time Workers (Prevention of Less Favourable Treatment) Regulations 2000. The equality of treatment is assessed by comparing the part time employee to a full time employee in the same establishment, and to be used as a comparator the full time employee will have to be carrying out similar work, and be of similar qualifications, skills and experience. The part time employee is entitled to be treated on a pro rata basis in their terms and conditions of employment, including pay and benefits, unless the employer can justify different treatment on objective grounds.

6.7   Duties of employer and employee

Once a contract of employment has been entered into, certain duties are imposed on both the employer and employee. The relationship is largely, but not entirely, governed by legislation. In addition to rules contained in legislation the employer/employee relationship is also governed by a number of important terms implied by the common law such as the duty of trust and confidence owed by the employer.

The employer has a duty to pay the agreed wages, and to pay expenses reasonably incurred by the employment. He or she has a duty to ensure that staff are reasonably safe, and shown appropriate respect and consideration.

The employee has a duty to render faithful service so as not to damage an employer's interests. This means making sure that self-interests do not conflict with those of the employer and that no secret profits are made. These, together with a duty not to compete with the employer, could be important where an employee undertakes private work and uses the firm's resources for it. Further complications could arise where the copyright in such work rests with the employer. Employees also have a duty to obey lawful and reasonable instructions, and to carry out all duties with reasonable care.

In general, employers assume a vicarious liability for the actions of employees, provided that the employees are doing what they are employed to do – however bad or negligent their performance of it. This vicarious liability will not normally extend to independent contractors, who are free to decide their own methods of working, nor would it extend to employees who indulge in frolics of their own outside the scope of their employment.

6.8   Self-employment

Being self-employed while undertaking work largely for one other practice may seem an attractive option to many architects. If offers a great deal of autonomy, with scope for taking on direct commissions, and perhaps starting and developing an independent practice. However, this must be handled very carefully. It may also seem an attractive proposition for the practice, which may hope that by arranging Schedule D contract terms it will avoid the financial effects of employing staff with proper PAYE (i.e. Schedule E) status and entitlements.

It should be understood that it is a matter of law whether a person is an employee or self-employed, not just a change of name in the relationship. The Inland Revenue has introduced very strict rules under IR35 to prevent self-employment being used as a method of avoiding or delaying paying tax, when the situation is really one of employment. Their guidelines for assessing this are set out at www.inlandrevenue.gov.uk. These are quite complex, and are based on such questions as the degree of control exerted by the practice over the 'self-employed' person (e.g. where and when work is done), whether the self-employed person has the right to provide a substitute, and whether the practice provides equipment and materials. It is quite possible that even where 'self-employed' arrangements have been made for payment and agreed in writing, the Inland Revenue would determine that the person was nevertheless an employee, and if this were the case the practice would be liable not only for the NI and PAYE, but also may be liable for penalties and subject to investigation by the Inland Revenue.

In addition to possible investigation of the 'employer' by the Inland Revenue, there are other disadvantages in opting to be self-employed. Rights relating to unfair dismissal and redundancy, for example, can only be claimed by employees. On the other hand, protection under the Sex Discrimination Acts 1975 and the Race Relations Act 1976 extends to the self-employed as well as to employees.

Self-employment and students

Much concern has being expressed by the RIBA at the plight of architecture students who are contracted on Schedule D contract terms so that the practice can avoid the financial effects of employing staff. The resultant savings in wage bills are then used to slash fees and undercut competitors, thereby damaging and depressing the market for architectural services generally. In such situations students are unlikely to have a planned programme of experience or receive supervision and guidance as advised under the RIBA Professional Training Scheme, and because of this periods of self-employment do not count towards the total requirement for periods of professional training at Part 3. Students in this position could also find themselves outside the protection of the practice's professional indemnity insurance cover. Students should realise that by accepting such conditions they may not only be casting aside the protection of employment law for themselves but are also driving wages down for others.

6.9   Health and safety

The Health and Safety at Work, etc Act 1974 is the principal legislation. Under it, Parliament has also introduced Regulations, including:

- Management of Health and Safety at Work Regulations 1999
- Workplace (Health, Safety and Welfare) Regulations 1992
- Manual Handling Operations Regulations 1992

- Health and Safety (Display Screen Equipment) Regulations 1992
- Personal Protective Equipment at Work Regulations 1992
- Provision and Use of Work Equipment Regulations 1992.

Section 2 (1) of the Health and Safety at Work, etc Act 1974 says:

'It shall be the duty of every employer to ensure so far as is reasonably practicable the health safety and welfare at work of all his employees.'

In addition, Section 3(1) of the Health and Safety at Work etc Act 1974 says:

'It shall be the duty of every employer to conduct his undertaking in such a way as to ensure, so far as is reasonably practicable, that persons in his employment who may be affected thereby are not thereby exposed to risks to their health and safety.'

Under the Act the employer has a statutory duty to provide a safe system of work, and not to expose employees or other persons to risks that could be foreseen by a reasonable person. The employer will be liable for all reasonably foreseeable consequences (such as injuries and loss of earnings) if he fails to meet this requirement. All employers have to be insured against claims by injured employees, and have to display a certificate confirming this insurance.

An employer of five or more employees must have a written statement of health and safety policy and details of how it is implemented. An employer must appoint or agree to the appointment of a safety representative in the firm, if requested to do so by one or more employees who are members of a trade union recognised in that place of work.

Employees have a duty to work in such a way as to maintain a safe system of work, but despite this duty the employer can be liable for the negligent acts of employees which cause injury to fellow employees in the course of their employment.

Architect-employers should refer to *Model Safety Policy with Safety Codes* (RIBA Publications, 2001) reproduced at Appendix B.

The model policy statement follows the advice given in the HSE publication *Writing a Policy Statement – Advice to Employers*, but each practice will need to analyse its own activities, identify the hazards that could arise both in the everyday running of the business and in emergency situations, such as a power cut or equipment failure. It is important to consult staff at all levels and take account of their views. The model safety codes included in the booklet can be adopted by practices as they stand, or modified to suit individual circumstances. Some practices may find it more appropriate to create their own code or codes.

Local authorities are responsible for health and safety inspections (usually by the environmental health department) of the office environment. They may be prepared to offer advice about specific safety issues, but responsibility for the developed policy statement rests with the practice itself.

6.9.1 Hazards in the office

Although at first sight architects' offices might not seem to be particularly dangerous places, there are potential hazards. These include:

- the removal of a duct cover for inspection;

- temporary obstruction of a fire exit;

- a paper guillotine;

- an ammonia dyeline machine;

- model-making machinery;

- heavy parcels or items of equipment which have to be moved.

Staff should be trained to use equipment correctly and advised of any operational hazards. All equipment should be regularly inspected and properly maintained, and this should be the responsibility of a nominated person.

6.9.2 Hazards outside the office

Visits to building sites, unoccupied buildings and construction operations are potentially dangerous. The likely hazards should always be kept in mind. Staff should be issued with a safety code and be required to follow it. (See section HS3 of the Model Safety Policy at Appendix B.)

Every office should have an inflexible rule which requires staff to give details of where they go when leaving the office on business, and when they expect to return. Someone at the office should know the whereabouts of all staff at all times.

6.9.3 First aid

To comply with Health and Safety legislation, practices must make provision for first-aid. This means that:

- first-aid equipment must be available;

- someone must be appointed to take charge in the event of an accident;

- in cases of special hazard or practices employing more than a certain number of persons, some staff must be trained and qualified as first-aiders;

- all these arrangements must be known to all the office.

Practices must also maintain a logbook for recording and reporting accidents.

6.9.4 Health and medical

Most people who work in offices are at risk from repetitive strain injury (RSI), eyestrain and exposure to video display units (VDUs). There may also be problems connected with reactions by staff to the internal environment.

It is prudent to have available at reception a list with the telephone numbers of the local hospital casualty department, the ambulance service, and a local doctor. A copy should also be kept somewhere where it can easily be found after normal working hours. This information should be included in the written health and safety policy.

Many practices encourage, and some arrange, periodic medical check-ups for senior and key members of staff.

6.9.5 Smoking at work

Many staff object to others smoking at work and are concerned about the dangers of passive smoking. The practice can try to improve matters by:

- improving ventilation;
- segregating smokers from non-smokers;
- designating certain areas as non-smoking.

It is best to consult all staff before instituting a non-smoking policy which means that smokers are excluded from the main work areas. New staff should be made aware of the policy at interview, so that they are forewarned.

6.9.6 Refreshments

Eating and drinking at the work station is not something to be encouraged. It gives a poor impression of the practice to visitors, and can cause hazards if there is spillage on floors or desks, particularly in the vicinity of electronic equipment. For example, a cup of coffee spilt over a computer keyboard will cause a malfunction immediately, and the subsequent cleaning operation will be very costly and is not likely to be covered by a maintenance contract.

If possible, an area should be designated for eating and drinking, and for making tea and coffee. If a vending machine is thought more appropriate, it should be sited at a suitable distance from work areas. Again, spillages are likely to be frequent nearby, making the floor surface slippery.

6.10   Staff training and development

A practice that actively works to realise the potential of its staff will be both meeting its professional obligations and enhancing its own calibre and effectiveness.

Training and development should not be regarded as something that stops once professional qualifications are obtained. Continuing professional development (CPD) is now an obligation on practices, and it is not sufficient just to pay lip service to the requirement. Where students undertaking professional experience are employed, the *Professional Experience Development Record* (*PEDR*) should include entries on any training or development events in which they have been participants or observers.

In a small practice where everyone is well known, it is relatively easy to plan career development for each staff member. In a larger practice, principals may have to be guided by their senior staff. Monitoring the performance of individuals is an important part of planning career development. This will help the staff partner to build up new teams as necessary with the appropriate known skills and experience.

6.10.1 Staff appraisals

Many practices conduct annual staff appraisals, which review performance over the previous 12 months, and discuss plans and objectives for the next 12. These should be carefully prepared for, with all parties fully aware of the purpose. They should be kept quite separate from salary reviews, as the staff appraisals should not be clouded with issues relating to money.

The appraiser will comment on past performance, and should be careful to give a very balanced view, and to keep the comments specific and work related. Appraisers should be careful to get all their facts right, particularly when discussing under performance, and should not rely on hearsay. He or she should aim to listen more than talk, and to make careful notes.

The appraisee should view the appraisal positively, and come prepared to discuss the previous 12 months in detail, to evaluate personal aims and goals within the context of the firm, and to acknowledge areas where there may be room for improvement.

The appraisee and appraiser should both sign the forms to indicate their agreement on the contents. The employee should be given a copy to keep and a separate copy should be placed in the employee's file.

6.10.2 Forms of training

As a practice develops, new areas of operation, skills, equipment and procedures may be needed, and to introduce them someone who knows the field in question might have to be recruited. Alternatively, the necessary expertise could be developed in-house. If new methods are to be effective they will have to be accepted by everyone; therefore their introduction, particularly by an 'outsider', needs careful handling.

Training can take the form of attending seminars and courses arranged by a commercial organisation, or as part of a CPD programme. Staff may be encouraged or detailed to attend those relevant to their own career development or to the needs of the practice.

For reasons of cost, it may only be feasible to allow one or two people to attend such events, so it is important to disseminate the information gathered at them. Conference papers and delegates' reports should be placed in the office library. Feedback from the event could be incorporated into the practice's in-house CPD programme, where the new knowledge or ideas could be considered in the practice context and proposals for follow-up developed if appropriate.

In-house training should be aimed primarily at:

- new staff, to familiarise them with the way the practice works;
- students in both periods of professional training, as part of the practice's training obligation;
- existing staff who need their knowledge and skills refreshing and updating.

For reasons of competence, sound practice and quality management, it is essential that proper time and care is given to this activity. In terms of cost benefit and educational effectiveness, the in-house approach to training has much to commend it.

The sessions should be at regular times and places when everyone can and will want to attend, and should be organised as a planned programme of events. Staff with particular interests or experience should be encouraged to develop exploratory sessions in their areas, while all staff should be encouraged to prepare case studies of current work for feeding into the programme. An occasional fun session or competition could be included.

It is important to monitor the results of a training programme. The questions to be asked are these:

- Are new ideas being tried out in the practice?
- Are people making fewer errors? Is there less wasted effort?
- How are individuals developing? Are they wiser, better motivated, more competent?

6.10.3 Individual study

From time to time staff may wish to undertake part-time courses of study, such as in landscape, conservation, urban design or business administration. This may mean day or block release, and it will inevitably divert some attention from the work of the practice. The individuals may also request sponsorship from the practice, as it may be assumed to be of benefit in the long term.

In all cases, it is important to consider whether the person is qualified to embark on the course proposed; whether he or she will still be able to give proper attention to the practice's work; and whether following the course is likely to be of direct benefit to the practice. Given the right circumstances, the office might well encourage this personal initiative and even consider financial help.

6.11   Recruitment

Recruitment can be a lengthy process. A minimum programme, where an advertisement is placed in the technical press, might entail six weeks from decision to advertise to making an offer; from offer to start date, up to three months. Contracts may have to be completed, notice worked, or relocation arranged. For some posts, it may be appropriate to have a two-stage interviewing process.

New staff can be recruited in a number of ways. The most usual is to advertise for them in the technical press or, if time is short, to use an architectural agency. For younger staff a school of architecture could be approached or, for special talent or expertise, some discreet head-hunting might be appropriate.

6.11.1 Advertising

Advertising is expensive, so it should be effective. Most architects looking for a job scan the technical press first, although they may also approach practices directly, or use the services of an agency.

A job advertisement should contain:

- the name, address and telephone number of the practice, and a name to ask for;
- the title of the job, a brief description of it, and where it is based;
- what attributes a successful applicant is likely to have;
- salary and benefits package, and whether this is negotiable;
- information about how to apply and whether to enclose a CV and details of portfolio.

The text should be succinct and should contain all the essential facts about the job being offered. Graphics are important in reflecting the practice's image and in giving the advertisement impact. Advertisements have a considerable PR value: they may be seen by prospective clients, other practices, other professions in the building industry, and by the practice's own staff, who will like to be seen as employees of a successful, high quality business.

6.11.2 Staff agencies

Using an agency can often produce a quicker result than placing an advertisement, and is useful when additional staff are needed at short notice. Agencies usually only expect to be paid if a candidate is appointed following an introduction by them. However, their fees are often high, and it is important to check the amount in advance, as conditions vary. The RIBA operates its own employment agency, which is open for business during normal working hours.

6.11.3 Employing students

Students from schools of architecture or colleges of technology sometimes seek casual work during vacations or because they have been advised to gain office experience before re-taking a part of their course. In such cases the student will approach the practice directly and the terms of the placement will be entirely a matter of agreement.

Students undertaking professional experience in accordance with the rules of the RIBA (see 2.8) can be very useful to an office, but it should not be forgotten that the work they do is part of their educational process. The programme, salary and other conditions should be established with this in mind. The placing of students still largely depends on students' own initiatives. Some schools of architecture have developed strong links with certain practices over many years, and maintain preferred lists for placings.

Students are normally required to undertake 12 months' professional experience after three years' education, and a further minimum of 12 months after graduating and before attempting the Examination in Professional Practice (the Part 3). Applications to offices are usually made during the Easter vacation, and availability starts in July. When taking professional experience students, enquiries should be made about any special requirements concerning assignments, recalls for school seminars, etc.

Some offices maintain links with particular schools, and this kind of continuity can bring advantages. It should certainly be worth establishing a personal contact with the Professional Studies Advisor from any school involved. Off the record information on an applicant's potential is usually available, and in the event of the placement not proving satisfactory, a hotline can be useful. Many schools visit students during their placement, and this will provide further opportunities for contact.

Offices wishing to bring job opportunities to the notice of students should contact the Professional Studies Advisors in good time, sending details of the vacancies in a form which can be displayed on the school's practice notice board.

6.11.4 Job descriptions

Job descriptions are useful for reference and comparison and one should be written for each post, non-technical as well as technical. Most jobs shift in scope or emphasis over the years, and the job description should be regularly reviewed so that it remains true and accurate and any necessary adjustments to wages and salaries can be made. The description can also be a point of reference if there is any dispute or grievance.

The job description should record the title, duties and responsibilities of the post, any special assignments or responsibilities relevant at the time of appointment, to whom the incumbent is accountable and the limit of any financial authority. The details should be updated each time there is a new appointee. Figure 6 shows the essentials.

A job description should not be confused with the written statement of the main terms and conditions of employment which has to be issued to all employees after they start employment (*see* 6.2).

6.12   Interviewing applicants

An employee should be nominated to receive written enquiries and field telephone enquiries. He or she should be welcoming, firm where necessary, and discreet. Telephone callers should be asked to send in a written application. Application forms (if available) and job descriptions should be sent out as necessary.

All applications should be acknowledged immediately, and those that are obviously unsuitable should be rejected at once. At the end of the stated period for receiving applications, the designated selection panel should consider all replies and make a shortlist of candidates for interview, keeping a few reserves in hand. The selection panel will normally consist of the staff partner or director and the post's immediate superior. If the post is senior, it is usual to have more than one principal on the panel.

A practice with a good reputation tends to receive a steady trickle of uninvited applications and will keep on ice any that indicate genuine talent until a vacancy occurs, when it can invite re-application.

6.12.1 The interview

A job interview is essentially a two-way exchange: the practice's primary objective is to gather enough information about an applicant to enable a judgement about him or her to be made, while the candidate has the opportunity to ask questions about the practice, its work, and the post in question. Notes should be taken discreetly during each interview, and developed

Figure 6: Specimen job description form

JOB TITLE	Job No. ....
Office/Department	Base ....

Summary of duties ....

....

....

Detailed duties ....

....

....

....

Special skills/experience needed ....

....

....

Special responsibilities ....
(*for staff, budget, etc*)

....

Accountable to ....

(This part for adminstrative records)

JOB TITLE	No ....

Holder of post ....

Salary	Start date ....

    Any special agreement, review? ....

....

How was post filled?

    (1) by advertisement in ....
        on (*date*)

    (2) by ....
        on (*date*)

afterwards into a form which can be kept on file. There are advantages in devising a standard record of interview form which can be used for all recruitment interviews.

The conduct of the interview should be planned in advance and agreed by all the members of the selection panel. Each should be clear about the part he or she is expected to play. If more than one person is conducting the interviews, a strategy should be agreed beforehand. The same structure should be adopted for each interview to ensure that all relevant areas are explored and that the results for each candidate can be compared within a consistent framework.

However experienced, interviewers should prepare thoroughly for each interview. There is nothing more disconcerting for applicants than to become aware that little thought has apparently been given to something that is of great importance to them and their future careers. Notes on the post advertised, and on the applicants, should be read again before the interview and questions or topics prepared which can be introduced to stimulate discussion. The relevant job description should be kept at hand, together with the CV and any other information supplied by the candidate.

The environment in which interviews are held should be free of distractions for the interviewers and encourage candidates to feel at ease. The layout of the room chosen should not be intimidating, and there should be a table or desk on which drawings can be spread out.

6.12.2 Selection

If only one applicant is seen, then the issue is simply whether or not the person is suitable. If there are several people interviewed for one post, then the question is which one is most suitable – bearing in mind, of course, that none may be suitable. Whatever the circumstances, it is essential to take time to make a proper decision. Unsuitable or hasty appointments can lead to problems later on and result in unnecessary expense.

The letter offering the post to the preferred candidate should state the principle terms of the offer and whether it is conditional upon anything, such as satisfactory references.

Once the candidate has accepted, the office should be informed and a work space prepared for the new arrival, and the unsuccessful candidates should be notified.

6.13 References

Employers are not obliged to provide references, but if they do so they have a duty to those who may be influenced by those references. Even though a practice may not wish to prejudice the chances of a job for a former employee, if it knows of something which may make the person unsuitable for another practice, it has an obligation, in the case of a written reference, to give a warning. An employer will not be liable for defamation provided that what is stated is true, and that the motive in supplying the reference is a genuine exercise of responsibility to another employer.

The two kinds of reference generally sought are character references and job references. For a character reference, the referee will be expected to have known the person in question for at least five years, and comments will be expected to relate to their personal qualities and an estimation of them as decent and trustworthy members of society. Employers who ask for a general reference are usually mainly concerned to discover whether the person in question is technically competent, honest and reliable.

A reference for a technical post might include details and remarks about:

- the period worked;
- the kind of projects worked on;
- duties and level of responsibility;
- financial authority;
- competence in performance;
- competence as a team member and/or leader;
- ability to cope with clients, consultants;
- health;
- loyalty and reliability;
- reason for leaving;
- the practice's willingness to re-employ;
- a caveat if the employment was some time ago.

If there have been problems, it may be better to indicate them rather than spell them out. It is then up to the prospective employer to pursue the matter.

References should be signed by a partner (the staff partner if there is one).

The offer of any job should be conditional upon the receipt of satisfactory references. This should be clearly stated in any job application form used, and at interview. However impressive the applicant is, it is important to take up references and evaluate them properly. It might be necessary to contact the referee and discuss the comments made. The applicant should be advised not to give notice to their current employer, if applicable, until they have received confirmation that satisfactory references have been received.

6.14 Induction

All staff should be informed about new appointments and their starting dates. If the practice has a newsletter, a few notes about the new employees could be included.

First impressions are important. Newcomers to the practice should be properly introduced and made to feel welcome. They should be given a copy of the office manual and an explanation of the various office procedures. Everyone should be encouraged to give their time to help new arrivals to settle in.

Where there are several new appointments, it may be useful to hold induction sessions on the practice's objectives and philosophy, past and present work, and technical and administrative procedures.

References and further reading

Birchall, K. 'Staff Appraisals', RIBA *Journal*, August 2000, p. 77, and September 2000, p. 94, with subsequent articles in the series such as time management (October 2000, p. 94).

McCrory, C. 'Work Permits', RIBA *Journal*, February 2001, p. 91.

Model Safety Policy for Architects, Engineers and Surveyors (2001) London, RIBA Publications.

Penton, J. H. (1999) *The Disability Discrimination Act: Inclusion*, London, RIBA Publications.

7 FINANCIAL MANAGEMENT

7.1 Managing practice finances
7.1.1 The capital requirement

7.2 Raising money
7.2.1 A business plan

7.3 The function of accounting

7.4 Accounting principles
7.4.1 Accounting entities

7.5 Standard financial reports
7.5.1 The balance sheet
7.5.2 The profit and loss account

7.6 The annual budget

7.7 Financial control
7.7.1 Controlling cash flow
7.7.2 Putting a price on time
7.7.3 Managing the workload
7.7.4 Speculative work
7.7.5 Job overruns
7.7.6 Day-to-day control
7.7.7 Book-keeping

7.8 Tax management

7.9 Making a profit

7.1 Managing practice finances

Accountants provide the essential financial accounting services that every business requires, but continuing financial information will also be needed to allow the firm's management to forecast, plan and make decisions. The provision of such information is the function of management accounting, and a primary decision to be made is who in the practice is to be responsible for producing it.

Large practices may have an in-house management accountant at the head of an accounts department. In a medium size practice, one of the partners may be responsible for managing finance with the help of an administrative assistant with book-keeping expertise and appropriate computer software. The senior (or sole) partner of a small practice will manage its finances, with or without human or electronic help in-house.

The development of standard accounting software has enabled businesses of all shapes and sizes to handle day-to-day book-keeping efficiently and to analyse and extrapolate financial information for the purposes of management and decision-making. However, it is important that architects recognise their limitations in this area and ensure that the practice's book-keeping system and accounting procedures are soundly based and appropriate, and are approved by the practice's accountant.

7.1.1 The capital requirement

Capital is the money invested in the firm by the owners themselves (equity capital), plus any long-term financing loans (debt capital).

In a partnership, each partner may have both a fixed capital account and a current capital account, which represent his or her share of the capital invested in the firm. The fixed capital account shows the amount of capital subscribed by each partner on entry to the partnership, and any additional capital contributions or withdrawals are recorded in it. The current capital account exists to record adjustments in respect of profit shares, partners' salaries, interest on subscribed capital and private drawings.

The amounts in the capital accounts can only be increased with the agreement of all the partners. Profits made by the firm are distributed into the partners' current accounts or are withdrawn as partners' drawings. If a partner wishes to realise his or her capital investment it will mean withdrawing cash from the partnership, which may be damaging.

A company's debt capital may include long-term loans, and bonds and debentures at a fixed rate of interest. In the case of a partnership, it usually takes the form of a long-term loan from the bank. Debt capital has to be repaid and attracts interest, whereas equity capital generally only has to be repaid if the firm ceases to exist.

Gearing

A primary decision to be made is what the gearing ratio is to be, which is an expression of the relationship between long-term debt and equity capital. If Business X has a gearing ratio of 3:1 it means that for every £1 of equity capital invested, there exists £3 of long-term debt (such as a bank loan). In the eyes of an investor, the higher the ratio, the riskier the investment in the business.

In times of recession, businesses with high gearing, i.e. a large proportion of long-term debt, can be far more prone to failure because interest payments, which are normally paid out of the cash receipts generated from trading, have to be paid regardless of the prevailing economic climate. Therefore if cash receipts fall – as they are likely to do during a recession – a business with a large amount of debt may find that it is not generating enough cash to meet the interest bill. However, the reverse can be true when substantial trading growth is experienced.

A company with a high proportion of equity capital can usually defer or reduce the payment of its annual dividend. This would certainly not be good news for shareholders, but if times are hard it should be possible to convince them of the need for reinvestment within the business.

How much capital?

Deciding how much capital is needed is never easy. For an architect considering setting up in practice for the first time and operating out of the spare room at home it might seem surprisingly little, but as soon as he or she considers taking on staff the picture changes. Staff need working space and equipment, which inevitably means finding office premises and, if these are to be acquired and fitted out, for most young practitioners it means borrowing money. But how much?

The primary operational consideration in business is cash flow (liquidity), and cash flow needs managing. The problem is timing. An architectural practice's staff is its main cost (about half of total practice costs), and staff have to be paid every month come what may. By contrast, fee income cannot be relied upon to come in regularly even when a practice institutes stringent credit control procedures for getting the money in, and in any case there is an unavoidable time lag between invoicing and payment. That time lag has to be financed.

The same considerations apply to an established practice that has decided to aim for an increase in turnover. More staff will be needed to cope with the additional work and will have to be equipped and paid. The practice will still have to find the extra finance to cover the period before the additional fee income materialises.

Before approaching any potential lenders it is important to seek financial advice and prepare a detailed financial plan so as to be prepared for the questions that will be asked about the practice's business objectives and its financial state of affairs. Lenders will want to know the likely costs of additional technical staff required to meet the workload envisaged and the increased overheads to support them. They will want to know the amount of partners' drawings, as opposed to the projected amount of profit, so that they can estimate how much can be ploughed back as working capital. However accurate the estimates are, it may be a long time before there is sufficient cash flow to meet the anticipated monthly expenditure, and this must be reflected in the size of the loan sought and the terms for its repayment. It is essential to obtain sound financial advice.

7.2   Raising money

Architects usually need to raise money to set up in practice. When established, they may need additional funds to allow expansion into larger premises or to refurbish an existing one, or to acquire some costly fixed asset such as a computer system. The usual route taken is to negotiate a loan or overdraf with the bank, but there are other ways of raising money. For example:

- by seeking venture capital from bankers, institutions or individuals;
- by using the office premises and assets to provide capital by sale and leaseback;
- by approaching an insurance company for a loan linked to a life assurance policy or pension;
- by converting a partnership into a limited company and raising capital by selling shares in the new company.

Venture capital funding is the investment of long-term risk equity to generate capital gain instead of interest or dividends. Venture funds are captive, i.e. linked to a bank or institution, or independent. The clearing banks all provide venture capital through their own fund vehicles, and so do merchant banks and various investment institutions. Merchant banks might seek to acquire an equity interest in the firm, but clearing banks are unlikely to be interested in acquiring equity stakes or providing unsecured loans.

There may also be government schemes and enterprise initiatives which might provide limited funding, or grants and development loans available locally and this should be investigated.

Any approach to a potential source of funds will need to be supported by adequate financial and general information about the practice and its objectives. This should be presented as the practice's business plan.

7.2.1 A business plan

In formulating a business plan it is important to consider who its readers will be, what form it should take, what it should say, and how it should be presented. These are the essential aspects of any form of business communication.

The plan should be well presented and easy to read. Its purpose is to persuade an external source to risk lending a sum of money and to reassure that source that the practice's finances and prospects are healthy enough to be able to sustain and service the loan. The interest rate charged on the loan will reflect the lenders' view of the state of the market and their estimate of the risk involved. There will also probably be a charge on property or other assets as security. Repayment of the loan and the interest usually starts at once, on a monthly or quarterly basis.

The first thing financiers look for is evidence of good management. They seldom know much about architects and their work but they will not hesitate to make judgements about them as business people, the quality of the information they present and the attitude they demonstrate towards business matters. This they expect to be serious, well-informed and clear-sighted; any temptation to exaggerate the practice's prospects or abilities should be firmly resisted. They will also be impressed by the reputation and quality of the practice's business advisors, whose help will have been sought in preparing the plan.

There are no rigid rules about the way to formulate a business plan, as this will depend upon the size of the practice and its reasons for seeking funds. The basic requirement is a summary statement which describes the practice and its objectives, how much it needs to borrow and when, and how it proposes to service/repay the loan. This summary will need to be supported by financial reports and statements and descriptive material about the practice's workload and personnel.

A suggested outline of contents is set out as Figure 7. As a general rule, the written information should be brief and the financial information presented in a form the potential lender will instantly recognise, typically a projected profit and loss account, balance sheet, a cash flow forecast and, if appropriate, the firm's audited accounts.

The business plan for a large practice might adopt a report format with a contents list and the body of the report divided into sections; a small practice might confine itself to a summary statement and two or three key financial statements. All business plans will need to be supported by appropriate documents and material about the practice and its work; these can either be bound in as appendices or presented separately.

Figure 7: Business plan: outline of contents

1 The practice
- A description of the firm, its personnel and premises.
- Its management structure.
- Its business advisors.

2 The service provided
- The type of work undertaken.
- The type of clients targeted.

3 The practice's position in the market-place
- An evaluation of its present position.
- Its anticipated position.

4 The practice's business philosophy
- Its objectives.
- Its views about competition, quality, profitability.

5 Marketing effort
- Initiatives, controls, feedback, results.

6 Financial performance
- Past and current state of affairs.
- A résumé of work in progress.

7 Business management and controls
- How the firm manages its finances.
- How it manages liquidity.
- How it gets the money in.

8 The financing required
- The amount needed and its timing.
- How it will be used.
- How the loan will be serviced and repaid.

Supporting material such as practice brochures, CVs of senior staff, financial statements, accounts, details of work in hand, project-related presentational material, videos.

Before preparing the plan for presentation it is essential to check for arithmetical errors and discrepancies and make sure that the written sections are well expressed and have been checked for spelling and typographical errors. Bankers and funds managers will have little confidence in borrowers who are incompetent communicators and whose numerical presentations are sloppy and inaccurate.

Attractive presentation is important. Depending on its length, the plan can be presented as a spiral-bound report or loose sheets in a folder. Only a limited number of copies of the plan should be prepared, and each copy should be numbered.

7.3   The function of accounting

At various times a practice needs to be able to communicate to its investors, creditors, advisors and managers information about its profitability, liquidity, financial viability and the soundness of its business strategy. The function of accountancy is to generate and present that information in a suitable form.

Day to day accounting procedures allow the activities of an enterprise to be compiled, recorded and analysed. Transactions are identified, measured in monetary terms, classified, and entered in a book-keeping system. They are subsequently summarised in financial statements presented in a form appropriate to the needs of the user.

Financial statements are used by government in the shape of the Inland Revenue (for tax purposes), and Customs & Excise (for VAT). Company accounts are filed at Companies House, where they are available for public inspection. Otherwise, the users of financial statements fall into three major categories: investors, creditors and managers. Architects could find their accounts reviewed by all three categories.

Investors are those who have a financial stake in the business, whilst creditors may be suppliers of goods who extend credit, or lending institutions such as banks. In addition, there are those who advise the business, or have a direct interest in it (e.g. staff, unions). Practice managers also use financial statements, together with various other reports compiled specifically for management purposes.

The different users of financial statements evaluate the information presented according to their particular needs. Investors or owners are primarily interested in trying to predict a return on their investment and in assessing the risks involved in that investment. They will concentrate on evaluating the firm's past performance and estimating its future profitability and overall financial strength. They will compare it with their other investments.

A creditor's primary concern is that the business should be able to repay its obligations (a concern that an architect might share when considering a potential client's financial status). Long-term creditors are therefore concerned with the company's long-term financial performance and strength; short-term creditors are more concerned with the solvency of the business in the near future, and tend to focus on its immediate liquidity. The practice manager will analyse the information about the firm's past to evaluate its present results so that corrective or other action can be taken.

The key factor in the analysis of financial information is comparability, because unless the present performance of the business can be compared with previous periods, or with the results of similar enterprises, or with a budget, a financial statement by itself is of limited informational value. Comparing results from previous years may reveal trends and provide a yardstick for evaluating current performance and financial strength. It is important to establish that the accounting policies and methods used remain constant over the relevant period. The value of the monetary unit fluctuates (with inflation, for example) so that only a rough comparison can be made year on year.

For architectural practices which trade as companies it may be particularly relevant to compare their financial results with those of others. However it should be noted that small companies need only provide abbreviated accounts which cannot effectively be used for this purpose.

7.4 Accounting principles

In accountancy, as in all professions, certain principles and conventions have been drawn up to establish norms and a consistent basis for operation. Accountants conduct their work in accordance with *Financial Reporting Standards* (*FRS*) and *Statements of Standard Accounting Practice* (*SSAP*).

There are four principles which need to be understood by anyone attempting to interpret financial statements:

1. Going concern

Accounts are generally based on the assumption that the firm is going to continue indefinitely. An entirely different set of figures would be used if its break-up value was being assessed.

2. Consistency

The same accounting policies are used each year and throughout each year. Any change in this respect has to be stated in the accounts and the accounts for the previous year amended for comparison.

3. Prudence

Accountants are often accused of taking a depressing view of events, but in financial statements they are required to exercise caution and restraint in recognising profits in order not to mislead the users of these statements.

4. Matching

The fundamental principle of accounting is to match expenses against revenues. Thus, if a cost occurs in one year but the revenue does not materialise until the next year, the cost is 'carried forward' and shown in the next year's accounts.

7.4.1 Accounting entities

An accountancy entity is not the equivalent of a legal entity. For example, in the case of a sole practitioner there is no distinction in law between the business and its owner – the owner is responsible for all debts incurred by the business regardless of how much he or she has invested in it. However, for accounting purposes there is a distinction between the sole practitioner's business and personal financial activities: the business is held to be an accounting entity separate from the owner.

In English law, a partnership is not an entity or persona, but in accounting it is recognised as a business entity distinct from the private financial dealings of the individual owners. A company, on the other hand, requires no such splits of personality for accounting purposes: it is a legal entity incorporated under the Companies Act 1985. It has an infinite life until and unless action is taken to dissolve it, regardless of whether its directors, managers or shareholders sell their shares, retire or die.

7.5 Standard financial reports

Standardised formats for financial accounting reports have been developed by the accounting profession. A set of statements for an accounting entity would cover:

- its financial position at the end of a period (the balance sheet);
- its revenue and expenses for the same period (the profit and loss account);
- for larger entities, its investments by and distribution to owners during that period
- its funds flow for the period;
- its statement of accounting policies;
- its auditors' report.

The two key statements are the balance sheet (*see* Figure 8), and the profit and loss (P & L) account (*see* Figure 9).

The balance sheet shows the financial position of a firm at a given point in time, whilst the P & L account shows its revenue and expenditure over a period. In the case of a company, the P & L account will also show the amount of profit that is re-invested in the company, the dividends that are paid to shareholders, the accumulated net profits from the previous year's trading, and the tax liabilities. In the case of a partnership, it will illustrate the amount of profit that has been transferred to the partners' current accounts (which show how the profit is distributed between the partners), what has been drawn, and what remains as capital.

7.5.1 The balance sheet

The balance sheet is made up of assets, liabilities, capital and reserves.

Assets

Assets are used to help generate, either directly or indirectly, future revenue for the firm. They can be tangible, like buildings and equipment, or intangible such as goodwill or current, such as money owed to the firm or work in progress. However, to be included in the balance sheet the value of every asset must be measurable in monetary terms.

Liabilities

Liabilities are debts, i.e. what the firm owes. They are claims by the creditors on the firm's assets. A creditor is someone who has provided an asset to a firm in exchange for future reimbursement, usually in the form of cash. Trade creditors in the balance sheet represent the amount owed to suppliers of goods and services. Other liabilities will be to the Inland Revenue, Customs and Excise, and will include bank loans, hire purchase and overdrafts. Liabilities are split into current and non-current. Current are expected to be met and satisfied within one year; non-current after one year.

Figure 8: Balance sheet: typical structure

Sparrow & Grebe Ltd: Balance Sheet as at 31 December 2001		
	£000s	£000s
FIXED ASSETS		
Land and buildings		100.0
Office equipment		60.0
		160.0
CURRENT ASSETS		
Stock, and work in progress	20.0	
Debtors	140.0	
Cash at bank	40.0	
	200.0	
Less		
CURRENT LIABILITIES		
(due within 1 year)		
Creditors	60.0	
		140.0
Net Current Assets		300.0
Less		
LONG-TERM LIABILITIES		
(due after 1 year)		
Bank loan		100.0
		200.0
CAPITAL AND RESERVES		
Share capital		60.0
Reserves		140.0
		200.0
Prepared January 2002		

Capital and reserves

In a partnership this will be represented by the partners' capital and current accounts, which shows the profits distributed to them from the P & L account, less any withdrawals that have been made. In a company's balance sheet this would be reflected in two principal items: share capital, and reserves.

7.5.2 The profit and loss account

The P & L account enables a firm's past financial performance to be evaluated. Whereas the balance sheet reflects its financial position at a point in time, the P & L account shows the in-flows and out-flows of resources over a period, expressed as revenues and expenses (*see* Figure 9).

In architectural practice, revenues are earned by providing services to clients. Expenses are costs incurred by the practice in the process of generating those revenues. All the revenues and all the expenses are added up to show the net result of the practice's operations over a period, i.e. its profit.

Published P & L accounts usually add all the operating expenses together, whereas those accounts used for internal management purposes analyse the operating expenses in greater detail under a range of budget headings (*see* Figure 10).

Figure 9: Profit & loss account: typical structure

Sparrow & Grebe Ltd: Profit & Loss Account for year ending 31 December 2001		£000s
Sales		640.0
Less: Cost of Sales		347.0
Office equipment	Gross Profit	293.0
Administrative expenses		192.2
	Operating Profit	100.8
Bank loan interest payable		23.8
	Net Profit before Tax	77.0
Tax		25.0
	Profit for Year	52.0
Dividends payable		30.0
		22.0
Plus: Reserves b/f		118.0
Reserves c/f		140.0
	Prepared January 2002	

Figure 10: Profit & loss account: management accounts

<u>Sparrow & Grebe Ltd: Profit & Loss Account</u>
<u>for year ending 31 December 2001</u>

	£000s	£000s)
<u>Income</u>		
Fee		640.0
Other		<u>nil</u>
Total:		<u>640.0</u>
<u>Direct costs</u>		
Technical salaries	(297.0)	
Consultants' fees	(25.0)	
Other expenses	(25.0)	(347.0)
GROSS PROFIT		<u>293.0</u>
<u>Premises expenses</u>		
Rent, rates, insurance	42.0	
Utilities	11.0	
Repair and renewal	<u>5.0</u>	(58.0)
<u>Administrative expenses</u>		
Staff salaries	52.1	
Staff training	4.5	
Staff pensions	4.2	
Cars	12.4	
Office equipment	16.6	
Printing, stationery	<u>7.0</u>	(96.8)
<u>Financial expenses</u>		
PI insurance	20.0	
Professional advisors	10.0	
Bank charges	3.2	
Bad debts	<u>4.2</u>	(<u>51.4</u>)
TOTAL EXPENSES		<u>192.2</u>
OPERATING PROFIT		100.8
<u>Less:</u> Bank loan interest payable		(<u>23.8</u>)
NET PROFIT BEFORE TAX		<u>77.0</u>

Prepared January 2002

Management accounts comprise the information provided by the ledgers and cash book presented in a way that enables decisions to be made about practice planning and operation. Their presentation and timing are determined by the needs of the practice and will relate to its size and the nature of its work. The function of the management accountant is to interpret and extrapolate information to monitor and control the direction and profitability of practice finances. The main aspects of his or her work are budgeting and financial control – in other words, where the practice is going and how to keep it on course.

7.6 The annual budget

The annual budget should represent a realistic forecast of total income and expenditure for the coming year. It is used to set targets for the level of fee income anticipated, staff salaries and other direct costs, logistical support, office overheads and, ultimately, profit for the year. It indicates how much money has been made available for marketing, training, new systems, furniture, equipment and books, etc.

The annual budget consists of a series of agreed budget headings (*see* Figure 11). The amount of fee income budgeted will represent the commissions expected to materialise during the year ahead. Direct costs include technical salaries, consultants' fees, drawing office materials and other recoverable expenses. Overheads (indirect costs) include all the costs of running the business that are not directly associated with projects. They typically consist of fixed or recurring charges (many of which are known in advance or can be realistically adjusted) such as rent, rates and utilities. Of the costs remaining, some can be estimated on the basis of previous expenditure, deducting any abnormal items and adding any known additional commitments.

The budget is set once a year, but the assumptions and forecasts on which it is based may well change in the course of the year, so that at strategic intervals it will be necessary to review and revise the budget to take account of any actual or expected changes.

The annual budget is the key control document for assessing overall profitability, and it can be used as the basis for quarterly or monthly analyses of income and expenditure. Any overspending on budget can be identified and corrected; conversely, if budget targets are not met for some particular initiative or commitment (staff training, for example) the reason should be investigated. It is important for accounts staff to be clear about who is responsible for authorising expenditure under the various budget heads, and they in turn should make sure that those with such authority are kept informed of the position each month.

The annual budget of a small practice can be broken down into monthly elements and supported by cash flow forecasts; a large practice will need more detailed information, which might include overhead costs analyses, performance indicators, forecast balance sheets and funds flow statements.

A level of overall profit will also be budgeted. A primary decision is how much is to be retained in the business as working capital and how much is to be distributed to partners or shareholders.

Figure 11: Annual budget: budgeted profit & loss account

Sparrow & Grebe Ltd: 2002 Annual Budget

	£000s	£000s)
Income		
Fee		600.1
Other		2.9
Total:		603.0
Direct costs		
Technical salaries	(260.0)	
Consultants' fees	(20.0)	
Other expenses	(20.0)	
GROSS PROFIT		303.0
Premises expenses		
Rent, rates, insurance	42.0	
Utilities	12.0	
Repair and renewal	6.0	
Administrative expenses		
Staff salaries	50.8	
Staff training	9.0	
Staff pensions	4.0	
Cars	12.4	
Office equipment	17.6	
Printing, stationery	6.2	
Financial expenses		
PI insurance	21.5	
Professional advisors	10.0	
Bank charges	3.5	
Bad debts	5.0	
TOTAL EXPENSES		200.0
OPERATING PROFIT		103.0
Less: Bank loan interest payable		(23.5)
NET PROFIT BEFORE TAX		79.5

Prepared January 2002

7.7 Financial control

The second and crucial aspect of management accounting is financial control – of cash flow, time and costs.

7.7.1 Controlling cash flow

Cash comes in to the firm in several ways, such as payment received against invoices, money invested in the firm, bank loans, and proceeds from the sale of the firm's assets. Cash goes out from the firm to pay staff, creditors, and to reward partners or shareholders.

In the section *How much capital?* (7.1) it was noted that the principal difficulty in architectural business is coping with the time lag between doing the work and being paid for it so as to maintain equilibrium in the bank balance, i.e. solvency. How can this situation be managed? It stands to reason that the best positive action is to be properly funded in the first place, and to control the factors that are capable of control, and the best defensive action is to anticipate the worst situation and know what to do if it arises.

Payments out

As far as outgoings are concerned, there are many peaks and troughs of expenditure that can be levelled out. It is often possible to arrange to pay annual bills such as rates in monthly instalments; the same applies to gas and electricity bills. Non-urgent orders for books, stationery, drawing office and computer supplies can be placed when the cash is available.

Payments in

Getting the money in is far more difficult. A basic business practice that architects are traditionally diffident about is establishing the creditworthiness of prospective clients. Discreet inquiries of professional contacts is often the most reliable indicator, but using a credit reference agency is inexpensive and anonymous and is certainly better than nothing. Checking creditworthiness should be done as a matter of routine with new clients, or where large additional costs are agreed when work is in progress.

There are certain disciplines that will help to get the money in regularly. An important one is to insist that clients pay on a monthly basis. Every appointment should clearly specify terms of payment, and these should always be recorded in writing. The arrangements agreed should suit the practice's accounting procedures and financial situation as well as the client's convenience.

Unfortunately, in business there are always some consistently late payers and a few who never pay at all. Practices need to establish a policy for dealing with both these situations and agree a cut-off point for work in the event of non-payment (say, three months). It is wise to put in place chase-up procedures to deal with late payers so that the problem does not become large-scale; unless the money comes in, the solvency of the practice will be threatened. Repeat work for bad or slow payers should be carefully considered and only undertaken if more effective controls can be put in place – or the job priced accordingly.

7 FINANCIAL MANAGEMENT

The cash flow situation

As well as establishing basic controls of this kind, the general cash flow situation should be constantly monitored, and this is done by means of cash flow forecasts (*see* Figure 12). One is usually prepared based on the annual budget to show the likely position at the end of the new accounting year and to serve as a check on the budget, and again at regular intervals throughout the year. It will highlight any surpluses or shortfalls, allowing decisions to be taken about possible investments or whether an additional loan or overdraft will need to be negotiated.

Figure 12: Cash flow forecast

Sparrow & Grebe Ltd: 2002 Annual Budget

	Jan–Mar £000s	Apr–Jun £000s	Jul–Sep £000s	Oct–Dec £000s
Receipts				
Fee income	125.0	132.8	181.2	149.3
Other	0.1	1.7	0.3	1.2
	125.1	134.5	181.5	150.5
Payments				
Capital expenditure	nil	nil	(15.6)	(24.2)
Salaries	(72.2)	72.1)	(84.6)	(95.8)
Fees	(14.7)	(3.2)	(15.3)	(14.9)
Rent & rates	(17.0)	(7.0)	(17.0)	nil
Stationery, etc	(2.8)	(1.0)	(3.0)	(1.7)
Insurance	nil	(1.5)	(30.0)	nil
Other	(10.4)	(5.7)	(42.0)	(21.9)
	(117.1)	(90.5)	(207.5)	(158.5)
NET CASH MOVEMENT	8.0	44.0	(26.0)	(8.0)
Plus: Opening balance	17.0	25.0	69.0	43.0
Closing balance	25.0	69.0	43.0	35.0

Prepared December 2001

Notes

1 Cash at the bank at the start of the year is £17,000.
2 Cash receipts in Jan–Mar are £125,000.
3 Cash payments in Jan–Mar are £117,000.
4 The net cash receipts are £125,000 less £117,100=£8,000.
5 Add the net receipts (£8,000) to the start of year cash (£17,000) and the total is £25,000.
6 At 31 March the balance is £25,000.
7 This process is repeated for each quarter in the year.

Bracketed figures are outgoings from the bank account.

The manager of a small practice might produce a cash flow forecast every three months. Larger practices usually need the interval to be shorter – probably monthly. Cash flow forecasts can relate to the practice's running costs and to its expected fee income. These can be combined to give an overall picture of liquidity over the year or be broken down to show the situation over shorter intervals.

7.7.2 Putting a price on time

Architects often have to provide fee quotations in competition with others and have to know exactly how low they can bid without sacrificing profits. This means that whatever the fee basis for a job is, they have to be able to assess and measure with precision its work content and the related staff effort needed to service it. It is essential for financial survival that the price charged for providing the professional service required by the client takes into account all the costs involved, direct and indirect, together with a margin for profit.

The only element of a professional service that can be measured is the time taken to provide it. This has nothing to do with the quality or value of that service or the competence of the people involved in its provision; these are things that have to be judged and assessed – they cannot be measured. Even where there is a tangible product such as a feasibility study or investigative report, the client pays for the time taken to produce it, not for the aptness or excellence of its recommendations. The intangible, but priceable, commodity of the service that architects provide is time.

The direct costs of a job arise from the amount and level of staff effort allocated to it. The time of an experienced job architect is considerably more expensive than that of a student, although both may expend the same amount of time on the same job. Failure to get the experience-inexperience balance right can reduce efficiency and, ultimately, profitability.

When a job comes in, it is necessary to calculate how much staff time will be needed to complete it and to put a price on that time. The crucial management tool in job costing is the time sheet.

The time of a full-time architect is spent in five principal ways:

- in carrying out project work;
- in looking for new business;
- in management and administration;
- in training and development;
- in legitimate absence.

Time spent on promotion and advertising would be included under new business, and CPD activities under training and development. Sickness, holidays and other legitimate absences have to be included in the reckoning.

All staff, non-technical as well as technical, should be asked to complete time sheets and hand them in each week. To allow time expenditure to be analysed, time sheets can be divided into the five major time categories described above, with individual projects listed under

Figure 13: Example time sheet

Sparrow & Grebe Ltd
Time Sheet

Name: _____ Week _____

Date completed _____ Signature _____

Project Work	Job no.	Monday hrs	Tuesday hrs	Wednesday hrs	Thursday hrs	Friday hrs	Total hrs	Overtime hrs
Partner i/c								
JR	927	5	3	6			14·0	
CJ	641		2·5		3	6	11·5	
Promotion/ business development					·5	1·0	1·5	
Management/ administration			2	1·5	·5	·5	4·5	
Training/ development		2·5					2·5	
Personal/ absences					3·5		3·5	

Notes
1 Working day is 7½ hours.
2 Minimum unit of time to be recorded is 15 minutes.
3 Overtime work to be agreed beforehand with project partner.
4 For job costing purposes, it is important to take into account agreed overtime rates.

'Project Work' and identified by job number and work stage where appropriate (*see* Figure 13). It must be made clear to everyone exactly what counts as 'project time' and what is the smallest unit of time that is to be recorded.

Time spent on project work is directly chargeable to each project, but time under the four other categories is not. The question therefore arises of how the cost of that other time is to be recovered. All the hours in the working day have a price; there is no 'free' time – salaries have to be paid and the costs of running the business have to be met.

Senior staff may spend about half their time on non-chargeable work: partners often as much as 80 per cent, and junior staff only ten to 15 per cent (*see* Figure 14). If 70 per cent of a job architect's time is fee-earning, the remaining 30 per cent has to be recovered by the price put on the job. If the ratio of chargeable to non-chargeable time can be improved, profitability should similarly improve. This ratio should be watched closely.

It is never easy to persuade staff of the need to complete time sheets, which is often seen as a tiresome chore imposed on busy people who consider they are already doing their best. Staff are more likely to comply if care is taken to explain why time sheets are needed – particularly if it is pointed out that they are a mechanism used to improve efficiency and profitability, which will bring benefits for the staff themselves.

The time of non-technical staff can sometimes be charged as a direct project cost, such as special research and secretarial back-up, computer time, or information provided by in-house specialists, but more often it cannot and in any case this is a matter that should be agreed with

Figure 14: Analysis of time expenditure by grade of staff

	Projects	Promotion/ business development	Management/ administration	Training/ development	Personal/ absences
	%	%	%	%	%
Principal	45	20	25	3	7
Associate	60	10	20	5	5
Senior professional	70	5	15	5	5
Professional	75	nil	10	10	5
Junior professional	85	nil	3	7	5

Notes

1 Read this Figure in conjunction with Figure 13 Example time sheet.
2 The percentages assume a working week of 5 days, and a working day of 7½ hours.

the client. However, it is still important for non-technical staff to complete time sheets as this often provides valuable information about the underlying costs of providing a professional service.

Calculating realistic hourly rates

A small practice will need to identify for each fee-earning member of staff an hourly rate that both recovers all the costs of employing that person and includes a margin for profit. For a larger practice it may be more appropriate to work out an average rate for each grade of staff.

Figure 15: Calculating the number of fee-earning hours

			Hours
Assumptions	A 5-day working week A $7\frac{1}{2}$-hour working day Paid annual leave: 20 days Paid public holidays: 8 days		
Total hours	Per year ($52 \times 5 \times 7\frac{1}{2}$)		1,950
	Minus		
	Public holidays ($8 \times 7\frac{1}{2}$)	60	
	Paid holiday ($20 \times 7\frac{1}{2}$)	150	
	Sick leave (say)	40	
		250	250
Fee-earning hours	Number of fee-earning hours per year per full-time member of staff:		**1,700**

The first step is to calculate the number of fee-earning hours available in a year (*see* Figure 15). Other information needed is:

- the percentage of fee-earning time given in Figure 16;
- details of staff salaries;
- the direct employment costs of each staff member;
- the practice budget.

The method of calculation* is given as Figure 16, and the explanatory notes included should be read. Taking time sheet data as its base, this approach enables the total cost of employing each grade of staff to be seen, the cost of each fee earning hour and, adding on an appropriate margin, the annual fee-earning potential of each grade. The point of the exercise is for architects to be able to know the real costs of employment each time they are required to put a price on a commission so as to be sure that these costs are going to be recovered. The RIBA-published fee scales and hourly rates are only indicative and do not remove the need for sound arithmetic based on up-to-date cost information for each new project.

*As advocated by Jonathan Lucas of Gray Lucas Management Consultancy, to whom the editors are indebted.

Figure 16: Calculating the employment costs of fee-earning staff

1	2	3	4	5	6	7	8	9	10
	Basic salary £	Other direct employment costs £	Indirect costs £	Total cost of employment p.a. £	Fee-earning percentage of time %	Fee-earning hours hrs	Cost per fee-earning hour £	Add 20% margin £	Fee-earning potential p.a. £
Principal	50,000	12,000	20,000	**82,000**	45	765	**107**	129	**98,400**
Associate senior professional	40,000	9,000	20,000	**69,000**	45	765	**90**	108	**82,620**
Senior professional	30,000	5,000	20,000	**55,000**	60	1,020	**54**	65	**66,300**
Professional	25,000	3,000	20,000	**48,000**	70	1,190	**40**	48	**57,120**
Junior professional	20,000	2,000	20,000	**42,000**	75	1,275	**33**	40	**51,000**

All figures given are purely illustrative and should not be taken as a realistic guide.

Notes
Column
3 Direct costs apart from salary include payroll costs such as bonus, employer's N.I. contributions, and benefits (car, pension, private health, etc). These will vary with the grade of staff.
4 Indirect costs ('overheads') include salaries of administrative staff, PI insurance and all costs of running the business that are not specifically project-related. They are divided equally amongst the five categories of staff (and see (**6**) below).
5 Column 2, 3 and 4 are added together to give column 5.
6 These are the assumed fee-earning percentages shown in Figure 14. In practice, the figure for principals will vary widely, and might be a low as 20% – even lower in some cases. In such cases it might be more realistic to redistribute all or part of principals' non-chargeable time as an overhead (i.e. included in column 4).
7 The column 6 percentages of assumed total available hours per year (i.e. 1,700, see Figure 15) are converted into hours.
8 The cost per fee-earning hour is calculated by dividing total employment costs (column 5) by the number of fee-earning hours (column 7).
9 The figures in column 8 with a 20% weighting. Obviously, the appropriate profit margin will vary according to the particular job.
10 The potential fee income for the grade of staff is calculated by multiplying the number of fee-earning hours (column 7) by the profit-weighted hourly rate (column 9).

Typically, the larger a practice becomes, the more time partners need to spend on management and looking for new business, and the less time they spend on direct project work. However, sooner or later the question will arise of how to rationalise in a job-costing system the relatively high salary of a partner with the relatively low percentage of his or her time that may be charged directly against the project. It may be more realistic to regard the non-chargeable element of a partner's time as a practice overhead. In the calculation, it would then be absorbed evenly by the other grades and is shown as indirect costs in column 4 of Figure 16.

It must be stressed that the method demonstrated is only one way of approaching the arithmetic and it is based on various arbitrary assumptions. It does not take into account the many variations in skill, seniority, efficiency and appetite for work between individual staff. Time spent on a job can be measured, but arithmetic says nothing about how effectively that time has been spent. The human factor should not be ignored.

7.7.3 Managing the workload

Calculating the practice's fee-earning potential has an important application as a strategic control in managing the practice's existing and expected workload. This requires a realistic forecast of fee income to be kept under review, so that action to recruit additional design or other staff can be taken as necessary.

The forecast could take the form of a schedule of all committed work, i.e. all workload continued, commissioned projects and any prospectives that are judged likely to materialise. The best way to monitor and control variable data of this kind is to use a computer spreadsheet. There are many add-on packages that work in conjunction with accounting software to forecast fee income on a monthly basis and record fees invoiced and received. In this way a running check can be kept on the status of each project and its performance against target. This allows fine tuning to be done if a lean period is indicated or a possible overrun means there may be a shortage of key staff to start on a new job. If similar information is compiled relating to the actual expenditure of practice overhead costs against budget, a picture of the overall liquidity and profitability of practice finances can be produced.

7.7.4 Speculative work

Carrying out work before a commission has been formalised is obviously risky, although most jobs start off as 'prospectives', to be converted to 'in progress' status when commissioned. In some cases, of course, the project does not proceed and the work done proves abortive. This is of no great consequence if it amounts to a few sketches and the odd meeting, but there must be a defined cut-off point for such 'free' work. Records should be kept of the amount of time spent, and at the cut-off point each should be given a prospective job number and budget. It will then at least be possible to assess the cost of the job realistically and, if it proceeds, even to recover the cost of some of the preliminary work.

7.7.5 Job overruns

As soon as a job overruns, its profits begin to be eroded. The reasons for the overrun must be stringently investigated. The fee quotation or time estimate may have been unrealistic, or the balance of staff assigned to the project may have been inappropriate or their performance inadequate. It may be that work additional to the original commission has 'crept' in. Whatever the reason, the lessons must be learned.

7.7.6 Day-to-day control

The practice's bank balance must be kept under constant review, so that credit is not exceeded or unnecessary loans maintained. Surplus funds should not be allowed to lie idle, and automatic transfer into an interest-earning account should be considered. Quarterly reviews are suitable for small practices; for larger firms they will need to be more frequent.

It is essential to know exactly where the money goes. A great deal is often lost by careless administration at a day-to-day level.

7.7.7 Book-keeping

In order to know the exact position at any given point in time it is essential to keep accurate records of day-to-day transactions (*see* Figue 17). This can be done manually, although there is an increasing tendency for firms to invest in book-keeping and accounting software packages, and larger practices will always handle these tasks using sophisticated computer based systems (these are discussed in Watson and Lockley's *A Guide to Managing IT*).

At the very least it is essential to maintain a cash book, a list of unpaid bills, and a list of unpaid fee invoices. The cash book records daily income and expenditure under pre-defined categories. It should be updated weekly and each month checked against bank statements (a process called 'reconciliation'), which will identify hidden expenditures such as direct debits, and identify possible bank errors. A separate 'petty cash' book should also be maintained.

In addition, a separate record of all payments to any employed staff should be maintained, together with tax deducted, PAYE, National Insurance, etc. This is usually done using a computerised system or a payroll bureau.

Book-keeping records should be studied and analysed; they will often reveal where waste is occurring and economies can be made, or where stricter control is needed.

An important management consideration is to identify who is responsible for authorising expenditure. Accounting procedures simply expedite the decisions of others; it must always be absolutely clear where the authority for expenditure lies, what limits there are, and to whom the authorising person is accountable.

Figure 17: A summary of book-keeping duties

Book-keeping duties are carried out daily, weekly, monthly, quarterly, and annually, and can be summarised as follows:

Daily
Deal with banking, petty cash.
Deal with items received in the mail.
Make appropriate entries in double entry system.
Raise invoices.

Weekly
Verify the situation at the bank.
Review petty cash activities.

Monthly
Send out fee accounts.
Prepare wages and/or send out salary notifications.
Deal with PAYE adjustments.
Settle month end accounts.
Pay office bills.

Compile, record and pay staff expenses.
Prepare financial statements as required for management accounting purposes. These might include:

- cash flows
- profit and loss matched against budget and previous year
- fees outstanding and amounts owing
- bank reconciliation.

Quarterly
Prepare VAT return.

Annually
Prepare annual accounts ready for audit by accountant.
Put away the year's files and prepare new.
Compare profit and loss with annual budget.
Prepare annual budget.
Prepare revised budgets (forecasts).

Accountancy software

There is a wide range of accountancy software, and it is essential that the staff who will be using it have, or acquire, a working knowledge of the basic principles of day-to-day financial accounting, i.e. book-keeping. Although most accountancy software programs are easy to use, those using them must understand what they are trying to produce and for what purpose. To use computing vernacular, what goes in as garbage will come out as garbage. Straightforward accounting packages are available from many manufacturers, the market leaders in the UK probably being the Sage Group and TAS software. Much more complex systems are available from companies such as Navision, Great Plains, Exchequer and Access Accounts.

7.8 Tax management

The tax situation changes from year to year, and needs to be kept under constant review. The taxation service provided by an accountant consists of tax compliance work and tax consultancy work. Tax compliance work is the service of preparing tax returns – typically the annual corporation tax return of a company or partnership, and the annual income tax returns of individuals. Tax consultancy work is the provision of advice on tax planning and management and is a highly complicated field. The accountant will aim to minimise a practice's tax liability making sure that any relief available is taken up, and will give advice about the least onerous way of meeting payments.

It is essential to have enough cash available to meet tax payments when they fall due. The various tax collectors have extensive powers of enforcing payment and punitive interest and even penalties will be charged on unpaid tax.

The main taxes affecting architectural practice are:

- Income tax (Schedule D, Classes I and II). Due in two half-yearly instalments in January and July.
- Schedule E (PAYE). Employers are responsible for deducting tax and NI contributions from wages and salaries.
- Corporation tax (payable by limited and unlimited companies on their profits).
- Value added tax (payable on goods and services sold). VAT returns are usually made quarterly.

There may also be implications for inheritance tax and capital gains tax in the case of some practices. It is also important to investigate taxes collected by the local authority, in particular those connected with rating business premises.

For a partnership, income tax is complex to calculate and administer and the advice of an accountant is essential. One of the advantages of conversion to trade as a company is that the income tax burden at least is simplified, as all employees, including directors, are subject to PAYE. Since 1998, individual taxation has been based on self assessment, which means it has been even more important to be meticulous about keeping records of all transactions.

7.8.1 VAT

A business is required to register for VAT if its 'taxable turnover' (which covers fee income) was greater than £54,000 in the preceding 12 months, or is anticipated to exceed that amount in the forthcoming 30 days. This is done using a registration form obtainable from the local VAT office.

After registration, VAT returns must be submitted to Customs and Excise every three months on forms sent to the practice. To prepare the VAT return, it is necessary to prepare an account of income and expenditure during the relevant period. VAT normally becomes due on a fee as soon as it is invoiced, regardless of whether the invoice has been paid. This VAT is referred to as 'output tax'. Practices whose taxable turnover is less than £600,000 may use the 'cash accounting scheme' which allows them to delay accounting for VAT until a fee is paid – practices intending to use this system should contact the VAT office for details. This clearly has cash flow advantages for small businesses.

VAT can be claimed on most business expenses, notable exceptions being entertainment expenses or the purchase of a car. The VAT (or 'input tax') can be recovered in the same period in which it is incurred. Once the quarterly account is drawn up, the amount payable to (or reclaimable from) HM Customs and Excise is normally the difference between the amount due on fees and the amount reclaimed on expenses. The position is more complicated, however, where some of the services supplied by the firm are not taxable, or where large purchases are made, such as land or buildings, or computer equipment, in which case specialist advice should be sought.

The VAT office is normally very helpful and a visit by a VAT inspector should not be treated as a cause for undue concern. Visits are normally arranged every few years, to check the books and records. If unsure about any details it is better to raise it with the VAT office rather than proceed in ignorance. One common mistake, for example, is to charge expenses net of VAT on fee invoices. The expense should be cited as the gross amount paid by the office, and then VAT charged on the total of fees plus expenses.

7.8.2 Company cars

Where a company car is provided to an employee, it is taxed as a benefit to the employee. The current system is to multiply the manufacturer's list price for the car by a percentage based on business mileage per annum, which is intended to reflect the degree to which the car is not really necessary for business use, and can genuinely be considered a 'benefit'.

It should be noted that the current system is to be replaced in April 2002 by a system where the percentage multiplier will depend on the rate of CO_2 emissions, with higher emission cars attracting a higher taxable benefit.

7.8.3 Self assessment

Under the new self assessment system, companies and individuals must record income and business transactions, compute the tax due and pay the relevant amount at the right time, regardless of whether they are provided with appropriate paperwork or contacted at all by the tax authorities. The Inland Revenue may demand to see documentation and information related to the calculation. If there is an error, additional tax may be demanded, together with interest and penalties, but a prosecution is only likely to arise where there has been serious fraud.

7.8.4 Pension schemes

Under new pensions legislation in force from April 2001, all practices employing more than four people must offer their employees a pension scheme. This must be a 'stakeholder compliant scheme', unless the employer already offers an occupational or grouped personal pension plan which satisfies requirements set down in the legislation. The stakeholder pension will be a simplified, low cost, highly flexible way for people to save for their retirement. There are severe penalties for not having a scheme in place.

Whatever kind of pension provision is being contemplated, two things are essential: first, to obtain expert advice on the tax implications and, second, to set up pension arrangements as early in one's career as possible so as to build up an adequate sum for retirement.

7.9   Making a profit

Profitability is not simply a matter of 'doing well' in the long term or achieving an increase in turnover; it should be seen as a quantifiable target for the performance of the business overall, as a target for each job in its own right and for each fee-earning person employed by the practice.

In times of high inflation, a practice that is breaking even on paper is, in real terms, operating at a loss; it follows that setting a level of overall profitability that relates realistically to the economic climate can be a matter of survival. In more stable market conditions, profitability is something that a practice might feel able to take a view about, in line with its character and philosophy.

The question of profit arises whenever a job opportunity materialises. On some jobs, costs can be reliably quantified and a profit margin set with confidence; others are less easy to evaluate. Sometimes it might be worth doing a job and keeping the profit margin low because there is a good prospect of more work coming in from the client. It is questionable whether it is ever worthwhile taking on a job where it seems that the best outcome will be to break even – and in a period of high inflation, even more doubtful.

Profits can be eaten away by sloppy commissioning procedures. The income expected from each project should be established in the terms of the commission agreed with the client and described in a properly formulated written agreement. If the client subsequently asks for additional services, the client must pay for them: the commission must not be allowed to 'creep' into something more than what was defined in the agreement. Profits are also dissipated by underestimating the time needed to complete a job and by allocating too much, or inappropriate, staff effort to it.

When assigning staff to projects a balance often has to be struck between skills, availability and costs. On some jobs, the first question might be who is the best project architect for this particular job; on another, who can the practice afford to put on it – or simply who is available?

Setting realistic profit margins depends upon a precise knowledge of costs – the cost of running the practice overall; the cost of running each job; and the chargeable and actual cost of each of the people employed by the practice (*see* 7.7). Previous experience of a particular type of job will help to indicate what level of profit can be targeted, but even where the situation is unknown a figure should still be set and job costs meticulously recorded.

Some jobs will be found to be less profitable than others and the reasons for this should be analysed. In some cases it may be the type of work involved, in others it may be the quality of the project team deployed – and there may be other reasons. It is important to read the signs and learn the lessons during a project as well as after its completion; if an unprofitable situation is revealed whilst a job is in progress it may be possible to take corrective action.

The varied and fluctuating nature of commissions does not permit architects to set a once-for-all pattern of costing that will assure profitability. Even if the arithmetic is sound, there is always the variability of human factors: key staff may leave or fall ill, there may be a disagreement on policy between partners, or a misunderstanding may arise with the client. Watchful and responsible management, supported and implemented by sound technical and financial procedures, will always be needed.

References and further reading

Baker B. *Tax Investigations Journal*, January 2001, pp. 80-1.

Conn, B. 'Value-added Tax', RIBA *Journal*, September 2000, pp. 85-6.

Gladdash, P. 'VAT', *The Capital Goods Scheme Journal*, November 2000, pp. 90-3.

RIBA Publications (2000) *A Guide to Painless Financial Management and Job Costing*, London, RIBA Publications, Small Practices series.

Thompson, R. *Company Cars Journal*, October 2000, pp. 99-100.

Watson, R. and Lockley, S. (2001) *A Guide to Managing IT*, London, RIBA Publications, Small Practices series.

8 INSURANCES AND RISK

8.1 Office insurances

8.2 Architect's liability

8.3 Risk avoidance

8.4 Professional indemnity insurance

8.1   Office insurances

Every practice has to face the possibility of financial loss arising from unexpected events. All the risks to which the practice may be exposed should first be identified and evaluated. The financing alternatives are then to carry the risk themselves by setting aside adequate financial reserves or self insuring to meet the unknown, or to pay someone else to take the risk (risk transfer) – for example, to insure.

Not all risks are insurable. The schedule of office insurances given as Figure 18 is intended as a helpful starting point, but the nature and level of risks will vary from practice to practice. It is always wise to seek the advice of an insurance broker.

Figure 18: Schedule of office insurance policies

---

1. Commercial combined material damage

Material damage (to buildings, contents and stock including glass breakage)

Business interruption (e.g. loss of insurable gross profit following material damage)

Computers

Legal liabilities (employers' and public/products)

Money (loss of or damage to cash and securities)

Fidelity guarantee (i.e. employee theft)

Elements of personal accident (e.g. to cover assaults under the money section or a specific personal accident/business travel section)

2. Liability policies

Employer's liability (compulsory cover)

Public liability

3. Travel policies

Emergency medical and additional expenses

Public liability ('personal liability' whilst travelling)

Personal accident

Baggage and personal effects

Personal money/documents

Cancellation and curtailment

Hijack

Delay/missed departure

Legal expenses

Figure 18 *continued*

---

4. Computer policies

Fire and theft

Accidental loss or damage

Breakdown

Business interruption following damage

5. Business interruption

6. Motor cars (third party liability is a compulsory cover)

7. Fires and extended perils: building (e.g. if in rented/non owned premises)

8. Liability for property overseas

A practice's risks should be re-evaluated regularly, preferably every year. Where possible, all policies should cover the legal expenses related to the defence of a claim. Policies should be checked to ensure there is no overlap of cover. Apart from obviously saving premiums, it will also avoid arguments between insurance companies in the event that 'contribution' from more than one insurer is required and possible delays in payment. ('Contribution' is one of the basic principles of insurance. Where there is dual insurance, insurers will contribute, generally on a proportion of loss basis, so that the insured does not receive more than indemnity, i.e. the claim will not be paid twice.)

Insurance contracts depend upon a basis of 'utmost good faith' where there must be total honesty in completing proposal forms and the insured (policyholder) has a duty of absolute disclosure in all matters, which continues throughout the term of the insurance policy. The proposal form will often ask you to warrant that what is stated is correct and that nothing is withheld. The insurance cover will be lost if this is not the case. A practice should be fully aware of all the other conditions included in policies held, for example the obligations to notify events which might lead to a claim, and not to admit liability to other parties without the consent of the insurers.

8.1.1 Employers' liability insurance

Under the Employers' Liability (Compulsory Insurance) Act 1969 and the relevant regulations (for example the Employers' Liability (Compulsory Insurance) Regulations 1998), it is compulsory for every 'employer' carrying on business to have employers' liability insurance. Without this cover, employees with a valid claim against an employer could find that the firm has no resources to satisfy that claim. The Act protects employees who work under a contract of service.

Under the Act, all employers (with some exceptions, e.g. local authorities and statutory bodies) must insure with an authorised insurer and maintain insurance currently for a minimum indemnity of £5 million arising out of any one occurrence in respect of claims which it is legally obliged to meet relating to any one or more employees arising out of their employment, and including whilst employees are temporarily overseas on the firm's business. The *Certificate of Insurance* issued under the Act must be displayed in a position accessible to all employees and retained by the practice as proof of cover for a period of 40 years.

Insurers will only pay out where a claim is one for which the employer has a 'legal liability', proven by the claimant/employee. Only incidents arising 'out of and in the course of the employment' are covered, but claims may be brought for death, personal injury and/or industrial disease, and may include compensation for pain and suffering ('general damages'), loss of earnings, out of pocket expenses, and legal costs. Claims may also be made if the employee is unable to resume the same type of occupation and thereby suffers loss of earning capacity.

8.1.2 Public liability insurance

Employers' liability insurance does not extend to 'third parties'. Whilst it is not compulsory for practices to insure against this type of liability, public liability insurance is something that should always be considered, depending on the nature of the work that the practice undertakes (e.g. ranging from injury to visitors to your own premises, to the potential to cause damage to property whilst on third parties'/customers' sites)

Public liability insurance covers 'legal liability' for death, injury or damage to property caused to third parties, subject to some exclusions, which will generally be caused through the negligence of the partner. It is recommended that a minimum indemnity of £5 million should be arranged, and the cover reassessed at regular intervals.

8.1.3 Personal accident, life and sickness insurance

In the course of employment, an employee may die, or become incapacitated by accident or sickness. The employer has lost the services of someone who may have to be replaced at considerable expense and at short notice.

The employee may have lost earning capacity permanently or temporarily. In the case of an accident, even though the incident may have occurred while the employee was travelling to or from work or was engaged in the employer's business, if the employer is not legally liable then the employee may have to look elsewhere for redress – to a builder, for example, if the incident happened on site and the contractor is liable.

It might be prudent to consider arranging personal accident policies for selected employees or for the entire staff. These can cover death, permanent total disablement, and temporary disablement, and may be extended to cover sickness. Premiums are based on the payroll and on the level of capital benefits to be provided, which may vary with the seniority of staff.

Lump sum benefits are usually payable in the event of death, loss of limbs and/or eyes or total permanent disablement, and 'temporary benefits' payable on a periodic basis (e.g. weekly) in the event of partial or temporary disablement.

A practice might consider a voluntary scheme whereby it arranges the insurance on behalf of staff who wish to participate and then recovers the premiums from them, e.g. via payroll.

8.1.4 Business travel

If employees have to travel frequently, particularly overseas where standards of health care vary and medical treatments can incur large bills, it would be wise to consider cover for:

- emergency medical expenses and repatriation expenses;
- emergency hotel and emergency baggage expenses (i.e. emergency travel expenses);
- curtailment and cancellation expenses;
- baggage, personal effects, and personal money;
- personal liability;
- personal accident;
- hijack;
- delay/missed departure; and
- legal expenses.

Temporary life cover would have to be established separately.

For overseas postings longer than three months, special packages for 'overseas secondees' should be considered which cover medical and repatriation expenses. The needs of each case should be discussed with the insurers.

Cars used for the firm's business

Cars owned and insured by the firm will be covered for business use. If employees use their own cars on the firm's business, their insurance will not be valid unless their policy is properly endorsed.

For those individuals that use their car for business use, the responsibility for insurance will fall to them. Such drivers will need to request 'Class 1' or 'Class 2' business use from their insurers.

- The normal private vehicle certificate covers use on 'social, domestic and pleasure' (which is often extended to include travel to and from the *policyholder's* usual place of work).
- Class 1 (or Class A) in addition includes personal business use by the *policyholder in person* (and may include the business of the policyholder's spouse) but excludes commercial travelling.
- Class 2 (or Class B1) also permits use on the insured's business by others (but not commercial travelling).
- Class 3 (or Class B2) in addition permits commercial travelling.

Class 1 allows the *policyholder only* to use the vehicle on business. For example, shared driving on a business trip where a colleague is driving is not covered.

Class 2 business use is necessary for shared business use of a private car.

It is wise to inspect the insurances of those who are to use their cars on the firm's business and if necessary pay an additional premium for the appropriate business cover.

The European Commission adopted the 4th EC Motor Directive in May 2000 and Member States have until July 2002 to make the Directive national law, with implementation occurring no later than January 2003. One of the objectives of the Directive is to solve the problems inherent in tracing an insurer or claiming in a foreign country against a local resident and insurance company. One of the requirements of the Directive stipulates the establishment of an information centre to retain details of all vehicles registered in the territory together with owner and insurer details. The database for recording private policy details has been set up and the fleet database is currently in development.

We understand a number of insurers are already declining to insure or renew fleet policies that include privately owned vehicles (partners' own cars, etc), because of the forthcoming Directive. The fleet database will have to be ready by the time the UK law becomes effective in July 2002. Whilst the administration involved with policies covering fleet and 'non fleet' vehicles may be more cumbersome, as more detailed information may have to be provided by the insurer, this will hopefully be overcome during the development stage, and should not be sufficient reason for an insurer to refuse a fleet renewal.

8.1.5 Permanent health insurance

If employees fall sick and are away from work for long periods, the practice may wish to continue making some payments to them. Permanent health insurance can be a relatively inexpensive add-on to pension packages. It will pay a proportion of a person's salary, after a qualifying period (usually three months) up to normal retiring age if necessary and will continue payment of the employee's pension contributions.

8.1.6 Premises and contents

Loss or damage to the premises and contents would be very serious for a busy architectural office, and it is good practice to insure against such losses. The basis of insurance should be for full reinstatement (i.e. with no deductions for dilapidation) and a full inventory of contents should be taken and regularly updated, with the policy allowing for the cost of, for example, re-drafting all drawings stored on the premises. Thought should be given to rights of subrogation, for example where the lease is held in the name of only one of the partners, whether the insurance policy should provide that the insurers waive their rights of subrogation against the other partners and employees.

8.1.7 Personal belongings

A practice's contents policy does not cover loss of, or damage to, employees' personal belongings or clothing. Employees' own household policies may include all risks cover for certain valuable articles temporarily removed from the house.

8.2   Architect's liability

Liability concerns matters for which the architect can be held accountable or responsible at law. Most claims against architects are for alleged breaches of contract, or for negligence in tort. The duty of care expected of a professional is usually that of exercising due skill, care and diligence. However, this can be modified and become more arduous or reduce in certain circumstances. It will depend largely on what the architect has undertaken to perform.

Liability arises in the context of common law obligations, and those duties which are founded in statute. For architects, it can be limited in the following ways:

- by adopting an appropriate form of practice;
- by incorporating appropriate terms in the appointing document and obtaining the client's agreement;
- by the intervention of statute (i.e. claims becoming statute-barred with the passage of time).

Some architects choose to practise in the form of a limited liability company, but this does not mean that the company and/or its directors and other employees are entirely protected from claims in negligence. (See 4.1, where the advantages and disadvantages of incorporation, and the attaching liabilities, are reviewed.)

It is possible to limit liability by only entering into tightly drafted contracts which clearly set out the extent of the services to be provided. These should restrict liability to that of the standard of reasonable skill and care normally to be expected of the professional. A simple contract is to be preferred, in that it has a shorter liability period than a deed.

Liability can be expressly excluded in some areas, or can at least be limited through the provisions of the contract. For example, current RIBA appointing documents provide in the Memorandum of Agreement for the architect's liability to be limited in time and amount. A clause allows for the insertion of any time that the parties might agree, and this should effectively override the limitation period arising from statute. There is also a 'net contribution' clause, which is an attempt to limit the architect's joint liability to his or her fair share. Another clause allows the insertion of an overall ceiling limit to liability, as a matter of normal commercial practice.

8.3   Risk avoidance

Architects should avoid unnecessarily widening the scope for claims by ensuring that they practise in a way that moderates risk. Risk potential is great if work which has a known bad record for claims is undertaken. Insurers have identified the following as areas of high risk:

- taking over someone else's work (or vice versa) on a partial service basis;
- structural related surveys;
- post-completion certification for building societies or other funders;

- one-off houses built by non-NHBC (National House Building Council) registered builders;
- working for some housing associations;
- design and build contracts, particularly those which do not limit design liability;
- approving drawings by specialists and sub-contractors;
- acting as a sub-consultant without a proper appointing document.

Responsibility for design, in the absence of anything expressly to the contrary, rests wholly with the architect and cannot be assigned or sub-let to others. The duty of the architect is a wide one, and may be interpreted to include a duty to warn in the case of innovative design or untried systems and materials. It applies equally to gratuitous advice, and has been held to extend to investigating alternative solutions and advising on relative costs.

Unfamiliar construction methods and new products have considerable risk potential. There is often a failure to investigate fully the durability of materials, components or systems relative to a required life cycle, the risks of differential movements or chemical reactions in particular circumstances or combinations. Typically, too much credence is given to manufacturers' claims, which are often based on tests under laboratory rather than real-life conditions.

To summarise, risks can be avoided or substantially reduced by:

- being sure that resources are adequate and available before making any commitment;
- making sure that the service offered is properly described and confirmed, and that the client's expectations are realistic;
- making sure that the fee or other remuneration is fixed before work starts and, unless agreed otherwise, work is never carried out 'at risk';
- making sure that the legal obligations are attainable and that the assessed risks are acceptable;
- making sure everything is systematically documented and recorded. In a dispute, the person with the best and most accurate records has a head start;
- checking and, if need be, questioning the brief at the outset;
- keeping the client fully informed about cost check procedures and the implications of any changes;
- only sub-letting specialist areas of design to consultants or sub-contractors with the client's authority and acceptance that such persons are solely liable for their design work;
- putting manufacturers' claims and test figures for new material or methods into the particular context, and never 'borrowing' attractive design ideas without fully investigating their suitability for the application intended.

Exposure to risks can be reduced generally by adopting sound practice management and establishing standard procedures for both projects and office business. A quality management system, regularly audited for effectiveness, will reduce a practice's overall risk potential and should be seriously considered by all practising units.

8.4   Professional indemnity insurance

All registered architects who undertake professional work are required to take out professional indemnity (PI) insurance, to protect both themselves and (indirectly) their clients. Under a PI insurance policy, insurers agree to indemnify the architect against damages and costs he or she becomes legally liable to pay arising out of the conduct of his or her professional business. The architect's clients (or third parties who have suffered loss) are not themselves covered but it is still reassuring for them to know that a fund will be there if it is needed, and they are not relying on the resources of the architect personally, or the practice. It is often now a condition of being appointed that there is adequate PI insurance in place.

Under the RIBA Code of Conduct, members undertake to inform clients whether or not they hold PI insurance. However, under the ARB Code of Professional Conduct and Practice Standard 8, all architects undertaking 'professional work' must have 'adequate and appropriate professional indemnity insurance'. The term 'professional work' is very broad, and the Standard applies to all architects, including those taking on work on a part-time basis (for example, in their spare time), and to employees. (The full text of Standard 8 is set out in section 2.4.) Employees should note that, in view of the recent case of *Merrett* v *Babb*, if appropriate insurance has not been put in place by their employer, then the employee might be responsible for outstanding liabilities. What is 'adequate' insurance will depend on the nature and size of the jobs undertaken. The ARB publishes guidelines as to the terms, conditions and coverage of PI insurance policies, the most recent at the time of writing being those published with the 2002 subscription renewal form. Under the new standard 8.3 the ARB requires that architects maintain minimum cover in accordance with these guidelines.

PI insurance is an annually renewable contract. To buy a policy, the architect will need an insurance broker, and it is recommended that a specialist (for example the RIBA Insurance Agency) is used. The broker's advice should be taken on the most appropriate policy and terms.

PI policies are always subject to a limit of indemnity, that is a maximum amount that insurers will pay. The limit may be on an 'each and every claim' basis (meaning that the limit will apply to each claim notified during the policy period) or an 'aggregate' basis (meaning that the limit of indemnity is only available once, in respect of all claims made). Policies are usually written on the former basis, and it should be noted that the ARB require the policy to be on 'an "any one/each and every claim" limit of indemnity unlimited in any one insurance period'.

At the time of writing, the ARB requires that the amount of cover should not be less than £250,000 for practices earning less than £100,000 per annum, £500,000 for practices earning between £100,000 and £200,000 per annum, and £1,000,000 for practices with annual fees of over £200,000. For practices with fees less than £10,000, there should be a minimum level of cover of £50,000. For larger projects many clients will ask for a minimum of £1 million, and often £5 million.

The architect will be required to bear the first part of any claim, that is the excess or deductible. As well as paying any sums that the architect has to pay the claimant, insurers will pay the costs of investigating and defending a claim (they will probably nominate their own solicitors and experts). Depending upon the terms of the policy, the excess may or may not be payable in respect of such 'defence costs and expenses'.

The architect is covered for claims made against him or her during the life of the policy only, irrespective of when the error was made or when the loss was suffered. That is, the policy is written on a 'claims made' basis, in contrast to most other types of insurance, which is written on a losses occurring or occurrence basis. The date when the negligence or breach of duty occurred is immaterial and once the policy lapses, so does the cover. It is therefore important to continue to take out insurance after ceasing to practise, or to arrange that the previous practice maintains insurance.

It is important to consider who should be covered, and this should be discussed with the broker. The policy should, if possible, cover the architect for all work he or she has done for which they might be sued (including for example work done as an employee in another practice); it should also cover all those working in the practice including past partners, employees, and self-employed staff or consultants. It is usual for the policy to waive subrogation rights against employees, but the position of self-employed staff should be considered.

It is also necessary to ensure that cover extends to all the work undertaken by the architect or practice, and again this should be discussed with the broker. For example, if work is undertaken abroad, as part of a partnering agreement or joint venture, or if the architect undertakes a different type of work from usual (as an expert witness, for example) insurers should be advised and confirmation obtained that cover is in place.

The cover afforded by different insurers using different policy wordings varies and it would be dangerous to assume that all policies are the same. It is essential to be clear about the protection offered and to understand the exclusions in the policy. For example, policies offering no retroactive cover – that is, no cover for work done before a certain date – should be avoided. All endorsements should be considered carefully.

Care should be taken in completing the proposal form, and assistance sought from the broker if need be. The architect seeking insurance is under an obligation to disclose all those facts regarded by the law as material which he knows or is presumed to know. Material facts are those which would influence a prudent insurer in deciding whether to accept the risk and if so on what terms, or in other words matters which might increase or alter the risk. Most architects' PI policies do include an innocent non-disclosure clause whereby insurers agree that they will not exercise their right to refuse indemnity as a result of non-disclosure (or other breach of policy conditions) provided that the architect can establish that the non-disclosure was innocent.

The level of premium will depend upon a number of factors, chiefly the fee income of the architect or practice seeking insurance and the prevailing level of premiums in the insurance market. For a number of years, the market has been very 'soft', meaning that premiums have been low; recently, however, the market has hardened noticeably, and premiums have risen steeply. The type and nature of work undertaken and claims recorded are also determining factors.

It is important that the policy requirements to notify claims timeously are observed. Generally, the policy will require that claims, or matters which could become a claim ('circumstances likely to given rise to a claim') are notified promptly. To be notifiable, a claim need not be in writing and it need not be justified. In broad terms, notifiable circumstances arise when there is a situation which could be reasonably expected to result in a claim. It is sometimes not easy to determine whether circumstances should be notified or not, but some examples are given below.

- the architect discovers that he or she has made a mistake, which will result in loss to the client;

- another member of the team (another consultant or the contractor, say) alleges that the architect has made a mistake;

- the architect's client refuses to pay fees and alleges negligence, even if the architect is confident that he or she has done nothing wrong.

The RIBA Insurance Agency provides a PI insurance scheme tailored to the needs of architects, which includes a 'compact' insurance policy to suit small practices, which has a number of benefits.

Information about the scheme can be obtained from the RIBA members' insurance line, or direct from RIBA Insurance Agency.

However good an architect is, he or she is at risk of a claim being made against him or her. If and when that happens, the architect will be glad to have the comfort of adequate insurance. It is time well spent to ensure that the appropriate cover is in place.

References and further reading

ARB (2001) PII Guidelines.

Employers' Liability (Compulsory Insurance) Act 1969.

Employers' Liability (Compulsory Insurance) Regulations 1998.

White, N. 'Cover Your Back', *Building*, 13 July 2001, p. 53.

9 OFFICE MANAGEMENT

9.1 Office manual

9.2 Quality management systems
9.2.1 System content and structure
9.2.2 Development, implementation and certification

9.3 Library services
9.3.1 Classification
9.3.2 RIBA Office Library Service
9.3.3 External reference sources
9.3.4 Annual audit

9.4 Files and records
9.4.1 Administrative
9.4.2 Project records
9.4.3 Databases
9.4.4 Promotional material

9.5 Archives

9.6 Computing and IT
9.6.1 How many machines?
9.6.2 Timescale
9.6.3 Type of hardware
9.6.4 Networking
9.6.5 The Internet

9.7 Drawings and CAD

9.1 Office manual

When an architect sets up in practice, a business entity is born with a definable philosophy and character, and with its own objectives, skills and ways of working. As the workload and staff complement grow, it becomes necessary to describe these attributes and activities in some formal manner, so that everyone in the practice can be certain about the way things should be done, where authority resides, and who is responsible for what.

In particular, practice will be concerned with the need to manage and maintain reference material, files and records, and archives. The paperless office confidently predicted some years ago remains an attractive theory. The popularity of the paper product continues because it is available, portable and can be circulated round the office. Its use does not depend on special equipment. That said, some practices now have most of their practice database information in electronic form and make use of on-line access to external information, and some have fully integrated information systems which can be accessed by everyone in the organisation. Management of all this information needs to be planned very carefully and the system of management understood by all staff.

Most practices meet these needs by compiling an office manual to which the staff can refer. Apart from its crucial role as the base document for developing a quality management system, the office manual is an excellent management tool in its own right, in that it provides support and guidance for staff, clarifies policies and responsibilities and ensures that working procedures and methods are coordinated and effective.

An architect starting up in practice can gradually compile a set of standard policies, formats and procedures, developing these as time goes by into an organised and authoritative collection of facts about the emerging firm and the way it operates, with statements about its aims and objectives and general philosophy. The contents could be arranged loose-leaf with card thumb guide dividers to demarcate sections; it is important to be able to update and revise the contents easily so that they remain current. Larger practices are likely to need several manuals covering the firm's activities and may well seek to implement a full quality management system (see below).

Compiling and keeping the office manual up to date is time-consuming and should be someone's designated responsibility; a principal or other senior member of the practice should be in overall charge of it. One or more copies should be kept available for reference by all staff.

A well-organised and informative office manual is an excellent vehicle for communication and an authoritative point of reference. In addition, it saves a great deal of management time by providing ready answers to a multitude of routine queries from staff at all levels. An outline contents list is given as Figure 19.

Figure 19: Outline contents for an office manual

---

1. **The practice**
   Organisation and structure.
   Aims and objectives.
   Responsibility and authority.
   Training and CPD.

2. **Office management procedures**
   Computer.
   Post.
   Correspondence.
   Filing.
   Library.
   Measuring equipment.
   Archiving and storage.

3. **Appointments procedures**
   Terms of engagement.
   Speculative work.
   Design team appointments.
   Reports and advisory work.

4. **Design management procedures**
   Design and production information.
   Specification writing.
   Design change control.
   Health and safety.

5. **Job administration and Plan of Work procedures**
   Work stage checklists.
   Health and safety.
   Permissions and approvals.
   Cost plans and monitoring.
   Architect's meetings.
   Reports to client.
   Job information records.
   Site visits.

6. **Building contract procedures**
   Standard forms.
   Contract correspondence.
   Instructions and certificates.

7. **General procedures**
   Corrective and preventive.
   Document control.
   Audits.
   Feedback.

9.2   Quality management systems

There are many reasons why a practice may wish to consider introducing a quality management system. It may be to give it a distinct marketing edge over its competitors. It may be that the client or potential clients are insisting on a system as a precondition for tendering for projects. In some cases it may be that there has been a growing awareness in the practice of an increasing frequency of unacceptable errors in work produced, and wasted man hours in retracing decisions and sorting out discrepancies.

An important objective for some practices will be to seek independent third party assessment and certification under the international quality management standard BS EN ISO 9001:2000, although it is, of course, possible to implement an effective quality management system without pursuing it to the extent of certification.

Clients are increasingly asking potential consultants for evidence of management capability, and a quality-managed practice, whether or not the full route to certification is to be followed, can offer assurance that it has achieved and intends to maintain a described level of quality, which it is able to demonstrate by means of well documented and regularly audited procedures.

9.2.1   System content and structure

A quality management system is a structured development of the office manual (*see* 9.1) into a comprehensive description of practice activities in a format that is suitable for regular review and audit. It enables the practice's overall management and detailed methods of working to be monitored, controlled and improved, and provides procedures used for managing and controlling projects.

It is important for the quality management system to describe what the practice actually does to be readily understandable. Procedures should be properly coded so that everyone in the office is clear about their application and revision status. The system should be lean, focused and effective; over-documentation should be avoided, or the system will become unwieldy and time-consuming to apply. Practices who do not feel confident about developing and instituting a system of their own can seek help from specialist consultants, or buy a ready-made system and customise it to suit their own needs.

Design professionals need a system that is appropriate, effective and easy to set up and administer. Tim Jeffries's *Model for a Quality Management System* published by RIBA Publications meets these requirements and has been well tried and tested in the construction industry. It is compatible both with this *Handbook* and with the *Architect's Job Book* (Seventh Edition, RIBA Publications). A transition document is currently being developed to pick up the requirements of the new BS EN ISO 9001:2000, which will enable the existing model to be used with a minimum of disruption. It will also allow certification to be obtained in compliance with the new standard, for which the deadline for systems that already exist is the end of 2003.

The model system, which complies with BS EN ISO 9001:1994, has three components: *The Quality Manual*, *Procedures for Practice Management* and *Project Control procedures for design management*.

Figure 20: Examples of possible practice aims and objectives

1 Provide a competent and comprehensive professional service to clients based on principles of quality and integrity.

2 Further individuals' aspirations both within the practice and in the context of their continuing professional development.

3 Manage and maintain the principles of environmental protection and eco design/management.

4 Maintain the development and implementation of quality management techniques.

5 Eliminate or minimise risks and hazards to health and safety during design processes.

6 Manage the design and building procurement process to meet the agreed needs of clients and end users.

7 Measure the efficiency of project information.

8 Develop lasting relationships between the practice and its clients.

9 Conduct the practice's business in such a way as to meet its responsibilities to employees, clients, end users, suppliers and the community as a whole.

10 Achieve the budgeted level of profit.

11 Encourage ideas for new and improved products and for new applications of technology.

Component 1: The Quality Manual

The quality manual is the only document that may be issued from the office, usually for marketing purposes. It is a comprehensive descriptive manual with information about:

- the practice, its establishment and areas of expertise;
- practice quality policy, and aims and objectives (*see* Figure 20);
- the people who run the practice, their roles and responsibilities;
- the services and disciplines offered by the practice;
- the design and related processes which the practice carries out;
- the quality system, its control, maintenance and implementation, and how it relates to the quality Standard.

Component 2: Procedures for practice management

These procedures will include:

- project registration;
- incoming and outgoing mail and communication;
- internal documents and filing;
- terms of appointment;
- sub-consultant selection and appointment;
- computer systems;
- measuring equipment;
- archiving;
- training and continuing professional development;
- library services.

In addition, the following system control and maintenance procedures are included in this section:

- management review;
- internal audit;
- corrective and preventive action;
- experience feedback;
- quality system control.

Component 3: Project control procedures for design management

These procedures will include:

- enquiries;
- design control;

- operations on site;

- completion and feedback;

- quality planning;

- design review and verification;

- appointment review;

- design change control;

- drawings, reports and specifications.

There will, of course, be many links and cross references between these procedures. For example 'appointment review' for a specific project, which is a proactive process to ensure that what the client expects the designers to do correlates with what the designers understand they are being paid to do, links to the 'terms of appointment' in the practice management section of the system. This procedure will set out the practice's most frequently used methods of negotiating and documenting terms of appointment, including, if appropriate, office-specific appointing documents.

9.2.2 Development, implementation and certification

An essential first step is to hold a practice discussion on the reasons for developing a quality management system, so that the practice objectives are clearly understood. In order that it is seen as being of central importance, someone senior, i.e. a principal, partner or director, should assume responsibility at an early stage for its development and implementation.

The system should evolve out of current procedures and other documents used in the office. A useful step is often to compile a carefully subdivided file of all existing standardised documentation, which can be used as an interim measure as a practice handbook, and which will provide a useful insight into how the practice currently works.

A budget and programme need to be worked out. Although a system can be implemented in a relatively short time it is more usual for it to be developed over a period of several months. Time needs to be allocated within normal office hours for development, review and implementation of the system. The practice needs to decide if it is going to seek outside help.

The next step may be to seek certification. The ISO 9000 series was developed in 1987 as a generic quality management systems standard. It sets out a model to follow in setting up and operating quality management procedures. Certification (or registration, the terms are used interchangeably) is against ISO 9001, or 9004 (enhanced performance), and must be carried out by an accredited certifying body. It should be noted that the ISO 9001 has recently been revised and now consolidates the 1994 versions of ISO 9001, 9002 and 9003.

If certification is required, then the practice should contact several of the accredited certifying bodies and invite them for interview. The practice should not be assessed until its system has been in place for several months, therefore a date needs to be discussed and agreed. The following issues should also be covered in the interviews:

- details of their accreditation status;

- experience in the practice's field of operation, with references;

- details of qualifications of Registered Lead Assessors;
- details of costs and expenses;
- length of assessment applicable and frequency/duration of subsequent surveillance visits;
- details of the Scope of Approval Certificate;
- period of notice to agree the appointment, in advance of the assessment taking place.

Following the interviews, the practice should invite one or more firms to provide a formal quotation. This will be followed by a formal agreement for signature. The practice should make sure that the dates are agreed and the entire practice is informed of when the audit will take place. Further details regarding implementation can be found in The Model Quality Plan and accompanying guidance book.

9.3 Library services

The practice library will be the source of most of the technical, trade, cost, practice and legal information needed by staff working on projects. It will be in constant use, and information must be sufficient and up to date. It must be properly resourced, both in terms of budget and staff. It must be clear who is responsible for maintaining library information. If there is no dedicated librarian, an appropriate member of staff should be put in charge to maintain a paper-based collection and where appropriate, subscriptions to commercial electronic services.

Libraries do not run themselves; there are tasks to be carried out on a day-to-day basis such as ordering, accessioning and maintaining periodical subscriptions, classifying, microfilming and indexing. Someone will need to spend a good deal of time monitoring construction industry events and developments in the provision of information, dealing with manufacturers' representatives and when necessary undertaking research. The librarian of a small practice may be required to compile the practice's brochure and other publicity material such as press releases, advertisements, directory entries, practice newsletters, etc (see Section 11). Another designated activity might be the storage and labelling of manufacturers' samples and yet another the compilation of in-house computer databases and maintenance of the practice web page. A checklist of library contents is given as Figure 21.

Library space and layout should be considered in relation to the practice's size and the nature of its premises. Accessibility is important and so is the provision of adequate shelving, bearing in mind that even the best-managed libraries expand – they never contract. Where possible, working space and a computer workstation should be provided, so that activities connected with cataloguing, publicity material and archiving can be carried out within the library area. Space may also be needed for computers to allow access to on-line information services, practice databases, and for microfilm and microfiche readers. Adequate user space must also be provided for browsing and reference.

9.3.1 Classification

An appropriate classification system should be used in the practice library. CI/SfB is in general use in the construction industry. However, it will be necessary to investigate the use of the more

Figure 21: Checklist of library contents

Quick reference collection
Items in constant use or of broad application, such as:
• CI/SfB manual/Uniclass manual
• Barbour Compendium
• RIBA Product Selector
• RIBA KeyFile Library
• dictionary
• telephone directories

Non-trade literature
Books
Pamphlets
Official publications
British Standards
Journal extracts/cuttings/research

Trade literature
Manufacturers' catalogues
Product data sheets

Samples
Materials, e.g.
• glass types
• timber species
• others
Products, e.g.
• bricks
• ironmongery
• others

Periodicals
Current (on display)
Back numbers (shelved)

Maps

In-house information
Central collection of the practice's own literature:
• promotional brochures
• office manual
• standard specification
• preferred details
• approved contractors lists
• technical data and feedback
• in-house magazines

Stock of standard forms
RIBA contract administration forms
In-house standard forms

Computers
Computers, modems and terminals for:
• internal indexes and databases
• RIBA disc
• CD-ROMs from external sources
• external on-line information systems
• internet access

Microfilm
Microfilm and fiche reader/printers for:
• commercial micro-file systems
• own archives

Visual aids
Wallcharts, posters, etc
Slide sets
Films
Videos

up-to-date Uniclass system of classification. This was developed for the Construction Project Information Committee (CPIC) by NBS Services and was published in 1997. Uniclass is more comprehensive and flexible than CI/SfB and is able to cover the many new categories of information which have developed since CI/SfB was introduced more than 30 years ago. An example table from Uniclass is included as Figure 22.

9.3.2 RIBA Office Library Service

As few practices can afford to employ a full time, in-house librarian, the RIBA Office Library Service is a reliable alternative used by numerous practices to maintain and up-date product literature. The OLS can also provide current information on publications and other services available from the RIBA and RIBA companies. [Contact: RIBA Office Library Service. Tel: 0141 332 6501. Website: www.ris.gb.com]

It may be more economical for a very small practice to use a freelance librarian from time to time. The Construction Industry Information Group (CIIG) can provide a directory of freelance members. [Contact: CIIG c/o the Building Centre, 26 Store Street, London, WC1 7BT.]

Figure 22: Uniclass table

Management Concise Table

C1	**Management theory, systems and activities**	**C5/C9**	**Management of construction activities/project management**
C11	Corporate strategy		
C12	Quality management		
C13	Security, industrial espionage, trade secrets	C50	General techniques/ information
C14	Objective setting		
C15	Decision making	C61	Inception/procurement
C16	Problem solving	C62	Feasibility
C17	Co-ordination	C63	Outline proposals/programme preparation
C18	Appraisal, assessment		
C19	Other	C64	Scheme design/costing
		C65	Detail design/costing
C2	**Management personnel**	C66	Production information
		C67	Bills of Quantities
C21	Top management, directors, partners	C68	Tender action
C22	Other levels of management	C71	Construction preparation/ project planning
C3	**Type of business/organisation**	C72	Construction operations on site
C31	Organisations by scale and location	C73	Completion
C32	Private enterprises	C81	Occupation/facilities management
C33	Mixed enterprises and partnerships	C83	Feedback
		C84	Refurbishment and recommissioning
C34	Government and related organisations		
C35	Public enterprises	C91	Decommissioning
C36	Non-profit-making organisations, charities	C92	Demolition, etc.
		C93	Redevelopment
C37	Industrial and commercial associations		
C38	Construction industry		
C39	Other types of organisation		
C4	**Specialist areas of management**		
C41	Management of office services		
C42	Marketing, selling		
C43	Research and development		
C44	Finance and accounting, business economics		
C45	Personnel management and industrial relations		
C46	Management of computing, information technology		

Some practices may find it cost effective to subscribe to one of the commercial providers of technical data, product/suppliers information, regulatory and standards information either on CD-ROM or on-line. [Contact: Technical Indexes Ltd. Tel: 01344 426311. Website: www.tionestop.com or Barbour Expert: Website: www.barbour-index.co.uk]

9.3.3 External reference sources

Practices should also take full advantage of the many outside information services that are available, some of them on-line. The British Architectural Library of the RIBA is undoubtedly the major professional institution library. The catalogue is available on the Internet at www.riba-library.com. It has compiled a useful directory of websites that is kept up to date at http://www.riba.org/library/rlinks.htm. The RIBA offers subscriber membership, one option of which includes reference use of its collection and free RIBAnet software to exchange information and ideas with other members.

Other sources are the National Art Library at the Victoria and Albert Museum, the National Monument Record Centre and local public libraries. In the United States the Avery Architectural and Fine Arts Library Columbia University, New York is the premier architectural library.

British Library

The British Library is a copyright deposit library and is the leading document provider in the world. It delivers a rapid and comprehensive document supply and interlibrary loan service from its extensive collection to researchers, libraries and other organisations. Details of services available can be accessed from the British Library website at www.bl.uk

9.3.4 Annual audit

An annual review of practice library services should be carried out, and the principal questions to be asked are:

- Is the practice being provided with the scope of information it needs?
- Is the information provided relevant, adequate and up to date?
- Are staff clear about who is in charge of library resources and activities?
- Is the library budget sufficient?

9.4 Files and records

A systematic approach to filing is essential if an office is to run smoothly and efficiently. It is important to set up a filing system that will serve the practice over a long period and can be expanded as its workload grows.

9.4.1 Administrative

Administrative documents are typically produced in-house and will be mainly to do with practice organisation, finance, staff matters, publicity and premises management. There will be a wide range of miscellaneous topics and related paperwork which may need temporary filing and which should be ruthlessly pruned out of the system if and when it becomes redundant. An alphabetical checklist for administration files is given in Figure 23, together with an indication of how CI/SfB or Uniclass might be used to provide a classified arrangement.

Figure 23: Filing arrangements for administrative documents

Administration filing:
Framework based on CI/SfB Table 4

Practice organisation
Communications
Preparation of documentation
Public relations
Controls and procedures
Personnel
Education, training, CPD
Research and development
Accommodation
Secretarial activities
Copying, photocopying
Filing
Finance
Projects

Administration filing:
Framework based on Uniclass

C1	Management theory and systems
C11	Corporate strategy
C12	Quality management
C123	Quality assurance
C19	Other
C193	Awards
C2	Management personnel
C4	Specialist areas of management
C41	Office services
C411	Switchboard
C412	Reception
C413	Security
C414	Secretarial
C415	Mail management
C416	Reprography
C417	Records management
C4171	Documentation/filing
C4172	Stationery, forms
C4173	Library/archives
C42	Marketing
C423	Promotion
C4231	Advertising
C4236	Press releases
C4237	Promotional publications
C43	Research and development

C44	Finance and accounting
C45	Personnel management
C452	Recruitment
C453	Training/CPD
C454	Communication
C455	Industrial relations
C456	Conditions of employment
C457	Remuneration
C458	Working conditions
C5/C9	Projects
C50	General techniques/ standard procedures
C81	Facilities management
C811	Premises
C812	Space management, equipment
C813	Contract office services
C814	Premises services
C8141	Catering
C8145	Transport/company cars
C8146	Communications/ mobile phones
C815	Maintenance and operation
C8153	Cleaning
C8159	Health and safety at work
C816	Emergency procedures

Administration filing:
Categories of financial documents

Original documents
Books of original entry
• day books
• cash books
Ledgers
Trial balances
Final accounts
Forecasts
Assessments
VAT records
Tax records
Administration
Reference*

*useful data such as interest rates, research notes, checklists

Figure 23: *continued*

Administration filing:	People, roles
A–Z checklist of subjects	Petty cash
	Post room
Administration	The practice
Archives	Practice control
Classification	Practice development
Commissions	Practice philosophy
Communications	Practice structure
Computers	Premises
Drawing office practice	Project control
Education, training, CPD	Project planning
Equipment	Publicity
Finance	Purchases
General administration	Quality assurance
General office routines	Quality control
Information system	Reprographics
Institutes and associations	Secretarial practice
Insurances	Staff
Library	Subscriptions
Management	Technical procedures
Marketing	Transport
Office organisation	Travel

9.4.2 Project records

Project records usually consist of paper items (correspondence, contract documents, forms, reports, instructions) and drawings, photographs and models. Some of these items are bulky and/or need special storage, and Figure 24 demonstrates a classified arrangement of project files that takes account of this.

Many disputes arise simply because there are inadequate written records. Good records, systematically stored and easily retrievable, are an essential part of risk management.

Records should be made and kept of all meetings, the advice given by consultants, including the architect, and of the considerations which influenced the many decisions taken during the design process. Architects constantly have to make difficult judgements and consider compromise solutions, and must be able to justify their decisions on the basis of contemporary records. Job and office diaries should be compiled legibly and systematically and kept with other project records for as long as the practice retains any liability for a project.

9.4.3 Databases

In-house computer databases for the storage and retrieval of information are widely used for job lists, job records, lists of clients, lists of contractors, indexes (of reports, files), library catalogue, etc. They may be part of an integrated management information system but it must be made clear who is responsible for their compilation and maintenance.

External databases can be accessed via various commercial on-line services or purchased CD-ROMs. Reference databases include bibliographic information, sometimes with abstracts, catalogues of library stock or library network, and directory information, e.g. names and addresses of organisations. Source databases contain the original source material in machine-readable form, e.g. newspaper stories, statistical surveys and company annual reports.

9.4.4 Promotional material

The items which will need to be collected and developed are considered under Section 11. In a small practice, responsibility for publicity and PR will need to be designated and may be included as part of library duties. Whatever the arrangement, there should be a separate budget allocation, and cost-effectiveness should be kept under review.

Figure 24: Filing arrangement for project documents

PART 1 **CORRESPONDENCE AND** **PAPERS** (mainly filed)	3.11 Health and safety 3.12 Highways 3.13 Means of escape Party walls 3.14 Public health 3.15 Town planning
0 GENERAL 0.1 General	**Miscellaneous** 3.16 …

1   CLIENT
1.0 General
1.1 Project manager
1.2 …
    (subdivide by departments as
    appropriate)
	04 PUBLIC SERVICES
	4.0 General, co-ordination
	4.1 Electricity
	4.2 Gas
	4.3 Post
	4.4 Refuse
	4.5 Sewer connection

2   DESIGN TEAM
2.1 Design team meetings and programme
2.2 Project manager
2.3 Architect
2.4 Quantity surveyor
2.5 Structural engineer
2.6 Building services engineer
2.7 Mechanical engineer
2.8 Electrical engineer
2.9 Lift engineer
2.10 Drainage engineer
2.11 Civil engineer
2.12 Windows consultant
2.13 Lighting consultant
2.14 Acoustic consultant
2.15 Interior designer
2.16 Landscape architect
2.17 Perspective artist
2.18 Modelmaker
2.19 Photographer
2.20 Planning supervisor
2.21 Principal contractor
	4.6 Street lighting
	4.7 Telephone
	4.8 Water
	4.9 Work on public highways and pavements
	
	5 MAIN CONTRACTOR
	5.0 General
	5.1 Touting from contractors
	5.2 Pre-tender enquiries
	5.3 Tendering
	5.4 Main contractor
	
	6 SUB-CONTRACTORS AND SUPPLIERS
	6.0 General
	6.1 Touting from sub-contractors and
	    suppliers (SCs and Ss)
	6.2 Enquiries and quotations
	6.3 Surveys and advance contracts
	6.4 Bulk quotations/bulk purchase/direct
	    supply
	6.5 Nominated SCs and Ss
	6.6 Named SCs and Ss
	6.7 Domestic SCs and Ss
	6.8 Works contractors
	6.9 Independent works and supplies

3 STATUTORY CONSENTS, NOTICES AND **CONSULTATIONS** 3.0 General	**7 CONTRACT ADMINISTRATION** 7.0 General
Client-related interests 3.1 Ministry 3.2 Landlord, etc 3.3 Funder 3.4 Insurers 3.5 Users, tenants, community 3.6 Adjoining owners	**Meetings and progress** 7.1 Briefing meetings 7.2 Site meetings 7.3 Programmes 7.4 Progress reports
Planning and construction 3.7 Building regulations and byelaws 3.8 Disabled access and facilities 3.9 Drainage 3.10 Fire	**Site staff communications** 7.5 Clerk of works' reports 7.6 Clerk of works' correspondence 7.7 Site staff correspondence 7.8 Site visits and inspections

Figure 24: *continued*

Instructions
7.9   Clerk of works' directions
7.10 Site instructions and draft instructions
7.11 Contractor's confirmation of verbal orders (CVOs)
7.12 Architect's instructions
7.13 Drawing issue notes

Quality control
7.14 Sample notes and test results
7.15 Defects schedules (pre-handover)
7.16 Handover and defects records
7.17 Making good defects records – buildings
7.18 Ditto – services
7.19 Ditto – landscape

Cost control
7.20 Cost control reports
7.21 Dayworks and overtime records

Claims
7.22 Claims records

Certificates
7.23 Valuations and certificates for payment
7.24 Certificates – extension of time
7.25 Ditto – practical completion
7.26 Ditto – making good defects
7.27 Ditto – others

Other
7.28 . . .

8   WORKING PAPERS
8.0   General
8.1   Brief and client's instructions record
8.2   Surveys and investigations
8.3   Specification notes and schedules
8.4   Quantities information
8.5   Calculation sheets
8.6   Information for maintenance manual
8.7   Data on project
8.8   Costing
8.9   Ceremonies
8.10 Awards
8.11 Publicity
8.12 Press cuttings
8.13 Internal memos
8.14 Miscellaneous correspondence
8.15 Miscellaneous meetings
8.16 Miscellaneous reports
8.17 Miscellaneous papers

9   LATE ADDITIONS AND SPECIAL EXERCISES
9.0   General
9.1   Post-completion filing
9.2   Specific claims, arbitrations, etc

**PART 2
SPECIAL DOCUMENTS**
(mainly bulky)

10   GENERAL DOCUMENTS
10.1 Job book/building record
10.2 Drawing register

11   LEGAL DOCUMENTS
11.1 Agreements (consultants)
11.2 Contracts (contractors)
11.3 Collateral warranties

12   PROJECT DOCUMENTS
12.1 Soil report
12.2 Design reports
12.3 Job literature (e.g. trade catalogues, official publications)
12.4 Specifications
12.5 Bills of Quantities and priced schedules
12.6 Site records
12.7 Weather records
12.8 Maintenance manual/tenant's handbook
12.9 Health and safety file
12.10 Final account
12.11 . . .

13   DRAWINGS
13.0 General
13.1 Site survey
13.2 Sketches
13.3 Design set
13.4 Special presentation or publicity drawings
13.5 Perspectives
13.6 Consents sets
13.7 BQ/tender set
13.8 Contract set
13.9 Site records
13.10 As-built sets
13.11 Drawings by others (sub-divide by originator and then sub-divide as above or keep in numerical order)
13.12 CAD records
13.13 CAD disks

14   PHOTOGRAPHS
14.0 General
14.1 Site
14.2 Design drawings
14.3 Model
14.4 Progress
14.5 Defects
14.6 As built
14.7 Publicity
14.8 . . .

15   MODELS
15.1 . . .

9.5   Archives

The storage of records that are no longer active needs special consideration. A policy should be developed as to how this is to be done and for what time period, and who is to be responsible for making such decisions. Some may need to be kept for a specified period for reasons of liability; some may be intrinsically valuable and need carefully preserving, perhaps by donating them appropriately – to the British Architectural Library, for example, or to CIRCA (Construction Industry Resource Centre Archive).

Storage is always a problem for architects, because each project generates a large quantity of documentation – drawings in particular, which are large and unwieldy. Most practices are short of storage space, and consideration may need to be given to storage out of house, or on computer or microfilm. There are many specialist firms offering secure storage, although they tend to be expensive. Storage on computer will suit some items, but duplicate hard copies will often be needed, and should be stored well away from the computer area in a fire-proof container (see Watson & Lockley's *A Guide to Managing IT*).

From the management point of view, it is essential that archived material can be accessed without difficulty when and if it is needed. This means developing clear procedures for indexing and the accessing and return of material. If the practice has no librarian, someone senior must be made responsible for controlling this important activity. Procedures should be set out in the office Quality Manual and audited regularly.

9.6   Computing and IT

There must be very few architects' practices that do not use some forms of computing or IT. In a recent survey of small practices (*Small Practice Survey 2000*, conducted for the RIBA small practice sub-committee) it was found that small practices own on average four computers per practice and that 95 per cent have access to the Internet.

In deciding to install or upgrade a practice's computing facilities, it is important, as with any major changes, to be clear as to the practice's objectives. A careful brief should be drawn up of the tasks which are to be performed. Consideration should be given to the following:

9.6.1 How many machines?

It is tempting to start by buying just one, often for use by one of the senior staff. This is rarely successful, and should be seen as only a temporary measure, in order to test what may be suitable for the office as a whole. Sharing terminals should be avoided, and the aim should be for all staff to be working on compatible machines.

9.6.2 Timescale

Both hardware and software develop quickly, so it is wise to assume that computers will need to be replaced on a regular basis, on anything between a two- and five-year cycle.

9.6.3 Type of hardware

A key decision is whether to purchase Apple Mackintosh machines or PCs. Before purchase it is essential to try using both, and to talk to users of both. It is very much a personal preference. Although very difficult to generalise as new machines are constantly being brought out, it is safe to say that Macs tend to be more reliable and user friendly, but there is a wider range of software available for the PC. A practice may not need this wider range, but the limitations should be explored carefully before a decision is made.

Macs have a long tradition of being used in the publishing world, and are favoured by graphic designers, whereas the engineering profession tends to use PCs. Although a Mac-based office may have had problems in the past communicating with consultants who were PC-based, these difficulties have been much reduced with many 'cross platform' software packages available. The editor's office is Mac based and seldom has difficulty in transferring either document or drawing files to PC based offices, provided the PCs are reasonably up to date.

9.6.4 Networking

A more critical decision is how much networking is envisaged, as this will determine the specification for the machines and their peripherals. For example, any older machines may be perfectly capable of performing word-processing and CAD functions, but as soon as they are connected to the Internet their limitations will become apparent as they will crash on attempting to access complex web pages, or on downloading large files of information.

Networking can be on several levels. Internally, individual machines can be linked together for the passing of files of information. With PCs this is done using Ethernet, and with Macs it can be done using either Ethernet or AppleTalk. The next step is to establish a 'server'. This is a dedicated machine on which all files are stored, to which all other machines in the practice are connected. It is essential in large offices, but should be given careful consideration in even the smallest of offices. There is logic in having one repository of files. It avoids separate and slightly different versions of documents appearing on different computers, and allows all the office files to be backed up quickly and efficiently, without having to back up all the separate machines, many of which will contain duplicate information. The disadvantage is that it involves one extra machine, but the additional cost will probably be recouped in the time saved through increased efficiency, especially where CAD is involved.

9.6.5 The Internet

Two things are needed to access the Internet: a physical connection, and an agreement with an Internet Service Provider (ISP).

The simplest way is to purchase a telephone modem, and to sign up with one of the many free ISPs. With this set up the practice will pay for the time on line, and if this time becomes extensive, it will be worth subscribing to a system which allow unlimited time for a flat monthly subscription.

Telephone modems are very limited in terms of the amount of information that can be sent in a given period of time – in other words they are 'slow'. This becomes very apparent when large files such as drawings are sent. It is possible to improve this by using packages which compress the files to a much smaller size before sending. The most widely used format for this is termed 'ZIP' but it is essential that the receiver has compatible software which can unzip the file.

A faster service can be obtained by using ISDN (Integrated Services Digital Network) such as the BT Office Highway service which, of course, involves a higher subscription. This is likely to be overtaken in the near future by ADSL (Asymmetric Digital Subscriber Line), which achieves speeds of ten times that of a normal modem. However, for the time being this system is only available in cities.

Once a rough outline of requirements is drawn up there will need to be some consultation and research. It is, of course, sensible to take advice from friends and colleges, but it may well be that independent expert advice is needed, in which case the advice of an IT consultant should be sought.

9.7 Drawings and CAD

All practices need a carefully thought out system for the preparation, format and storage of drawings, usually set out in the office manual. Sir Michael Latham in *Constructing the Team* recommended the adoption of Coordinated Project Information (CPI) for all projects regardless of procurement method. The CPI publication *Production Drawings: A Code of Procedure for Building Works,* should be followed wherever possible when preparing technical drawings. The Code is for use by all members of the design team who have the task of preparing and issuing production drawings. It is complementary to BS 1192:1984, Construction Drawing Practice.

All drawings must show the following, set out in a 'title block':

- name of the practice;
- telephone, address, fax and e-mail;
- project title;
- drawing title;
- drawing number;
- revision number and date;
- scale of drawing and north point on plans;
- key to symbols used.

In the CPI system the written notes on the drawing are kept to a minimum, and detailed information is indicated by a reference to the specification.

Architects' drawings are best structured as follows:

Location drawings (e.g. block plan, site plan, general arrangement plans, sections, elevations)

Where the project is so large that at a suitable scale these will not fit easily on to single sheets, it might be necessary to split the project into suitable blocks or zones. They should enable users to gain an overall picture of the building, give setting-out dimensions, locate and identify the parts of the building, and refer to more specific information.

Assembly drawings

These will be divided into groups representing parts of the building, e.g. walls, stairs, roofs, openings, ceilings, fittings and external works. They should show the construction of the building, particularly at selected junctions, and refer out to more specific information as necessary.

Component drawings (e.g. purpose-made windows, doors)

These should be referred to from the location drawings. They should show the shape, dimensions and assembly of various parts, and identify components which are not described adequately elsewhere.

By far the majority of practices now have at least some CAD systems. This can range from one dedicated station to a CAD workstation for every member of staff. As with computer systems generally, the most important thing is to define clearly what you are aiming to achieve. There are two main areas which should be considered. CAD is an extremely efficient way of producing 2D technical drawings, allowing them to be adjusted and reproduced with infinite flexibility. For many offices this will be the prime function of CAD systems. There are many simple and inexpensive packages that can fulfil this with ease, without the need to invest in elaborate software. A package such as MiniCad can be useful for small offices; if something more sophisticated is needed AutoCAD, Microstation and ArchiCAD should be investigated. The practice should check before investing that the output is compatible with the systems used by its consultants. This is much less likely to be a problem now than it was a few years ago.

The other key area is in presentation drawings, including 3D and rendered drawings, and in animations such as 'walk-throughs'. This is a particularly specialist area, about which expert advice should be taken. The packages can take a long time to learn, therefore a considerable investment may be needed by the practice before any results appear. If these types of drawings are not needed very often, it may be more efficient to sub-contract their production to a specialist firm.

The storage of CAD drawings must be organised very carefully. It is all too easy for two members of staff to make two different amendments to a base drawing and issue two different 'revision A's', something which was far less likely to occur with hand drafted negatives.

References and further reading

BS1192: Part 1 (1984) *Construction Drawing Practice*, HMSO.

Co-ordinating Committee for Project Information (1987) *Production Drawings: a code of procedure for building works,* London, CCPI.

Hill, M. (1999) *Drawn Information*, London, RIBA Publications, Small Practices series.

Jeffries, T. (1999) *A Model for a Quality Management System,* London, RIBA Publications.

Lupton, S. (ed.) (2000) *Architect's Job Book,* London, RIBA Publications.

Small Practice Survey 2000 (can be downloaded from www.riba.org)

Uniclass, *Unified Classification for the Construction Industry,* London, RIBA Publications, (1997).

Watson, R. and Lockley, S. (2001) *A Guide to Managing IT,* London, RIBA Publications, Small Practices series.

10 COMMUNICATION

10.1 Channels of communication

10.2 The purpose of meetings

10.3 Chairing meetings

10.4 Minuting meetings

10.5 In-house talks and seminars

10.6 Making presentations

10.7 Telephones, faxes and e-mails

10.8 Dealing with the post

10.9 Writing letters

10.10 Responding to letters

10.11 Contractual correspondence

10.12 Formal report writing

10.12.1 Preliminary items

10.12.2 Main text

10.12.3 Appendices, etc

10.12.4 Content and style

10.13 Checking the report

10.14 Technical reports

10.14.1 Surveys

10.14.2 Feasibility studies

10.14.3 Design development

10.14.4 Work in progress

10.14.5 Site inspection reports

10.15 Reports for litigation

10.16 Presentation of reports

10.17 Feedback

10.1   Channels of communication

In offices, oral and written communications often have to pass through various people and processes, and can easily become distorted in transit. If they are not clearly formulated at source and properly directed, they will have little chance of being received and understood, let alone acted upon. In management, it is essential to be certain of the following:

- what information is needed;
- who needs it;
- what form it should take;
- that it will be understood.

Instructions should always be transmitted along designated and recognised channels of authority. If the proper route is bypassed, authority is undermined, the validity of the instruction is in question, and the result is uncertainty and confusion. Whatever the style of management, the procedure for transmitting instructions must be clearly defined and must be followed at all times.

Information tends to proliferate in offices, much of it trivial and unnecessary, and unless priorities are identified and pursued, channels of communication can become overloaded, resulting in delay and frustration. Principals need to keep the situation under constant review, otherwise they may find themselves talking to everyone but failing to communicate with anyone.

10.2   The purpose of meetings

It should be clear to all participants why a meeting is necessary and what it seeks to achieve. A great deal of time can be wasted if the objectives of the meeting are not identified, as it will be all too easy for the participants to steer the meeting towards their own personal concerns. An agenda should be sent out in good time before the meeting, which makes it clear what those objectives are. This not only focuses the minds of the people attending on the issues to be discussed but provides a framework of control for the meeting itself. The agenda is normally prepared by the chair. A model general purpose notice and agenda is given as Figure 25.

Thought should be given as to who should attend. It is tempting to invite everyone who may have an input in the matters to be discussed. However, where the input is limited to only one or two items, this may waste a person's time, and it may be possible to deal with the input by asking for a short written submission, and by circulating the minutes to the person for comment.

In architectural practice, meetings are typically called to review progress and get decisions approved. The people who attend should have the appropriate authority to act in accordance with the decisions taken. The meetings that job architects normally call, chair and minute include:

- the initial design team meeting;
- the initial project team meeting;

- any site inspectorate briefing meeting needed;
- the architects' regular progress meetings.

If attending a meeting, be sure to be clear as to its purpose, and if necessary raise queries in writing. If you wish to raise relevant matters which are not shown on the agenda, make this clear to the chair beforehand so that time can be allowed under 'any other business'. Nobody welcomes someone introducing major new matters unexpectedly, no matter how important these are, as they will prolong the meeting at a stage when most people will be looking at their watches and will have started to think about their next appointment.

At the meeting, be sure you are clear as to who is present, and do not be nervous to ask for names to be repeated if they are not clear. If new to the group, make sure that you are introduced. It is a good idea to arrive early and introduce yourself to the chairman before it starts. Attending important meetings can be quite daunting, especially to Part 3 students or the newly qualified. However, do not be too nervous of asking for clarification where issues seem confused, it can often help the meeting to backtrack slightly and set out the recent history regarding a particular matter. Avoid doing this continuously, however, as it will bring the meeting to a halt! It would be better to take careful notes and do some background reading so that at the next meeting you are more fully informed.

Figure 25: Specimen notice and agenda

NOTICE OF MEETING AND AGENDA

Name of project   **Job no.**

Type of meeting   **Meeting no.**

This meeting will be held at Sparrow & Grebe's offices at (*time*) on (*date*). It is expected to end at (*time*).

There will be a (*forty minute*) break for lunch/A sandwich lunch will be provided during the meeting.

Apologies, names of replacements should be notified to (*name of architect or secretary*).

AGENDA

1   Minutes of last meeting

2   Matters arising

3   (Item for discussion)

4   ditto

5   ditto, etc.

6   Any other business

7   Date of next meeting (*if any, with details of time and place*)

Distribution: (names of people or organisations invited/expected to attend)

Date: (agenda was issued)

10.3   Chairing meetings

It is essential to keep control, otherwise the purpose of the meeting may be defeated and a great deal of time wasted. Confining discussion to the points at issue usually requires good humour and diplomacy, but it may sometimes be desirable to allow grievances to be aired and to encourage the less articulate and self-confident to have their say. If it is appreciated that the chairperson is prepared to be reasonable and considerate but will not tolerate time-wasting and pointless argument, the meeting is more likely to run smoothly.

Meetings should start on time, with the chair calling the room to order firmly but pleasantly. Then he or she should identify those present, introduce newcomers or replacements, including making clear the reason for their attendance. This is extremely important, as a great deal of time can be wasted and mistakes made through misunderstandings regarding the identity or role of those present. The chair should then ask for apologies for absence and mention any already received. The minutes of the last meeting should then be accepted, with any agreed corrections noted. Their acceptance as a fair record of the previous meeting is usually recorded as item one of the new set of minutes. In the case of formal meetings it is very important to follow these procedures so as to achieve a true and agreed record which those present cannot dispute at a later date.

It is then usual to take Matters Arising from the previous minutes. Discussion of these should be strictly limited, and any attempt to introduce a new topic or an agenda item at this stage should be resisted – new items should be raised under Any Other Business at the end of the meeting, and agenda items should not be discussed out of sequence. A note should be made of any important points made and these should be included in the next set of minutes under Matters Arising with their previous numerical references.

Agenda items should be taken in their set order, only departing from this if there is some cogent reason for doing so. It is useful to sum up at the end of each item, especially if discussion has been lengthy, and to repeat the decisions made and actions to be taken. If the chair is also taking the minutes, time should be allowed to check that an adequate note has been made before taking the next agenda item. When these have all been properly dealt with, new issues may be raised under Any Other Business.

Lastly, the chair should thank those present for attending, make sure that notes taken are in good order and that he or she has a copy of anything tabled at the meeting in preparation for writing up the minutes.

10.4   Minuting meetings

Minutes are a written record of the significant items of business transacted at a meeting. They have a number of important functions:

- they record why the meeting was called, what it achieved, and what further actions are needed;
- they provide a record by which future progress can be measured;

- they are a means of reporting the proceedings to interested parties;
- they constitute a record which may be relied upon in the future.

Architects, especially in their early years of professional life, often have to chair meetings and minute them, and many find this difficult and worrying. Fortunately, minuting is a skill that improves with practice, although it always needs a high degree of concentration. If the meeting itself is run competently, minuting it will be that much easier.

It is important to draft minutes while the meeting is still fresh in one's mind. The primary decision to be made is what to include and what to exclude, as a full record is rarely appropriate. The art is to identify priorities. It is essential to record some things (decisions, actions to be taken) and relevant to record others (changes in situation, strongly opposing views). It may be desirable to include some parts of the remaining proceedings – and equally desirable to exclude others. This is where discretion must be exercised.

When writing up minutes, care should be taken to link people with views expressed and actions to be taken. An Actions column running down the page to the right of the text is a good way of focusing the attention of recipients on follow-up actions. Formal meetings are written in 'reported speech', i.e. events are put into the past and the style is observational. Although many of the meetings connected with architectural practice are informal or semi-formal in character and will not require stringent grammatical attention, it is no less important for them to provide a well-expressed and unambiguous record that can be relied on in the future.

The aim should always be to issue minutes within a few days of the meeting, and in any case well in advance of the next, if this is a series of meetings. The sooner the minutes are issued, the more time people will have to take the action or obtain the information required of them, and the more likely they are to make a satisfactory contribution to the next meeting.

10.5   In-house talks and seminars

Practices may consider holding occasional, or even a series of in-house talks or seminars to disseminate project or research information, or as a matter of continuing professional development. These need to be well managed, and consideration should be given to the following:

- the structure and content of the programme overall, and who is expected to attend or participate;
- who is to be responsible for the programme overall and each event on the day;
- the likely costs and what budget should be allowed;
- the timing of events;
- finding a suitable venue with adequate facilities;
- identifying speakers or presenters with the appropriate expertise and knowledge;
- ways of promoting the programme so as to attract speakers and ensure a good attendance.

Figure 26: Organising an in-house event

1. Who is it for? Students, mid-career architects, management, non-technical staff	**5. Running the event** Make room booking, hire equipment Prepare questionnaires for feedback Brief the chair about speakers, timetable *On the day:* Prepare and check the venue Check that equipment functions properly Do a dry run of the event
2. What are the options? Do it yourself Collaborate with other practices Bring in external organisers	
3. What kind of programme? *The approach*: reactive, proactive, anecdotal *The event*: talk, workshop, forum, video etc	**6. The role of the chair** Introduce the event Manage speakers and audience Keep to the timetable Wind up
4. Organisation and planning Decide who is to be responsible Set a budget Decide timing and venue Plan necessary publicity Assess what clerical and catering support is needed Approach speakers, presenters	**7. How did it go?** Issue questionnaires to participants and audience Evaluate the event as a whole Report the event as appropriate Learn the lessons for next time

Figure 26 is a checklist. Any kind of learning programme may be intrinsically useful and valuable to the participants, but it will only be of real benefit when the lessons can be applied while they are still clearly in mind. With in-house events, this should be relatively easy to achieve because the participants will probably be dealing with topics which are of immediate concern to the practice. Otherwise, every effort should be made to capitalise on newly acquired skills, information and interests. If this is left untapped for too long, the real impact and benefit may be lost.

Job architects spend a great deal of their time engaged in writing project reports of various kinds. A client who is kept properly informed and involved will be able to deal promptly with report recommendations and give appropriate instructions. Prior to design development, reports normally fall into two main categories: surveys and feasibility studies. Once a full architectural service has been commissioned, there will be regular reports to be made to the client at the completion of work stages.

10.6   Making presentations

Making presentations, and indeed any form of public speaking, can be terrifying for the inexperienced. However, it is virtually unavoidable in practice, and a very useful skill to develop. Architectural students are normally required to present their work at crits, but they rarely attend formal courses in oral presentation, and the jump to more formal internal or public presentations can seem quite daunting.

As with most things, the only way to get good at it is to practise, so although it may seem an unattractive proposition it is worth volunteering when there is an opportunity. Practice helps not only with technique but also, and perhaps more importantly, with confidence.

Careful preparation is important, even for informal occasions. Everyone develops their own system, but it is generally worth writing out what you are going to say in full, and then running through it in private before hand, keeping an eye on the time. Normally speakers are given a specific time allowance, and it is important to be confident that you will keep within it. Have a few additional points to hand in case you finish early – this can happen if you rush due to first time nerves. Try to envisage what queries may be raised, and prepare the answers in advance.

Prior to the day, assemble all your material carefully. Make sure you know what the room will be like and what facilities are to hand. Some people prefer to summarise their presentation on cards, as they are easier to hold. Others highlight key points in their notes and talk round those. It is a good idea to indicate the time on your notes, for example for a half-hour talk mark the point in the material you should have reached every five minutes, as this gives a good early warning if your are rushing or going too slowly. Organise all visual material (slides, overhead transparencies) in the order in which it will be needed. Keep it very simple until you have had some practice. Computer assisted presentations are very impressive, but as they seem to be plagued by technological hitches, it is imperative to have a fall back plan, and they may be best avoided by beginners as they are just one more thing to worry about!

On the day itself makes sure you arrive in plenty of time so that you can get used to the venue and sort out any technical problems. If you are one of several speakers, talk to the other speakers and offer to help if appropriate (e.g. turning over their overheads, setting up their laptop). This is not only useful for them, but also a good trick to reduce nerves as it takes your mind off your own presentation. If you are the only speaker, talk to the organiser of the event, and to the audience as they arrive – avoid sitting in silence!

When you address the audience, make an effort to speak distinctly, and more slowly and louder than you normally would in conversation. It may feel awkward, but it comes across much more clearly than something mumbled or rushed. If you start to run out of time, do not rush, just summarise what you had intended to say. Most people do not remember the majority of what they hear at a presentation, therefore covering all the ground is not nearly as important as making two or three key points clearly.

10.7 Telephones, faxes and e-mails

A record should be made of all telephone calls that relate to the administration of projects within the office, and of most other calls which relate to business or professional matters. With projects, the simplest method is to make a note of the date and time of the call, the person to whom the call was made or from whom it was received, and the main points agreed, and to file this in the job file for the project. If important matters were discussed, these should be confirmed by letter.

Some office management packages for computers have direct dialling facilities, which allow the user to search for the number in the computer's files and then use it to dial out. The call will then be logged, and there may be provision for noting the details of the conversation. These should be transferred to the job file on a regular basis.

Careful thought should always be given to whether the telephone is the best means of communication in any situation. Unless it has been pre-arranged, the recipient is likely to be busy on some other task and will not welcome the interruption. There is a limit to how much information most people can absorb over the telephone; therefore it should not be used as a substitute for a formal letter. It is generally better to send as much information as possible in written form, and then to follow up it up with a call to discuss what was sent, and then follow the call with a confirming letter. Calls should be made personally. It is very irritating to receive calls from secretaries or assistants on someone's behalf, and then be put through (or possibly not!) after a pause. It implies that the receiver's time waiting for the call to be put through is less valuable than that of the person who made the call. The caller is the one taking the initiative, if anyone has to wait is should be the caller.

Many smaller practices operate without a receptionist or telephonist, and therefore any member of staff could answer calls. It is normal practice to state the name of the practice on answering. If the person called is not available, an accurate record of the enquiry should be made including the telephone number of the caller, their name, the subject of the call, and the date and time of the call. All messages should be returned very promptly; it creates a very bad impression of the practice if its staff have to be continually chased for a reply.

Faxes are invaluable for sending information that is needed very urgently, for example for sending drawings to site. A computer package which sends and receives faxes direct is a great help as it avoids paper copies and fax machine breakdowns, and it also keeps a record of transmissions. Nevertheless, faxes should always be followed by a copy sent by post, as it is likely that the fax will not be accepted as evidence of the communication for legal purposes. Some practices tend to send everything by fax with a copy by post. This should be avoided because of the duplication of paperwork and possible confusions that could arise, and it is generally better to keep faxes for matters of real urgency.

E-mail is undoubtedly the most exciting recent development in communication. It is possible to send very large amounts of information virtually instantaneously, and to send it simultaneously to many recipients. The information can be in a very wide variety of formats, and can include text and drawings. Thought should be given before sending as to whether the sender wishes the receiver to be able to alter the document. Sometimes this is acceptable, but if this is not the case there are now a variety of ways of 'fixing' the information, such as the formation of 'pdf' files from drawings. It appears that in the near future the development of 'electronic signatures' may make the need for posting hard copies redundant, as the transmission will be accepted as evidence in court, but in the meantime all documents should also be sent by 'snail mail'.

10.8 Dealing with the post

It is important for this to be handled systematically. One person only should open all the post and deal with it as appropriate. There should be a set of procedures drawn up for receipt and distribution and these should be complied with by all staff. They should be set out in the office or quality management manual, and regularly audited to make sure they remain effective (*see* Figure 27).

Figure 27: Dealing with incoming and outgoing mail

> **Incoming**
> Procedures should be put in place to ensure that:
>
> - letters, packets, parcels, etc are opened, date-stamped, and recorded;
> - items are marked for action and distributed as appropriate;
> - drawings received are entered in the appropriate register;
> - courier deliveries are signed for and logged, with receipts retained, and recipients alerted about arrival;
> - faxes are photocopied and the originals destroyed;
> - items marked 'personal' or 'confidential' are given unopened to addressees, but are returned for logging, etc if practice-related;
> - invoices are passed promptly to accounting staff.
>
> **Outgoing**
> Procedures for controlling outgoing mail should ensure that items:
>
> - are checked and signed by originators;
> - have the right enclosures or attachments;
> - are correctly franked or stamped;
> - are collected for postal or courier transmittal as appropriate;
> - achieve intended delivery dates and times.
> - are logged as despatched in the correct list or register.

In small practices a principal usually opens the post, but in larger practices the task may be delegated to a practice administrator. Whoever is responsible must be capable of identifying important and urgent items that need immediate attention. Professional practices get inundated with letters and literature of all kinds, much of it speculative, and it is important that whoever deals with the daily post is not side-tracked by irrelevant items and can be relied upon to discard time-wasting rubbish.

An incoming letter should be read, initialled and date-stamped, and a decision made whether it needs immediate action, whether it can or should wait, or whether it can be filed.

10.9   Writing letters

The conventional wisdom that letters require a beginning, a middle and an end is based on sound common sense. Each element has a distinct and proper function. Figure 28 is a checklist.

Letters should be dated correctly, include the relevant references, and give the name and full address of the intended recipient. Informal letters begin 'Dear Ms/Mr Jones' and end 'Yours sincerely'. Formal letters begin 'Dear Sir/Madam' and end 'Yours faithfully'. It is important to check that the addressee's name and title are correctly spelt; if in doubt, ring up their office and ask, or consult the relevant directory.

All letters should have their subject headings typed in capital letters or bold so that they can be quickly identified, and to make filing and retrieval easier. The heading can include the in-house job number. Avoid using 'Re' before the heading: this is old fashioned and unnecessary.

Figure 28: Elements of a letter

Date

Your ref
Our ref (*may include project number*)

(*Name*)
(*Address*)

Dear ...

(*Name of project*)

(*Beginning of letter*)
Thank you for letter of (date)
State context of request

(*Middle of letter*)
Reply as requested, or
Make request for information, state action required

(*End of letter*)
Sum up
Restate view, request
Final greeting

Yours ...

(*Your name and title*)
Encs (or Atts) ...

Copies to: ...

The preferred style of layout is blocked to the left of the page, i.e. there are no indented paragraphs (*see* Figures 31 and 32). Punctuation is not included in dates and addresses. Where a choice is available, use a clear typeface such as Times Roman or Helvetica for business correspondence. Be sparing with italic script: it is not easy to read in quantity and is best used to emphasise or highlight words, phrases and short items.

Check through the letters after typing or processing and make sure that all enclosures or attachments have been prepared for posting, and appropriate copies made and marked up. Figure 29 is a checklist. A compliments slip with the name of the intended recipient should be attached to copies that do not show the office address and other details. Note that compliments slips should not be used where transmittal needs to be recorded, particularly in the case of drawings. The issue, description and despatch of drawings should be carefully recorded in the appropriate register.

After signing the letter, initial all the copies including the file copy. This is always advisable with formal correspondence and is a good habit to cultivate as a matter of risk management. The

Figure 29: Checklist before despatch of letter

1. **Does it include**
   correct title, name, address of recipient
   references (theirs and yours)
   job number, date?

2. **Is the mode correct**
   formal/informal?

3. **Have I referred correctly to their letter**
   date, heading?

4. **Have I said what I wanted to say clearly, concisely and appropriately?**

   Will they know
   what I am talking about?
   what they have to do now?
   whether I expect a response and, if so, when?

5. **Should I remind or reassure them about anything before I sign off?**

   Is the final greeting correct and appropriate?

   Have the proper enclosures been added?

   Has the letter been copied
   to the right people?
   at the right addresses?

6. **Has the letter been properly laid out?**
   Is it pleasing to look at?
   Has the spelling been checked?
   Have necessary corrections been made?

7. **Is the file copy exactly the same as the despatched version?**

8. **Have I signed the letter and initialled the copies?**

writer's name and status should be typed under his or her signature. Lastly, read through the letter and consider it from the recipient's point of view.

- Is its purpose clear?

- Is it well expressed?

- Will they know what action, if any, they should now take?

10.10 Responding to letters

When replying to letters, the first rule is always to respond promptly, even if this is only by way of acknowledging receipt while considering how to respond. Pre-printed acknowledgement cards are not recommended for use by professional practices: they give an impression of remoteness, tend to get lost or ignored, and are awkward to file.

The second rule is to reply politely – even when the writer seems rude, or is 'fishing', or trying to exert pressure for whatever reason. The temptation to respond to rude people with

Figure 30: Reminders

Letter one: (Heading)
We do not seem to have received a reply to our letter of (date) about this matter/enclosing our invoice, etc. Would you please confirm that you have received it and that you are giving it your attention?

Letter two: (Heading)
We refer to our letters of (date) and (date). Would you please let us have your reply by the (date)/end of the week?

Letter three: (Heading)
We are sorry to note that you have not replied to our letters of (date), (date) and (date). In such circumstances, our standard practice is to withdraw service/credit/instruct solicitor, etc. We are reluctant to do so in your case, and hope that your immediate response will make such action unnecessary.

Figure 31: Letter to newly appointed clerk of works

Mr B Finch
72 Old Common
Wargrave
Berks
RG2 8PJ

Our ref.: BL/HM/Appts01/F
26 June 2001

Dear Mr Finch

APPOINTMENT OF CLERK OF WORKS:
'Treetops' Estate, Chorley

We are pleased to tell you that the employer, (name), has instructed us to confirm your appointment on the terms agreed at interview and as described in the enclosed contract of employment and description of your duties and authority as clerk of works.

Please read these documents carefully and then sign, date and return the contract to us in the enclosed envelope. If there are any matters that you would like to discuss further before signing the contract, please telephone us.

So that you can familiarise yourself with the project, we enclose a set of drawings, bills and specifications as issued to the main contractor.

There is to be an initial project meeting on (date), which you should attend. An agenda is attached. You will see that your duties and responsibilities as clerk of works are to be discussed under (items x and x).

On your first day, please report to the project architect, (name), at this office, and collect a pad of weekly report forms, a daily diary, and a pad of Directions.

We hope that you will enjoy your work on the 'Treetops' project and look forward to your joining us on (date).

Yours sincerely

(name)
Encs
Copy to: (employer)

Figure 32: Letter of refusal

Mr B Finch
72 Old Common
Wargrave
Berks
RG2 8PJ

Our ref.: BL/HM/Appts01/neg
26 June 2001

Dear Mr Finch

APPOINTMENT OF CLERK OF WORKS:
'Treetops' Estate, Chorley

Thank you for coming in for an interview yesterday. I am sorry to tell you that your application has not been successful.

However, we were impressed by your knowledge of the building industry and your interest and enthusiasm, and we will keep you in mind when and if other appointments are being made.

Yours sincerely

(name)

'put-down' one-liners should be resisted; a bland reply is often more deflating. Similarly, a fishing letter is best dealt with by a little exposure, such as 'I suspect that what you are really asking me is ... and, if so, I am afraid I can't help you ...'. A letter refusing some product or service should be firm and unequivocal, otherwise a long and time-consuming correspondence may ensue.

It is good practice to have a standard procedure for issuing reminder letters, such as the set of examples given in Figure 30. After sending the third letter, give them a few days' grace, and then be sure to take the action threatened.

A formal letter of appointment should refer to the firm as 'we'. It should confirm the discussion and agreement reached at interview, and may have attachments such as a contract of employment or a statement of working conditions. As examples, two specimen letters connected with the appointment of a clerk of works are given as Figures 31 and 32.

10.11 Contractual correspondence

Letters, architect's instructions, site meeting minutes and notes of inspections connected with contract works are part of the history of that contract, and if there is any subsequent court action, they will be part of the evidence. Therefore it is crucial for them to be clearly expressed and unambiguous. Many disputes arise simply because letters and instructions are misunderstood. Figure 33 is a checklist.

Figure 33: Checklist for contractual correspondence

Use a formal style
Letters connected with contractual matters are always formal. Start and end them *Dear Sir –
Yours faithfully*. Be sure to refer to yourself as *We*, not *I*.

Get the references right
The main heading will be the name of the contract works and any project number. Always date
the document as the date of issue, not the date it was drafted.

State the relevant clause in the contract
Quote the clause number in the contract that relates to the subject of the letter or AI with the
name of the form of contract under which the works are being carried out. (*This request is made
in accordance with Clause ... of IFC 98.*) Check that you have got it right.

Quote drawing numbers correctly
It is equally important to quote drawing numbers and their titles exactly and fully.

Refer to events precisely
State the relevant date and where necessary, the location.

Keep sentences short and language simple
Contract provisions are often expressed in a convoluted way and this tends to creep into the rest
of the correspondence. Write as clearly as possible.

Remember to send copies to all the relevant parties
Some architects believe in copying all job-related correspondence to the client as a matter of
course. You *must* copy all contract-related correspondence to the client.

Consult your solicitor
Be sure to do this whenever a situation arises where there may be legal repercussions; he or she
will advise you in the light of the particular circumstances.

Advise your insurers
Similarly, you must advise your insurers immediately of any circumstances likely to give rise to
a claim. Failure to notify in good time can be a valid reason for their refusing to indemnify you.

Don't ignore claims
Respond if claims or allegations are made, but always take legal advice about the form of your
reply.

'Powers' and 'duties'
Under a building contract, the architect has 'powers' and 'duties'. Make sure that you know the
difference between them. A power is usually expressed as *the architect may;* a duty as *the
architect shall.*

'Without prejudice'
It is a common misconception that heading a letter 'Without Prejudice' in some way protects the
author from its contents. *It only does this in certain, special circumstances.* For the purposes of
business correspondence, always assume that it does *not*. Again, consult your solicitor.

10.12 Formal report writing

At some time in their professional lives, most architects will be required to present a formal
commissioned report and need to know how to tackle what is often a demanding task.

Reports commissions are formally accepted in writing and their cost is negotiated and agreed,
usually on a time-charge basis. Their contents are the property of the commissioning person

Figure 34: Outline report structure

	Title page
	Summary of report
	Contents page
	Glossary

1.0	**Introduction**
1.1	The brief
1.2	Background
1.3	Scope of report
1.4	Methodology
2.0	**Findings**
2.1	Site
2.2	Buildings, etc
3.0	**Conclusions and recommendations**
3.1	Conclusions
3.2	Recommendations
4.0	**Remedial proposals**
4.1	Options available
4.2	Costs
4.3	Recommendations

	References
	Appendices
	Bibliography

or organisation and are kept confidential. This may be important for commercial reasons, or the report may concern an investigation into alleged defects which could give rise to litigation. Such work is often unexpectedly time-consuming, and should only be taken on after fully considering the implications in terms of staff effort and availability and what repercussions there may be on other work in progress.

All reports have a basic structure and rationale, regardless of the complexity or otherwise of their content. As can be seen in Figure 34, a formal report consists of a main text preceded by introductory items, and followed by supporting material.

10.12.1 Preliminary items

Title page

This should show the report's title and job number, status (draft, interim, final, etc), date, and the name and address of the client. Report covers can become detached with handling or during storage and may be lost. As a result, the report may be difficult to identify, particularly if a considerable time has elapsed since it was written or if it was one of a series. Therefore, as well as giving full details of origination on the title page, this should be repeated at the end of the report after the appropriate signatures.

Summary of report

A separate summary of findings, conclusions and recommendations is sometimes attached to the front of the report immediately after the title page. This can be useful where the report is lengthy, makes numerous recommendations, or is for the use of a committee. In the very rare case of the report's findings being newsworthy, such a summary could be used as a press handout, and can be written in the manner of a news item.

Contents list

All the contents of the report should be listed, including any appended items.

Glossary

When a report contains numerous specialist or technical terms, it is sensible to include a glossary to explain them. It is most helpful if it appears at the front of the report, usually just after the contents page. List the items alphabetically and make sure that the explanations are clearly given in plain English.

10.12.2 Main text

Introduction

The introductory section establishes the terms of reference for the report, gives relevant background information to put it in context, defines its scope and describes the way the investigation has been tackled.

The Brief

The instructions from the client constitute the terms of reference for the report. They will state:

- who the report is for;
- why it has been commissioned;
- what it is about;
- when it will be completed;
- who will be writing it.

There may also be instructions about the way it should be presented.

It is usual to include an account of the commissioning process in this section, on the following lines:

'On [date] we were instructed by Mr E. C. Jay, Estates Officer for ABACUS (UK) Developments Ltd to carry out an investigation of ... ... and present our findings as a draft report to be submitted to the Corfield Housing Committee on [date]. We accepted this commission by letter on [date], saying that the investigation would be made by C. J. Perrin DipArch and W. C. Lea DipArch.'

Where desirable, copies of the exchange of commissioning letters may be included in an appendix.

Background information

This section is sometimes called History of the Project. It contains information about why the report has been commissioned, so that it can be read in its proper context. For example, the subject of the report might be an unpopular housing estate where there had been a long history of vandalism and neglect and where many attempts had been made to mitigate its problems. It would be relevant to say what those problems are or were, what solutions were tried out, by whom and to what effect. It might be appropriate to include a map of the locality.

Scope of report

For example:

'The report covers all the two-storey terraced dwellings in Phases 1 and 2 of the development, but excludes all the 3-storey dwellings in Phase 2. It was agreed [with the client] that the extensive condensation observed in many of the flats should be the subject of a separate report.'

The report may have been commissioned in stages. There may need to be a preliminary report and then an interim report, both to be superseded eventually by a final report. The preliminary report may just state the findings, the interim may discuss the options available and explore cost alternatives, while the final report will review the situation in the light of the client's reactions and the latest cost estimate and make final recommendations.

Methodology

This section relates how the investigation was tackled. For example, three visits to site may have been made. Describe them in chronological order, saying who was present at each, what actions the reporter(s) took, whether tests were made and if so why, where and by whom. Add whether any supporting research (for example, into local history, social conditions, climate, water table, etc) was carried out. If any appendices are included, say why and in what respect they may be useful to readers.

Then briefly describe how the material in the report has been organised:

'This report consists of four main sections. In Section 1 we describe the events which led to this commission and the way we have tackled the work. Section 2 records our findings, and

Section 3 sets out the conclusions we deduce and our recommendations for action. In Section 4 we discuss the remedial solutions available and compare and cost the proposed options. We conclude this Section with recommendations. The appendices contain items and information which support and validate our findings and recommendations.'

Findings

The findings should be a clear statement of facts; any temptation to comment or draw early conclusions or propose solutions should be firmly resisted.

This section of the report will go into some detail, breaking down the inspection of a building into, say, an element-by-element description (preferably illustrated). It will say who was present during the survey, what the weather conditions were then and had been recently (e.g. heavy rain the night before). It will record in detail any opening-up procedures, borescope inspections, dye or spray tests and so on. Some photographs may be included, but if they are numerous it is probably better to present them in an appendix.

Because of the technical detail included it is useful to conclude the section with a summary and to illustrate the material wherever possible. One good illustration can give the reader more information than several pages of text.

Conclusions and recommendations

After analysing the situation, draw conclusions and then, if asked to do so in the Brief, suggest a course of future action, explaining the salient aspects of various alternatives and the financial and other implications.

Set out conclusions clearly as itemised points. State the options available as (a), (b), (c), etc so that they can be referred to thereafter as Option (a), etc without having to recapitulate them extensively.

Some investigative reports end at this point. Where the Brief asks for proposals for remedial solutions, another part is added.

Remedial proposals

The options described, costed and compared will have been chosen because of their suitability within the context of any budget set. Recommendations must be performable as well as cost-effective, and it is essential at this stage to draw attention to any limitations or disadvantages of the remedies proposed.

10.12.3 Appendices, etc

References

Publications or sources of information are often referred to in the body of the report. Each item should be given a number (superscribed or in brackets), and a related list of numbered references should follow immediately after the main text. It may be convenient to use footnotes for references while drafting the report, but in the final version the convenience of the reader is paramount, and a separate list is generally more useful.

Appended material

Although nothing crucial to the theme should be banished into an appendix, it is important not to allow the main text to become clogged with extraneous material. In some reports it may be necessary to include copies of relevant correspondence, notices, extracts from codes and standards or related literature – even translations of foreign research papers on occasion. These can all be appended items.

Appendices should be listed on the contents page at the front of the report. Each should have its own title page and number and its own internal page numbering. Paragraphs should be numbered in a similar style to the main text.

Bibliography

In the context of report writing, a bibliography is a list of sources of information consulted by the author in the course of preparing the report. It is a category of information in its own right and should be kept separate from appendices. Sometimes more than one kind of bibliography is appropriate: for example, a selected bibliography to support the main text, and a detailed bibliography for a topic discussed in detail in an appendix. Reports which have required extensive literature searches or which are research based must have full bibliographies to validate them.

Index

Technical reports rarely need an index because their scope of enquiry is relatively limited. If an index does seem desirable, it should be the very last item included in the report.

10.12.4 Content and style

It is important to assess the recipient's level of knowledge accurately. If it is underestimated, at least some of the content of the report may be superfluous, which will probably irritate the reader; if it is overestimated, the report may be largely unintelligible, which will doubtless infuriate. It is best to steer a middle course, particularly where the client is a committee consisting of, say, members of various professions, local authority officers, and lay people. Whatever mix of readers is expected, it is good practice to sum up at the end of sections in the main text, particularly where the subject matter is complex or technical.

As to writing style, in report writing special efforts have to be made to achieve a style that is clear and unequivocal, businesslike, free of subjective judgements, reactions and comments, and suited to the disciplined structure of the report format. The linguistic peccadilloes and inelegances that sometime characterise practice correspondence will not be overlooked or forgiven if they appear in reports. They will erode the validity of the opinions expressed and do little to reassure the client of the excellence of the writer's professional judgement. Figure 35 contains some guidance for report writers.

Figure 35: An appropriate writing style

Be businesslike
Your tone should be consistently helpful and pleasant, neither chatty nor clinically remote. Do not lecture your readers. Decide how to refer to yourself as the author of the report. The safest advice is to use *we*, meaning your firm.

Be concise and accurate
Remove weak modifiers such as *quite, rather, somewhat, about.* To say that *the bricks were rather/somewhat/wet* tells the reader nothing about the *degree* of wetness, just that the bricks were wet. Similarly, prune out monitoring phrases such as *as it were, so it seems, all things being equal, to all intents and purposes, more or less.* These can weaken or actually defeat what you are trying to say.

Be specific
Generalities such as *Flashings generally blow off in bad weather* are not helpful and will make you look foolish. Beware of making value judgments, such as *This is a good way to fix tiles, The contractor made a bad decision.* In reports in particular, statements should be validated.

Be relevant
Do not include superfluous or distracting themes and details. As a check, re-read the Brief at the end of each section and ask yourself whether what you have written is useful and relevant. Keep to the point.

Be intelligible
If you cannot avoid using technical or specialist terms, make sure that you add explanations where necessary, and sum up frequently in plain English. If necessary, include a glossary of terms at the front of the report.

Be digestible
The more difficult a subject is to grasp, the more important it is to present material in appetising chunks by making paragraph breaks at logical points in the argument or discussion. Paragraph headings relieve the monotony of a long text and help readers find specific topics. Make sure that they are relevant and keep them short.

Rephrase
Many linguistic knots can be untied by rephrasing sentences (or whole passages) instead of trying to find a precise change of word or construction. You can 'free' a dense sentence by introducing more clauses and sentence division.

Example:
(a) Built in 1932, Hoopers Park, a Tudor-style development with houses arranged around a central courtyard, was recently designated a Grade II listed building.

(b) The Hoopers Park development was built in 1932. The houses, which are Tudor-style, are arranged around a central courtyard. Hoopers Park has recently been awarded Grade II listed building status.

10.13 Checking the report

Checking should be carried out at three stages:

First check

Before the report is processed, the writer should revisit the brief and check that all its requirements have been understood and met, and that the response to it is adequate and comprehensible. Reading the text out loud to a colleague can be a good test of intelligibility and will expose any lack of coherence and clarity of expression.

Second check

Before photocopying and binding, check:

- for typing and spelling errors;
- that the report looks well presented;
- that the contents list corresponds with the actual contents, paragraph numbers and headings, and that page numbers are correct;
- that all the items to be included are assembled in the proper order;
- that the report has been signed, dated and referenced.

Reports must always be signed and dated by the writer and countersigned by a principal, who is thereby assumed to have read the report and approved its contents. It is essential that this happens: it has been known for a practice to be separately commissioned to present expert advice on behalf of opposing parties and for this only to have been picked up at the time of that crucial final reading.

Third check

Before despatch, check:

- that the right number of copies has been prepared (remembering the requirements of the library, filing system, etc);
- that each copy has been correctly collated, with no skewed or defective pages included;
- that the necessary identifying information has been included and is clearly visible;
- that the report handles well;
- that any separate items have been properly prepared and are clearly identified.

Whatever the pressures of work and time, this final check must be thorough.

10.14 Technical reports

10.14.1 Surveys

Surveys commonly undertaken by job architects will be to do with the land or the site and/or existing buildings. The subject is well covered in the *Architect's Job Book,* to which reference should be made. The advice included on conducting and reporting a survey of an existing building is given here as Figure 36.

Specially commissioned surveys such as those for prospective house purchasers, building societies, commercial enterprises and church authorities may also be undertaken, but these often carry risks for architects which should be properly understood (*see* 8.3).

Figure 36: Guidance on surveys of existing buildings

It is essential that the architect personally walks through every room in the building to be surveyed, regardless of whether the survey is being done by in-house personnel or by a surveying firm. It is important to perceive the architectural character of a building and the way it has been constructed.

The measured survey drawings might show:

- plans, sections, elevations;
- elevational features, e.g. plinths, string courses, openings;
- precise levels at floors, datum, thickness and construction;
- levels of external ground;
- details of decoration, profiles, false columns, etc;
- finishes and colours;
- loose equipment, landlord's fittings, etc.

A written report might include information that cannot be shown graphically, such as:

- structural and other defects and their causes;
- dry rot, damp penetration, condensation;
- infestation by rodents, beetles and other insects;
- recent repairs and decoration;
- settlement cracks, mis-shapen openings, gaps at skirtings and windows;
- walls that are misaligned or have bulges;
- sagging roofs, defective roof coverings;
- deflection of beams or lintels, cracks at beam bearings.

The architects/surveyors should state whether or not they were able to see inside the structure of the building and how much they were able to see. It is important not to infer the state of the whole building from sight of one part of it. A statement on the following lines should appear at the end of the relevant part of the report (as stipulated in most professional indemnity policies):

'It has not been possible to make a detailed examination of the floor or roof construction except at the positions described because material damage would have been caused in gaining access. It is therefore impossible to make any statement about the condition of the unexamined structure.'

Where appropriate, the client should be advised to call in specialists, e.g. mechanical, electrical, timber treatment, and should be asked for instructions regarding any fees, expenses and inconvenience arising from their investigations.

10.14.2 Feasibility studies

The Stage B project feasibility report is especially important, since the client's decision whether or not to proceed will be based on what it says. Depending on the project's complexity, feasibility may need investigating by means of various and sometimes numerous exploratory studies. These can range from simple assessments of possibilities to sophisticated and extensive research into social, industrial and economic factors. Only some of these areas will be within the average architect's expertise. It is important to recognise one's limitations and not to try to take on unsuitable work which could overstretch the practice and even put it at risk.

In broad terms, the Stage B report will consist of:

- a statement of its purpose;
- its findings;
- its proposals and recommendations;

- the decisions required from the client;
- any supporting material.

10.14.3 Design development

At the completion of each of Work Stages C, D and E, a report will be sent to the client advising progress and seeking approval to proceed to the next stage. It will summarise the present position on the brief, site matters, consents and approvals, and relevant contractual matters (*see* Figure 37).

Reports to the client should be clear, concise and well presented. It is important to pursue a consistent structure and format and maintain it throughout the series of reports. A judgement should be made about the client's level of technical knowledge and explanations included as necessary. Each Stage report should have a covering letter requesting the client's written approval of the report and its proposals, and asking for instructions to proceed.

Figure 37: Stages C, D and E reports

Stage C
At the close of Stage C, the report to the client might:

- summarise the design work so far;
- present outline proposals;
- make recommendations including an approximation of cost and an outline programme for the project;
- suggest a method of procurement;
- append relevant supporting information and drawings.

Stage D
At the close of Stage D, the report to the client might show the development of the scheme in respect of:

- planning permission;
- the appearance of the building;
- materials and methods of construction;
- services systems;
- outline specifications;
- special features as required;
- a cost estimate and a programme for the project.

Stage E
The report at the close of Stage E might:

- confirm completion of the detailed Brief in line with the outline specification and agreed materials and methods of construction;
- describe how the client's specific requirements for plant, equipment, services, layouts, and the fitting out of special areas are to be met;
- report on statutory approvals;
- include revised cost estimates and a programme for the project.

Figure 38: Specimen financial report to client

Job no: _____ Job title: _____

Financial report to client

To end of (month)	(year)	Savings £	Extras £	£
Financial approvals	Contract sum as adjusted	_____	_____	_____
	Additional approvals to date of last report	_____	_____	_____
	Total approvals to date of last report	_____	_____	_____
Adjustments	Contract sum as adjusted including contingencies	_____	_____	_____
	Cost adjustment on PC sums ordered	_____	_____	_____
	Cost adjustment on provisional sums	_____	_____	_____
	Value of AIs issued to date	_____	_____	_____
	Changes of work anticipated	_____	_____	_____
Contingencies	Original contingencies sum £	_____	_____	_____
	Estimated proportion £ absorbed to date	_____	_____	_____
	Estimated remainder £	_____	_____	_____
Cost of works	Estimated cost of works £ including contingencies sum	_____	_____	_____
Reconciliation	Variations instructed by the employer since last report	_____	_____	_____
	(a) [addition] estimated cost	_____	_____	_____
	(b) [omission] estimated saving	_____	_____	_____
	Additional approvals to last report	_____	_____	_____
Final estimate	Estimated final expenditure on present information	_____	_____	_____
	Not included in assessments: VAT, fees, other works (eg piling, landscape, advance orders)			

Figure 39: Specimen site visit report

Job no:	Job title:

Site visit report

Date _____ No. of visits scheduled _____

Visit by _____ Visit no. _____

Purpose

_____
_____
_____
_____
_____
_____
_____
_____
_____

Observed

_____
_____
_____
_____
_____
_____
_____
_____
_____
_____
_____
_____
_____
_____
_____
_____
_____

Checked

Samples _____

Verification of tests _____

Vouchers _____

Records _____

Recorded

Photos _____

_____

Video _____

Other _____

Summary

☐ Work properly executed

☐ Materials properly stored and protected

☐ Proceeding in workmanlike manner

☐ Progress to programme

10.14.4 Work in progress

Once site operations commence, the client will expect to be kept informed about the progress of the work, usually in the form of a report at regular intervals with a detailed statement of expenditure, an appraisal of the current position and a forecast of total costs. Cost reports are normally prepared by the quantity surveyor, but where no QS has been appointed (e.g. for minor works), these may have to be prepared by the architect. A specimen financial report to client is given as Figure 38.

The client should always be sent a copy of the minutes of architect's progress meetings and copies of correspondence relating to notices of delay and the award of any extensions of time. Similarly the client should be kept informed of any problems concerning materials and workmanship where it becomes necessary to issue architect's instructions. He or she should also be advised in good time about such matters as maintenance contracts and any need to instruct staff about the operation of installations.

10.14.5 Site inspection reports

The purpose of site visits is to observe and comment. Checks of a general nature might include:

- whether quality complies with the provisions of the contract;
- whether progress accords with the contractor's master programme;
- whether essential parts of the design have been or are being carried out in accordance with contract provisions.

Reports of site visits are not usually sent to the client, but they should be prepared to a consistent format and written up as soon after the visit as possible. Record photographs (dated), notes and sketches should be attached and carefully filed. Figure 39 is a specimen site visit report form.

10.15   Reports for litigation

Architects are increasingly being retained as expert witnesses in construction disputes. From the management point of view it is important, when asked to undertake such a commission, to consider what impact this will have on one's own and the practice's workload. Acting as an expert witness, particularly if the technical matters at issue are complex, can be extremely time-consuming. Expert reports may need to be revised and redrafted many times, there may be numerous meetings with lawyers and with experts from the other side to agree matters pre-trial. Then there can be many days spent in court, some of them simply in an advisory capacity. While this kind of work is usually lucrative and enhances a firm's credibility, its uncertain timescale may well have unwelcome repercussions on the work of the practice as a whole.

The function of an expert witness is to assist a court or an inquiry to arrive at fair and just decisions. In Britain, the expert witness is not an advocate for the client: he or she has been retained to give independent and objective evidence. To be accepted by the court as an expert witness able to deal with the particular issues in question, an architect has to be able to demonstrate special authority derived from qualifications and experience.

An architect's involvement in litigation often starts with an instruction to report on the condition of a building, and this can be done using the report format already described. In addition, he or she may be asked to give an opinion about the attribution of responsibilities.

On the basis of this advisory report, a client may decide to initiate legal proceedings and ask the architect to act as an expert witness. The case will often be heard in the Queen's Bench Division of the High Court and will be Official Referee's business. The judge will have special jurisdiction to hear cases which involve complex technical matters.

An expert report is not to be confused with a proof of evidence. This is a formal written statement in which someone sets out facts and matters which he or she can swear are within his or her personal direct knowledge. By contrast, the expert report is evidence of opinion. Lawyers may have a view about the way the expert report is to be structured and presented, but will usually leave this to the discretion of the writer. It is likely that the draft report will be revised a number of times before a final version is agreed. The report should be validated by supporting documentary evidence, such as copies of extracts from codes or standards or relevant manufacturers, or other literature.

Reports by expert witnesses are usually written in the first person and signed by that person only, as the expert recognised by the Court. Therefore countersigning by a practice principal is not appropriate and may even call into question the expert's claim to exclusive authorship.

Professional standing and experience add weight to the expert evidence given. At the beginning of the report the expert has to declare who he or she is and state relevant qualifications and experience. This preamble is usually written in the first person.

'I am Cecilia Brown, partner of Smith and Brown, architects and party wall consultants, of [address]. I am retained as expert witness on behalf of ...'

Then give a résumé of qualifications, work experience and anything else of particular relevance to the action being brought.

The report will be structured formally, beginning with details of the Brief, background information and a description of the way the investigation was tackled. Then items of claim and response are listed in the order they appear on the Scott Schedule (if there is one) and comments given, followed by comments on the remedial work required and the related costs. Lastly the expert sets out his or her conclusions. A further report may be required later, after the expert has studied the other side's reports.

10.16 Presentation of reports

Reports may be an important element of a firm's output and an important aspect of its public image. The way reports are organised and presented will be influenced by the firm's house style. Details may be set out in its office manual.

Reports must handle well and all the contents must be easily visible. This means that left hand margins must be particularly generous if the report is to be tightly bound at the spine. Spiral binding is generally suitable for reports, but poses problems where frequent redrafting is likely, as the product has to be pulled apart and reassembled. However, usability is excellent, as spiral-bound documents can be opened completely flat, and illustrative material such as photographs can be seen properly. Any items difficult to bind into the report could accompany it in a separate folder or large envelope. Some can be put in a plastic wallet and bound into the report as an appendix. Ring binders and lever arch files are convenient where large texts need frequent redrafting and the hard covers give durable protection.

Some practices invest heavily in facilities for producing and binding reports, brochures and booklets to achieve a high quality finish and businesslike image for all the firm's output. An alternative is to put this kind of work out to a printer or one of the many firms that offer drawing office services.

Processing

Use double spacing whenever the report has draft status, or is likely to need redrafting by any of the parties involved. Reports commissioned by the legal profession should always be double-spaced, and paragraphs numbered throughout in sequential whole numbers. The final version of a report can be presented single-spaced with the pages backed up.

10.17 Feedback

As a practice develops, so its library of reports will develop. It is often forgotten that this collection of researched information is a valuable asset which all professional and technical staff should be encouraged to share and study. In the course of preparing and researching a report an architect may encounter some new state of the art information or discover a fresh perspective on solving some problem, or be faced with some aspect of design which they had never considered before.

None of this information should be allowed to disappear from the collective memory of the practice, which should develop an effective system for disseminating as well as gathering information. Reports should be circulated to suitable staff as a matter of continuing professional development, and some of the topics covered might also be taken as the subject of an in-house talk or seminar (*see* 10.5).

References and further reading

Chappell, D. (1996) *Report Writing for Architects,* Oxford, Blackwell Science.

Chappell, D. (1996) *Contractual Correspondence for Architects and Project Managers,* Oxford, Blackwell Science.

Hamilton. A. (1988) *Writing Matters,* London, RIBA Publications.

Lupton, S. (ed.) (2000) *Architect's Job Book,* London, RIBA Publications.

11 SELF-PROMOTION AND ATTRACTING WORK

11.1 The need for marketing

11.2 The Codes and self-promotion

11.3 Marketing methods
11.3.1 Using the RIBA
11.3.2 Direct approach to clients
11.3.3 Direct approach to other parties
11.3.4 Advertisement
11.3.5 Press coverage
11.3.6 Competitions

11.4 A marketing plan
11.4.1 A marketing budget
11.4.2 Managing marketing
11.4.3 Marketing tools and techniques
11.4.4 Measuring performance

11.1 The need for marketing

The Institute of Marketing has defined marketing as 'the management process responsible for identifying, anticipating and satisfying customer requirements profitably'. It is the process of exploring the market place and matching or developing skills and services to meet its demands.

There is often some reluctance by practices, particularly smaller practices, to engage in any active marketing. Perhaps they are extremely busy and feel they have no need to encourage new clients. Or they believe they have a good reputation – the standard of their projects is self-evident and needs no further promotion. Many architects feel self-conscious about 'selling' themselves and prefer to rely on the satisfaction of existing clients and personal recommendation. Many practices feel it to be an expensive waste of time.

However, it is quite clear from the above definition that marketing is about more than simply 'advertising'. It includes not only self-promotion, but also the development of skills to meet the demands of an identified market sector, and the satisfaction of existing as well as potential client requirements. Most practices already spend time and energy on these activities. This will be more efficient if it is directed and planned. The next step is to make the process more transparent to outsiders, so that it is clearly evident how the practice has and can meet client needs.

All practices need to develop a strategy for this process. Even busy practices would benefit from a higher profile, and the higher fees that would result. Also, no matter how busy a practice might be, the construction industry is notoriously volatile, and workloads can drop with surprising speed. Practices which have worked hard at nurturing existing clients and at identifying markets, developing contacts and skills, and at reinforcing existing potential clients' perceptions of what the practice can offer, will fare much better in times of economic recession than those who leave these matters to chance.

11.2 The Codes and self-promotion

The professional codes and standards are now relatively relaxed over what used to be referred to as the 'advertising' of professional services.

By the RIBA Code of Professional Conduct, members undertake:

- not to offer discounts, commissions, gifts or other inducements in order to secure an introduction (undertaking 3.1);
- not to quote a fee without receiving an invitation (undertaking 3.2);
- not to revise a fee quotation in order to undercut another architect (undertaking 3.3);
- not to attempt to oust another architect (undertaking 3.4).

The only direct reference to advertising is in an undertaking by the member not to allow his or her name to be used in advertisements for services or products associated with the construction industry (undertaking 2.7). Presumably this allows architects to feature in advertisements for other products, and perhaps this wider exposure might serve to attract potential clients

By the ARB Code, Standard 3 requires all advertising of professional services to be conducted in a truthful and responsible manner. It also requires that advertising conforms to the codes and standards of the industry (e.g. British Code of Advertising Practice, ITC and Radio Code of Advertising Standards and Practice) as relevant. Before any approaches to clients are made, architects should take steps to establish that they have the necessary expertise, competence and resources, and that there are unlikely to be conflicts of interest.

11.3   Marketing methods

There is, of course, no simple answer to the question of how best to attract work. However, there are many well-tried approaches to clients, both direct and indirect, which might usefully be considered. Amongst these are:

11.3.1 Using the RIBA

All firms should consider applying for entry to the RIBA *Register of Practices*. This is the database which is used by the RIBA Client Services to compile the RIBA *Directory of Practices*, to maintain a fully searchable web directory (www.ribafind.org) and to match the client enquiries it receives to a suitable practice. To be listed, practices have to provide the following:

- evidence of adequate professional indemnity insurance;
- evidence of adequate practice management procedures;
- evidence of compliance with CPD and Code obligations;
- information about the practice, submitted to a prescribed format;
- an annual registration fee.

The RIBA *Directory of Practices*, published annually, is sent to some 5,000 clients or potential client bodies. To register the practice should telephone 020 7307 3800 or e-mail register2002@inst.riba.org. In addition, some RIBA Regions publish regional directories, and if practices wish to be listed they should contact their regional office.

RIBA Client Services helps clients to find an architect by providing a shortlist of practices suitable for the type, size and location of the project under consideration. The practice should be prepared to respond immediately to any enquiries from clients, and should develop a practice policy for dealing with such enquiries as part of their market plan.

11.3.2 Direct approach to clients

This would need to be preceded by careful research identifying likely clients, preferably by building up a database of information. The approach can be by telephone, fax, e-mail, or by letter. It is ideally targeted at a particular individual or group of individuals, and it should be clear to the client that the practice is aware of their background and that they have been approached for specific reasons. Such a move might spring from a casual introduction or social conversation, or be generated by reliable intelligence reports, or simply be a routine follow-up to earlier commissions. A practice brochure, regularly updated and capable of being assembled with a particular interest in mind, is an indispensable marketing tool in such situations (see below).

An alternative method is to identify a potential project, for example to prepare proposals for developing derelict or under-used land, or finding new uses for redundant buildings, etc and then to target specific clients on the strength of the proposed scheme. This could be a speculative move, which would create interest from firms known to have sympathy with such initiatives (e.g. contractors, developers, conservation bodies). It might be a loss leader and would need to be kept under tight control, but it could generate some welcome publicity and spin-off benefits.

If the practice has invested in the development of specific expertise in areas of topical concern, then this will be a great help in directing the approach. This could be in an operational respect (e.g. as energy consultants, planning supervisors, specialists in upgrading premises to health and safety requirements, specialists in adapting buildings for disabled access, etc). It could also be in respect of building types (e.g. health centres, housing association work, building conservation, community architecture, etc), particularly where these accord with current political strategy or seem likely to feature in funding programmes.

11.3.3 Direct approach to other parties

These days the architect may not be the first point of contact for a client considering investing in a building project. Bearing this in mind, it may well be wise to broaden the catchment from commissioners of building projects to include other members of the procurement team.

The approach could either be to contracting organisations, perhaps offering a package approach – preferably design-led. Such a partnering could broaden the client base, but would need close control. It could also extend to working with construction management contractors. Many contractors are the lead organisation in putting together bids for PFI projects, and may consider approaches from practices that can demonstrate special skills or a track record in particular building types. Careful research, particularly on the Internet, will identify contractors that are likely candidates.

Another method is to approach other construction professionals, lead consultants or project managers, to secure a sub-consultant's role. This could result in longer-term relationships. Simply working as sub-consultants to another firm of architects might be expedient, but the work is likely to be unpredictable, needed at short notice, and accompanied by considerable pressures.

Alternatively, many consultants are grouping together to put in joint bids for projects. Careful research will pay dividends as it will enable the practice to demonstrate a clear need for the specific contribution the practice can make to the team. Before making any approach it is important for the practice to become familiar with new forms of procurement used for larger projects, and to be clear as to what terms of appointment it is prepared to accept. If in any doubt as to the proposed arrangements the practice should take legal advice.

11.3.4 Advertisement

Advertising in the *Yellow Pages* (or equivalent) telephone directories, trade directories, etc can produce some enquiries but the returns are often small compared with the (sometimes considerable) expense involved. Inclusion in the RIBA Corporate Boxed advertisement in *Yellow Pages* is normally handled on a regional basis and restricted to practices which are listed in the RIBA Register of Practices. Any entry in trade directories is likely to prove of limited direct benefit, but it might at least draw attention to the name of the practice. Architects should take a cautious view of any unsolicited mailshots inviting entries (usually for a considerable sum of money). In the UK, the Unsolicited Goods and Services Act 1971 controls such practices, but operators elsewhere are sometimes not so constrained.

More useful are approaches for inclusion on a register of approved consultants such as those held by the DTLR, local government or other public bodies. Such lists are usually reviewed and updated annually. Inclusion in them is often a first stage to an invitation to bid for a professional engagement, an approach popularised by the US Brooks Method of selecting consultants.

11.3.5 Press coverage

Press coverage can be a very useful way of obtaining publicity for the practice. The first step is to obtain the client's agreement to publishing the project. They usually have no objection, and may even contribute if they feel the publicity would benefit their business. The next stage is to identify a possible publication. Architects tend to focus mainly on the architectural journals, as coverage in such journals carries status amongst their peers. Articles about specific projects or about the practice in general are, of course, a useful marketing tool, as offprints or good quality copies can be sent to existing or prospective clients. However, it is worth considering other publications, such as local press, technical journals, or business journals, as these may reach a larger a number of potential clients than the architectural press.

Clearly any approach to the press has to bear in mind the agenda and needs of the publication targeted. It may be that the scheme is of particular interest locally, or that it exploits new technology that would interest a particular trade journal. It helps to have a specific 'angle' to interest the editor, and it is essential to have a clear summary of the key information readily to hand that can be submitted at very short notice. *A Guide to Marketing on a Shoestring* gives very useful guidance on the various approaches that could be made to different types of journal. Practices might also wish to access the RIBA membership service 'Media Matters Toolkit' on www.site.yahoo.net/press-services/mediamatters.html.

11.3.6 Competitions

Many practices seek new work and also publicity through entering competitions. These should preferably not be the informal type where an unscrupulous client seeks to obtain the maximum amount of free information. A competition should be regarded as unacceptable if it is not possible to elicit:

- the scope of the competition and a design brief;
- the terms and conditions of the competition;
- the conditions upon which the fee (if any) is based;
- the number of practices invited to take part;
- the time available for a stated (and reasonable) amount of design.

Under the RIBA *Code of Professional Conduct,* members undertake not to enter any architectural competition which the Institute has declared to be unacceptable (Undertaking 3.5). Current information on competitions, both in the UK and internationally, is held by the RIBA Competitions Office. It publishes a regular newsletter, *Competition Hotline,* available on subscription, or can be accessed on the Internet at www.ribacompetitions.com. The newsletter and web page contain information about the briefing documents, submission requirements and assessors for each approved competition.

11.4   A marketing plan

A natural development of the practice's established business strategy will be the identification of a marketing plan and allocation of a marketing budget. Then the practice will need to choose the marketing methods that best suit its objectives and will reach the right people. However, it is important to remember that no matter what marketing goals are set, the priority is to maintain the flow of work in the immediate short term.

The first step in developing a marketing plan is to analyse the previous year's workload, broken down into three categories:

- carry-over work: commissions already in progress carried over from the previous year;
- repeat and referral work: repeat work for former clients, and work received by referral with little marketing effort;
- new business: work obtained by actively seeking it.

Carry-over work from existing commissions is likely to remain roughly constant as a percentage of turnover from year to year as completed commissions are replaced by new ones.

Repeat and referral work is a substantial part of most architects' workload, with repeat work from existing clients of particular importance. Although repeats and referrals are the result of the practice's successful previous work and good reputation, it is still essential to maintain contact with clients to make sure that this satisfactory state of affairs continues. Even though the requirements of such clients are likely to be well known, they should still be carefully targeted.

New business must be actively sought, both in familiar areas of work and in any new areas defined in the practice's business strategy. The plan adopted can aim at a single market, or target several. A single target plan aims at one market only, for example, healthcare projects or restoration work. It can be a way of introducing a new area of work into the practice in a limited way, or of concentrating effort on a single important market.

Figure 40: Example of a composite marketing plan based on Weld Coxe's approach in *Marketing Architectural and Engineering Services*

		Health Service	Local Authority	General	Industrial and commercial
Markets	Present clients	21	5	80	1
	Potential clients (to be contacted)	–	3	–	50
Process	Message	Our track record	Our track record	We are local	We are better and cheaper
	Market method	Referral	Repeat and prospecting	Housing Association	Prospect
	Sales tools	Present brochure	Present brochure	Newsletter	New brochure
Organisation	Staff member	AB	CA	JB	BC
	Staff effort	4 hours/week	8 hours/week	12 hours/week	16 hours/week
	Direct costs £	2,500	800	5,000	7,000
	% of total effort	10	20	30	40
	% of total budget	10	10	50	30
Goal	Targeted income £	6 new / 250,000	75,000	100,000	2 new / 75,000
Long range plan	% of present workload	50	15	20	15
	Priority	3	4	2	1
	% of future workload	30	15	20	35

When a practice is undertaking a comprehensive review of several markets, a marketing plan will be needed for each; these can then be combined into a composite plan which allows comparisons to be made between the individual plans, and adjustments made to ensure that resources are used to the best advantage.

A framework for a composite marketing plan is given as Figure 40, while Figure 41 summarises the points for consideration when approaching the task.

11.4.1 A marketing budget

The marketing budget will need to reflect accurately the effort the practice plans to put into getting work, and needs to be set in the early stages of drawing up the marketing plan. All direct expenses, and the amount of staff time expended, should be recorded on time sheets so that it is possible to monitor and assess cost-effectiveness. The budget should be kept under review and will probably need upgrading – the natural tendency is to underestimate the marketing requirement in the hope that the targeted work will soon come rolling in. It is important to maintain marketing activities through good times as well as bad, and the marketing budget should be regarded as a continuing commitment when planning the deployment of practice finances.

Figure 41: Developing a marketing plan

Market
What types of client, types of project, and geographical location are to be covered?

Capability
What services and strengths can the practice offer?

Message
What particular message does the practice wish to convey; is it offering anything special?

Contacts
What past, present or potential clients have already been identified?

Methods
What methods will the practice use for research, lead-finding, courting prospects and presenting the firm's credentials? Will the approach be passive or aggressive?

Tools
What sales tools (promotional literature, publicity, advertising, etc) will be appropriate?

Organisation
What tasks and roles will be required, and who will be responsible for organising the marketing initiative? What time should be allocated? What budget should be allowed?

Goals
What results are desired, and how will they be measured?

11.4.2 Managing marketing

Three important decisions to be made are:

- Who is to be in charge of the marketing drive?

- How is it to be organised?

- Who will carry it out?

Most architects have only limited experience of marketing, although some may have a natural flair for various aspects of it. Marketing expertise can be brought in, and firms of marketing consultants abound, although only a few have any special knowledge or experience of the needs of architectural practices. One of these could be briefed to carry out the whole marketing operation, find clients and 'deliver' them to the practice principals. Alternatively, they could be used to support an in-house marketing effort, where practice principals and senior design staff play the leading roles.

If it is decided to institute and organise a marketing force in-house, careful consideration will have to be given to what level of effort is needed, whether the practice has sufficient and appropriate resources, and whether this is the most cost-effective way of meeting its marketing needs.

A large practice might consider appointing a marketing director with a number of full-time staff, or a marketing manager with or without supporting staff. Smaller practices might make a member of staff responsible for marketing activities on a part-time basis, or one of the principals might devote some of his or her time to marketing.

The tasks involved in a marketing drive are various. In a small practice one person will probably have to carry them all out, but a larger practice may be able to match people to tasks and roles to which they are particularly suited (*see* Figure 42). This makes the best use of available skills, as well as spreading the load.

It should be remembered that a practice that embarks on a marketing exercise is asking to be assessed and evaluated in public, and it is bad for morale, as well as business, to be seen to fail. If the marketing effort is poorly executed, there is little hope of impressing clients about the quality of the professional service being offered.

Figure 42: Marketing roles and tasks

Lead finding

Task: explore the market, find out whom to contact, make contact, introduce to the practice.

Person: must know where to look, have a good nose for prospects, persevere although work can be tedious and unrewarding.

Development

Task: develop good understanding and convince client of practice's abilities.

Person: must be authoritative and carry conviction – probably a principal. Each principal could deal with a group of clients.

Success

Task: present the practice's proposal to client and win commission.

Person: a principal, with full authority and knowledge. Client may expect him/her to manage the project as well.

Co-ordination

Task: maintain marketing 'tools', put together publicity material, proposals and presentations.

Person: a full-time job if the practice has 15–20 staff. Should be well-organised, quick to respond, good writer.

Management

Task: to make sure it all happens.

Person: an appointed 'marketing director' or a principal responsible for directing the marketing drive. Could be a manager/facilitator with an integrated support service.

11.4.3 Marketing tools and techniques

Once the marketing aims are clear and decisions have been made about who is to manage the marketing drive, the various tools and techniques needed have to be considered. It is important to channel effort and expenditure into the most cost-effective directions.

An expanded entry in the RIBA's *Directory of Practices* is sensible if the practice is looking for new work. Press releases about significant new commissions or completions may result in some valuable (and free) publicity in the locality. Placing an advertisement can sometimes be stunningly successful as a one-off 'impact' event, but advertising is relatively expensive and can seldom be afforded on a regular basis.

Marketing will make use of a wide range of documents and generate yet more. The collection could include:

- information about practice – its history, personnel;
- information about projects: job records, competitions and awards, photographs and slides;

- promotional brochures and leaflets;
- project brochures, presentations and models;
- press cuttings; market research and reports, directory entries, etc.

There should be a database for recording details of clients and potential clients, and the production and issue of marketing material. Equipment will also be needed for printing and binding documents, for producing visual materials, and for storing files, photographs and slides, brochures, models and exhibition material.

In a small practice, whoever acts as librarian could be responsible for looking after such material. A large practice with a vigorous marketing department might consider making a special appointment.

11.4.4 Measuring performance

In simple terms, the success of a marketing plan can be quantified in terms of the commissions won and the fees earned. However, there are intangible benefits, such as 'potential' and 'goodwill', which are not directly attributable either to the excellence of the people involved in the exercise or to the accuracy of the targeting. Even if the only identifiable result of the whole operation is that the practice has become better known in the locality, it will not have wasted its energies entirely. That said, marketing activities must be monitored and judgements made about their effectiveness, so that corrective measures can be taken if necessary and money is not wasted.

As a matter of quality management, marketing operations should be audited at regular intervals to make sure that the plan is on target, being operated properly, and that any weaknesses are identified and corrected. The questions to ask are:

- Is the overall programme being maintained?
- Are the right staff, in the right numbers, being used?
- Are they performing their tasks effectively?
- Is the budget set at the right level?
- Are the promotional aids sufficient and of the right quality? Are presentations well prepared and executed?
- Have the right targets been identified?
- Is action being taken to address future needs?
- How effective are the marketing tools and techniques?
- What are the quantifiable results so far?

The long-term implications of the results will need to be evaluated to allow forecasts of:

- future workload and staffing;
- any change in financial commitment;
- the kind of marketing required in the future.

References and further reading

Coxe, W. (1983) *Marketing Architectural and Engineering Services*, London, Van Norstrand Reinhold.

Martin, I. (1999) *A Guide to Marketing on a Shoestring*, London, RIBA Publications, Small Practices series.

12 ARCHITECT-CLIENT RELATIONSHIP

12.1 Client identity

12.2 Client perceptions

12.3 Client guidance

12.4 Professional advice

12.5 Professional duty

12.6 The appointment

12.7 Standard forms
12.7.1 SFA/99
12.7.2 CE/99
12.7.3 SW/99
12.7.4 SC/99
12.7.5 DB1/99
12.7.6 DB2/99
12.7.7 PS/99
12.7.8 PM/99

12.8 Copyright

12.9 Collateral warranties

12.10 Other consultants

12.11 Rejecting the impossible

12.12 Other consultancy services

12.13 Additional services with risk aspects

12.1 Client identity

The architect will need to discover the true facts about a client's requirements, expectations and sources of finance, and whether there are any constraints on time and budget critical to the project's success. Architects should not feel diffident about making discreet checks on the financial status of new clients before accepting a commission and, if circumstances suggest it, even asking for money up front. They need to be confident that clients are creditworthy, particularly where large sums of money might be at risk.

An important first step is to clarify the identity and status of the client in relation to the project. For example, if the client is a company it is vital to know whether it is the parent company, a holding company, or just a subsidiary – a subsidiary may be more vulnerable to insolvency. With corporate clients it is essential to have a single point of contact, one named person who can be held accountable and have authority to act. The client organisation needs to be studied – how is it structured and how does it function?

The client might be an unincorporated body. It could be a church or club or some other association. If the client is a committee or board, it is important that there is one named person authorised to make decisions, convey instructions and sign cheques.

The client might simply be an individual looking to build an extension to his own house for his own occupation. However, if 'the client' seems to be a couple, it is essential to establish which one will give instructions, sign the agreement and cheques, etc – or will they both insist on doing this, and could there be potential for friction and delay?

It is also important to find out where the client is 'coming from' in relation to the project. Clients build for different reasons and purposes, and their degree of interest in the project will vary accordingly. A client might see development as a speculative initiative or investment, and be interested primarily in the financial return; matters of building design and construction may largely pass the client by. On some projects there might be a commissioning client, and a user client who could be the eventual purchaser of the completed work – or even an occupier under a pre-let agreement. The client may have backing from a funding organisation which will seek to secure safeguards by way of collateral agreements. It is wise to establish in the early days of the architect-client relationship just what and whose interests have to be taken into account.

12.2 Client perceptions

Normally clients have personal aspirations about their projects as well as a shopping list of the functional and operational requirements to be satisfied, and architects should make a point of discovering what these are and identifying with them. With most building projects a compromise has to be made between cost, speed of completion and quality, so it is essential to understand the client's real objectives and priorities.

In this respect there are lessons to be learned from some of the conclusions reached in the RIBA *Strategic Study of the Profession* concerning architects and clients, which were that:

- practices were too often introverted;

- practices were 'more concerned with rationalising their own processes than explaining the power of design';

- clients were disappointed by 'the gap between the aspirations they had been encouraged to harbour and the realities of poor delivery';

- architects should 'replace perceived arrogance and disappointment with mutual respect';

- architects should devote as much energy to managing relations with clients as they devote to designing buildings.

Clients who have built before should have a relatively clear idea of their needs, and what the chosen procurement method will entail. A client who has not built before is likely to lean heavily on the guidance of advisors and consultants. It is worth remembering that in several legal cases it has been held that a professional's duty of care relates to the known experience or inexperience of the client. A client new to building may not realise that he or she will have to be accessible for the duration of the project, make decisions quickly when necessary and abide by them, and respond to requests for information promptly. The implications of disregarding critical points in the agreed programme will need spelling out.

12.3   Client guidance

It is important to explain to clients at the outset that every building project involves some degree of risk, and that it is rarely possible for their aspirations about time, cost and quality to be realised without some compromise being necessary.

To help identify and explain the services architects can provide, and to remove areas of potential misunderstanding, the RIBA publishes a series of client guides ('yellow books') on engaging an architect. Titles to date include:

- *Guidance for Clients to Quality Based Selection;*

- *A Client's Guide to Engaging an Architect including guidance on fees;*

- *A Client's Guide to Engaging an Architect (Small Works) including guidance on fees;*

- *Guidance for Clients on Health and Safety – the CDM Regulations 1994;*

- *Guidance for Clients on Party Wall Procedures: the Party Wall, etc Act 1996.*

The guides offer concise and constructive advice and are addressed directly to the client. Sending an appropriate guide under a covering letter early in the relationship is a convenient and helpful way of informing clients about important aspects of their project.

The range of advice expected from architects today can be wide and varied, depending on the type of client and the nature and scope of the services to be provided. The architect may be appointed to act in various capacities, with varying measures of accountability and liability.

12.4 Professional advice

When giving professional advice, as for example when reporting on the potential of a development proposal, or when preparing design drawings, the architect will be expected to exercise a duty of care – i.e. to use reasonable skill and care. This is a duty in tort, but will probably also be a contractual obligation. Some essential points to bear in mind follow.

- Architects should not attempt to advise on matters beyond their expertise. This is not just contravention of the RIBA *Code of Professional Conduct*, it could amount to misrepresentation.

- Architects should not attempt to advise or make recommendations on matters which are beyond their control (e.g. that a particular result will be achieved, or that a particular contractor will 'do a first class job').

- Architects should not volunteer advice gratuitously, or offer advice that goes beyond contractual obligations or what is required under legislation, without first assessing the risk.

- The professional duty to exercise reasonable skill and care is based on an objective standard, but the degree of skill and care which can be expected in particular circumstances can vary.

- Advice should always be based on the best information obtainable at the time. Any caveats or conditions meant to be taken into account should be clearly stated and explained if necessary.

- The extent to which the architect may be expected to give advice should be set down in the terms of the professional appointment, which should be clear and unambiguous. In cases where such matters are not covered expressly and assumptions made, the courts have been known to decide that terms were implied, particularly where the parties had contracted previously.

- The RIBA *Code of Professional Conduct* requires members, when acting between parties or when giving professional advice, to exercise independent judgement impartially to the best of their ability and understanding (Undertaking 1.1). Furthermore, members are required to seek appropriate advice when faced with a situation which is outside their experience or knowledge.

- The ARB *Code of Professional Conduct and Practice* requires registered persons to exercise due skill and care and diligence, and to carry out professional work without undue delay and, as appropriate, within any agreed time limit.

12.5 Professional duty

There may be situations where the architect has accepted more than the normal duty of care. Liability in tort could co-exist with a duty of result – for example, where a 'fitness for purpose' warranty is given. In such situations, merely exercising skill and care may prove insufficient if the intended purpose is not achieved.

Although the architect's duty will normally relate to the client in tort and in contract, a tortious duty may also arise with third parties who have no contractual relationship. For example, a contractor might be able to sue an architect in tort where there has been advice culminating in intended interference in the running of the building contract, as a result of which the contractor has suffered loss. There will also be a tortious and contractual duty to third parties, e.g. funders, lessees, etc where collateral warranties have been given.

From the earliest stage of negotiation, everything agreed with the client should be set down in writing and filed. When the work is in progress, all instructions, approvals and decisions should be meticulously recorded. It is important not to assume everlasting goodwill, even where the client is well known to the practice, or the personal friend of a principal. Records can be produced as evidence in years to come, whereas good will can vanish in a moment.

Claims still commonly arise against architects because the original commission was not properly defined and recorded – in some cases, not recorded at all. The RIBA *Code of Professional Conduct* requires members 'to have defined beyond reasonable doubt and recorded the terms of the engagement' (Undertaking 1.2), whilst the ARB Standard requires architects not to undertake professional work unless the parties have agreed in writing specific terms of their agreement; including scope of work, responsibilities and fees (Standard 11, *see* 2.4).

12.6 The appointment

The client's agreement in writing to all the conditions of appointment must be obtained. Any departures from standard conditions should be clearly stated in the document used. Architects should never proceed with any work until they are sure that a proper basis for the commission has been established with the client and recorded in writing, and that they have the necessary authority to proceed. Architects should take particular care, when dealing with clients acting as consumers, to explain all terms to them clearly, as otherwise the client may not be bound by any terms deemed 'unfair' under the Unfair Terms in Consumer Contract Regulations 1994 (see 3.5).

Clients should always be given an explanation of the need and purpose of each work stage; if they do not wish to pay for a full service, they then have the choice of making other arrangements. However, providing a 'partial' service can have dangers if the scope of the service is not clearly defined, and architects would be wise to state clearly what this does not cover, in order to avoid any misunderstanding. Where the client's own organisation provides part of the service, or an architect is asked to take over work started previously by others, both the scope and the limits of responsibility should be set out in writing.

It is always advisable to use a Standard Form of Appointment. At the time of writing, the RIBA publishes appointing documents for use in traditional procurement which relate (very approximately) to major commissions under JCT 98 (SFA/99), less complex projects under the Intermediate Form IFC 98 (CE/99), and commissions of up £100,000, possibly under the Minor Works Agreement (SW/99). It also produces appointing documents for use with design and build (DB/1 and DB/2), for use when acting as a sub-consultant (SC/99) or project manager (PM/99). A complete list is set out in 12.7.

All the RIBA appointing documents have a similar and logical structure which consist of a memorandum of agreement (or a model letter of aappointment) and schedules which set out the services to be provided, the fees to be charged and how these are calculated, and details of any other appointments necessary for the project. Each document also includes the conditions of appointment applying to the project. The RIBA publishes accompanying guidance on the use and completion of its forms of appointment.

Where the prospective client is proposing amendments to a standard form, or proposing their own terms of appointment it is essential to seek advice from the practice's professional indemnity insurers. If the architect agrees to terms without the insurer's approval or without taking legal advice, the insurer may refuse to provide cover should there be a claim. Areas which can cause problems are where the architect accepts a strict obligation to perform a task, rather than an obligation to carry out the task with reasonable skill and care, common ones being where the promises to ensure that no deleterious materials are used, or that the building when complete will perform as per the client's brief. Another area of difficulty is where the architect fails to incorporate limitations on liability required by the insurers, for example an overall cap on liability.

SFA/99 provides for an absolute cap on liability. It also includes a 'net contribution clause' which some insurers now insist on. Where several consultants are involved in a project, this limits the liability of the architect to a proportion of the losses recoverable by the client, the proportion reflecting the extent of the architect's responsibility within the team. If the form did not contain such a clause, the client would be able to pursue the architect for the whole of its loss, and the architect would have to recover the balance from the other consultants.

Where there are ad-hoc terms, it is also important to check that the extent of the services is defined accurately, and that the provisions for suspension, termination and dispute resolution are detailed and fair. The appointment will be subject to various statutes (*see* 3.5) and compliance should be checked. It will normally be necessary to have expert advice on all these matters.

12.7   Standard forms

The RIBA publishes a comprehensive range of appointment documents as follows:

SFA/99   Standard Form of Agreement for the Appointment of an Architect

CE/99   Conditions of Engagement for the Appointment of an Architect

SW/99   Small Works

SC/99   Form of Appointment as a Sub-Consultant

DB1/99   Employer's Requirements

DB2/99   Contractor's Proposals

PS/99   Form of Appointment as Planning Supervisor

PM/99   Form of Appointment as Project Manager

12.7.1 SFA/99

This is the core document from which all the other standard forms of appointment are derived. It is suitable for use where an architect is to provide services for a fully designed building project in a wide range of sizes and complexity and/or to provide other professional services. It includes notes on completion and an optional services supplement. There are articles of agreement and an attestation with provision for the agreement to be executed as a deed. The form can be adapted where the applicable law is the law of Scotland using text published by the RIAS for this purpose.

SFA/99 is clearly suitable for use on large projects following a traditional procurement route. In addition, unlike CE/99 and SW/99 this form differentiates between the role of architect as designer, design leader, lead consultant and contract administrator. This splitting of functions means that this form can be used in more complex or unusual procurement routes, for example construction management, where the architect is acting as design leader but the role of contract administrator may be performed by a separately appointed project manager.

If, after the appointment is agreed, it is decided to use a design build procurement, the parties can amend the agreement by executing DB/1 (see below).

12.7.2 CE/99

Suitable for use where an architect is to provide services for a fully designed building project and/or to provide other professional services where a letter of appointment is preferred to the articles of agreement in SFA/99. It includes notes on completion, a draft model letter and an optional (modified) services supplement. The form can be adapted where the applicable law is the law of Scotland using notes and model letter published by the RIAS for this purpose.

CE/99 would normally only be used for straightforward projects using traditional procurement, and where there is no requirement to have the appointment executed as a deed. If necessary, it can be adapted for design and build (appointment by employer client only) by use of DB1/99.

The agreement comprises a letter of appointment from the architect to the client, to which a copy of the form is attached after completion of the schedules. The model letter should be carefully adapted for the particular circumstances of the project. Amongst other things, it deals with professional indemnity insurance and dispute resolution matters, in other words it covers the items included in the appendix to the conditions in SFA/99.

In the absence of signed articles, obtaining a written reply from the client accepting the terms set out in the letter of appointment is an important safeguard.

12.7.3 SW/99

Suitable for use where an architect is to provide services for a fully designed building project and/or to provide other professional services and where a letter of appointment is preferred to articles of agreement. It is suitable where:

- the services are of a relatively straightforward nature;
- the cost of the construction works is not expected to exceed £150,000;

- use of the JCT *Agreement for Minor Works* is appropriate;

- there is no requirement to have the contract executed under seal;

- the applicable law is the law of England and Wales (the notes clearly state that it is not suitable for use where the applicable law is the law of Scotland).

The agreement comprises a letter of appointment from the architect to the client, to which is annexed the conditions of appointment for small works and the printed schedule of services for small works, with other activities (not services) listed on the reverse. SW/99 includes notes on completion, and a draft model letter which must be carefully adapted to suit the project. As with CE/99, obtaining a written reply from the client accepting the terms set out in the letter of appointment is an important safeguard.

12.7.4 SC/99

Suitable for use where a consultant wishes another consultant (sub-consultant) to perform part of his or her responsibility, but not for use where the intention is for the client to appoint consultants directly. It is used with articles of agreement and includes notes on completion and a draft form of warranty to the client. SC/99 is very similar to SFA/99, with the terms 'client' and 'architect' being replaced with 'consultant' and 'sub-consultant'.The form can be adapted where the applicable law is the law of Scotland using text published by the RIAS for this purpose.

The form is compatible with SFA/99, and with modification could be used with CE/99. The notes point out the importance of ensuring that the services are compatible with the services being provided under the head agreement, and that the warranty terms are harmonised with the head agreement and with any other warranties being provided.

12.7.5 DB1/99

An amendment for SFA/99 and CE/99 where an architect is employed by the employer client to prepare employer's requirements for a design and build contract such as the *JCT Standard Form of Building Contract with Contractor's Design* (JCT WCD98), and to act as the employer's agent during construction if required. It includes some modified definitions and work stages to suit the procurement method and a replacement services supplement. The notes give guidance on the procedure at initial appointment, on the need to vary the agreement where a change to design and build has occurred after initial appointment, and on use with SFA/99 where 'consultant switch' or 'novation' is contemplated.

A 'consultant switch' arises where the employer requires the contractor to make a separate follow-on agreement with the contractor for professional services. After the consultant switch takes effect:

- the architect's services will be performed for the benefit of the contractor;

- the architect will remain liable to the employer client for services previously undertaken for the benefit of the employer client;

- the architect will not be liable to the employer client for services undertaken for the contractor (unless a warranty is executed).

A 'novation' arises where the employer requires the contractor to take over the employer's agreement with the architect. In a true novation the terms of the agreement would remain unchanged but in practice the novation is often conditional. After the novation:

- the architect becomes liable to the contractor client for services already performed and to be performed in the future by the architect;

- the architect will not be liable to the employer client for services already undertaken or to be undertaken for the contractor (unless a warranty is executed).

In either arrangement a supplementary or tri-partite agreement will be needed, and the employer client may require a warranty. Model clauses for both of these are included in *The Architect's Contract: a guide to the RIBA standard forms of appointment*. However these are only intended as a basis for discussion and neither of these arrangements should be entered into without taking legal advice.

12.7.6 DB2/99

An amendment for SFA/99 where an architect is employed by the contractor client to prepare contractor's proposals for a design and build contract such as JCT WCD98, or in connection with the *Contractor's Designed Portion Supplement*. (Use with CE/99 is not recommended.) It includes replacement articles, appendix and services supplement and notes on completion for initial appointment and for 'consultant switch' and 'novation'.

12.7.7 PS/99

Used for the appointment as planning supervisor under the CDM Regulations 1994 of suitably qualified construction professionals. An appointment as a planning supervisor is distinct from the provision of architectural services under other RIBA forms of appointment. It is used with articles of agreement and includes notes on completion. The form can be adapted where the applicable law is the law of Scotland using text published by the RIAS for this purpose.

12.7.8 PM/99

This will be for use where the client wishes to appoint a project manager to provide a management and/or other professional services. It is intended that this will not duplicate or conflict with the services as defined in other RIBA forms, particularly with the architect as design leader, lead consultant or contract administrator as set out in SFA/99.

12.8 Copyright

It is important that any terms of appointment agreed include adequate protection of copyright. The Copyright Designs and Patents Act 1988 protects copyright in drawings, and 'works of architecture, being buildings or models for buildings', which prevents copying of drawings, models or completed buildings (or parts of any of these) without the architect's permission.

Under the RIBA standard forms of appointment the architect retains copyright and the client is given a license to copy and use drawings for specified purposes relating to the project. This right is subject to the payment of a licence fee (if specified), and the licence can be suspended in the event of default in the payment of fees by the client.

Even with such clauses, however, it is difficult – if not impossible – to protect against the copying of ideas. In the case of *Jones* v *London Borough of Tower Hamlets* (2000), Jones was the original architect engaged on a project by a developer, who later went into liquidation. The project was taken over by Tower Hamlets, whose own designers submitted a scheme for planning permission which was very similar to the one developed by Jones. Jones attempted to sue for breach of copyright, but Tower Hamlets claimed that the similarities were an inevitable consequence of the tight site restrictions and the strict brief. The court decided that there had been no infringement of copyright. The only practicable solution to problems such as this is to ensure that the fee structure agreed should reflect this risk, i.e. to ensure the fees for early stages adequately remunerate the intellectual input into the project. The implications of the case are yet another reason to resist the temptation to work on the early stages of projects 'at risk' or for very low fees.

12.9   Collateral warranties

Architects are often put under pressure to give collateral warranties to third parties; these may be institutional funding organisations, or prospective purchasers or tenants. It is uncertain what effect warranties may have in respect of future claims on the profession, but they certainly increase risk and should be avoided if possible. Insurers must always be informed about any warranties proposed and asked whether they are prepared to cover the additional risk. Not all insurance policies cover claims arising from contracts with third parties. The RIBA scheme insurers have stated that they will cover, without further reference to them, claims arising from the use, unamended, of the *Form of Warranty in Favour of Funder Issued Jointly by the RIBA and the British Property Federation (BPF)*. It should be borne in mind that cover for these additional risks might well affect the practice's professional indemnity insurance premiums in future years as well as the current year.

Collateral warranties to persons providing finance for a project usually require the architect to act for the third party if that party becomes the owner of the project before completion. It is crucial for architects to retain their rights of termination. Often the third party will only come into ownership through the failure of the original client and there may well be a legacy of ill will affecting all the professional advisors. Continuing to work for the third party under strained circumstances can lead to trouble.

Forms of collateral warranty can sometimes introduce obligations greater than those set out in the original contract. The wording of 'duty of care agreements' and any attempts to obtain 'fitness for purpose' undertakings should be treated with great caution and be checked by a lawyer. Architects who sign documents incautiously may find themselves in breach of their insurance policy conditions, and without professional indemnity insurance cover as a result.

12.10 Other consultants

Many claims arise partly or wholly from an action, or a failure to act, by other consultants. Consultants should preferably be appointed directly by the client, who will hold them responsible for the service they provide. Where the client insists on a single appointment for all professional services, architects should establish a proper structure of control and only accept their own nominees.

Architects should insist on the right to check the terms of appointment and services of consultants and, if necessary, ask for them to be changed. If the client disagrees, the architect should put a disclaimer of responsibility in writing. The terms under which consultants are appointed should state their responsibility for complying with the architect's requirements regarding time and programme.

Clients are increasingly reluctant to make individual and separate appointments, and often insist that the architect appoints and accepts responsibility for the whole professional team. An architect who refuses to do so may risk losing the job, but that is a matter of commercial judgement.

Every architect who undertakes a commission exposes him or herself to some degree of risk, because this is the nature of business. It is always necessary to balance an assessment of the risks entailed against a judgement about the potential for profit. Risks can be reduced by acquiring a good understanding of job costing, making sure that arrangements for paying fees are clearly set down in the terms of the commission, and by instituting and operating strict administrative procedures for the issuing of invoices and for their prompt payment.

12.11 Rejecting the impossible

Commissions that are clearly impossible should not be accepted. Prospective clients frequently lay down a brief, with a budget and a timescale, as a precondition of appointment. These may be incompatible and one or other of them even unattainable. As a result there may be a claim – or the architect will not be paid. A commission should never be accepted under one set of terms and operated under another. Changes to the conditions of a contract require the agreement of both parties in writing.

Similarly, it is essential to avoid over-committing practice resources. As well as sound commonsense, it is a requirement of the ARB and RIBA *Codes of Professional Conduct* that architects undertake to establish that their competence and resources are adequate before accepting a commission. Over-commitment can lead to an inadequate service, a dissatisfied client and eventual claims.

The tendency has increased in recent years for clients to offer commissions to architects on their own purpose-made terms. These often seek to transfer all risks to consultants, and sometimes include requirements which are uninsurable. Architects should study the terms and conditions carefully and consult their legal advisers and insurers before accepting the appointment.

Another situation to watch out for is the 'creeping commission' – one that gradually becomes something far in excess of what was originally agreed, often without any recognition that adjustments need to be made to the appointment to reflect the true situation, and the architect's fee increased accordingly.

12.12 Other consultancy services

RIBA appointing documents typically include a range of services which could be provided by the architect in addition to services specific to building projects. Of these 'other services', some are advisory in character whilst others are directly related to sites or buildings investigation. Many of the latter can be accommodated under the appropriate standard appointing document, whilst many of the listed consultancy services require a separate agreement outwith the normal RIBA appointing documents.

Professional services for which architects could be appointed include:

- to act as expert witness;
- to act as arbitrator under the Arbitration Act 1996;
- to act as adjudicator under Part II of the Housing Grants, Construction and Regeneration Act 1996;
- to act as expert (i.e. not as arbitrator) in dispute resolution;
- to act as party wall surveyor under the Party Wall, etc Act 1996.

Some of these appointments may need an agreement specially drafted by a lawyer, since a simple exchange of letters is rarely adequate. In all cases where non standard terms are being proposed the architect should inform his or her insurers. For certain specific roles the following forms may be useful:

- Adjudicator: The JCT publishes a form of appointment for an adjudicator (with a version for a named adjudicator) which must be used where an adjudicator is appointed in a dispute relating to a JCT form. The CIC *Model Adjudication Procedure* includes an agreement on appointment of an adjudicator which may be used in relation to other disputes.
- Arbitrator: normally arbitrators set their own terms of appointment.
- Conciliator: the RIBA has a standard form for use with the RIBA *Conciliation Procedure*.
- Party Wall Surveyor: this should be dealt with using a specially drafted letter or document. Guidance is set out in *Architect's Guide to Job Administration, the Party Wall, etc Act 1996*, which includes a letter of authorisation which must be obtained from the Appointing Owner before proceeding.
- Clerks of Works: the Institute of Clerks of Works publishes an appointment document.
- Historic Buildings: SFA/99 and CE/99 can be adapted for work on historic buildings. *The Achitect's Contract: a guide to the RIBA standard forms of appointment* includes a schedule of special services for this purpose.

- Community Architecture: SFA/99 and CE/99 can be adapted to community architecture projects. *The Architect's Contract: a guide to the RIBA standard forms of appointment* includes a schedule of special services for this purpose.

Some services often undertaken by architects can have pitfalls, and should be regarded with a degree of caution. They are extensive, and examples of some are described in the following sections.

12.12.1 House surveys

Structural surveys for the house purchaser are a major area of risk for most small practices. Unless this kind of work is to be a regular and major source of income, architects are best advised to avoid it. Any architect who does undertake house surveys should establish some sound procedures to be followed in all cases.

A house purchaser commissions a survey for one reason only: he wants a realistic indication of his likely future commitment. However enthusiastic he may be about the property at the time he commissions the survey, if faced with an unexpected cost some time in the future, his first reaction will be to try to recoup his costs from the surveyor. And if he is insured against, say, subsidence, then his insurers will bring an action in his name to recover their loss. In recent years, judicial findings on what constitutes professional negligence in surveys have been extremely punitive. Architects should remember the following points:

- They should never carry out a survey for a friend for a reduced fee, or for no fee at all. Responsibility is not limited by the size of the fee.
- Any warning required by their indemnity insurers should be included in all reports. An architect who fails to do so is likely to carry the whole burden of any claim.
- The report should include a statement about the physical and climatic conditions under which the survey was carried out and the vantage points from which inaccessible parts of the property were viewed, e.g. roof slopes. It should be made clear what was not inspected, or where it was not possible to inspect.
- They should have available a full complement of instruments and tools with them on site so that the condition of the property can be properly established.
- There must be access to all the principle parts of the property, particularly roof spaces and drains. It may be necessary to ask for the attendance of a builder to provide access and opening up; if so, this should be arranged in advance.
- It is best to work to a tried and tested checklist. Many good ones are published, and can be adapted to suit particular circumstances.
- Architects should not allow their judgement to be clouded by explanations from the owner or his agent about obvious defects.
- If any doubt remains about any aspect, the architect's report should include a recommendation that there should be further inspections by specialists (*see also* 12.12.2 below).

Architects should remember, particularly when surveying unoccupied properties alone, to avoid hazardous situations where it might be difficult to get out again. They should make sure that the office knows where they have gone and what time they expect to return. Recommended health and safety guidelines should be followed (*see* 6.9 and Appendix B).

12.12.2 Building society inspections

Building society and similar inspections of existing properties are usually carried out for a considerably smaller fee than full house surveys. The reports are usually recorded on a standard form provided by the society. The drafting quality of these pro formas and the degree of responsibility that they place upon the surveyor can vary widely. Some are made available to the purchaser, and some are not. Even in the latter case, the courts have decided that the purchaser can rely on them.

Architects should not hesitate to delete words or paragraphs that are inappropriate to the inspection they have carried out, or to add caveats. The point from which visual observations are made should be stated, e.g. 'The condition of the roof, when viewed from the ground only, was ...'.

As well as inspections and reports on existing buildings, architects are sometimes approached to carry out inspections in connection with mortgage advances on new property. Building societies or banks often stipulate that money will be advanced in instalments upon completion of certain stages, subject to inspection by an architect or surveyor who is required to submit an inspection report and ultimately sign a certificate. Provided the architect is approached before work starts on site, inspection may be reasonably undertaken, but the client must alert the architect that a stage is ready for inspection before any covering up of work takes place. Where the architect is approached late during construction, it might prove impossible to complete stage reports and certification.

It is important for architects involved in such work to understand the difficulties and recognise the dangers. Inspection can only be on the basis of periodic visits to check generally the quality and progress of the work to the extent that this is possible by visual inspection. Any statements which might amount to absolute warranties (and these frequently appear in standard certificates produced by building societies) are unacceptable. They go far beyond the legal duty to use reasonable skill and care, and should be resisted.

12.12.3 Surveys of commercial buildings

These surveys are usually carried out either before purchase or when entering into a lease. They present less of a risk to architects because of the nature of the client and because an adequate fee can usually be charged to allow the job to be properly resourced. On all major buildings it is usual to employ specialists to report on services. The same general rules apply as with house surveys, but some additional caution is required.

- With newly constructed property, architects should establish the rights of the purchaser in relation to the latent defects provisions of the building contract. If the rights are not to be assigned, they may be unenforceable.

- With leased property, architects should always insist on having a copy of the lease so that the full responsibilities of the lessee can be established, if necessary by taking legal advice. Repairing leases can be onerous.

Even where only part of a building is being leased, it is still essential to inspect the whole building, paying particular attention to the roof and main services, as the tenant will almost certainly bear a proportion of any costs of repair and maintenance.

12.12.4 Quinquennial church inspections

The 1955 Inspection of Churches Measure requires that every parish church in the Church of England is the subject of an inspection and report by a 'suitably qualified' architect, at least every five years. This is work usually undertaken by a sole practitioner, or by a named architect. It is specialised work, and it is important to make sure that a policy of professional indemnity insurance covers the person actually doing the work. In some cases this work will be the firm's work, but in others it will be a personal appointment and the named architect is acting in an individual capacity. This should be checked with insurers.

A Guide to Church Inspection and Repair is published by the Council for the Care of Churches, and gives sound and helpful advice.

12.13 Additional services with risk aspects

Architects are sometimes asked to certify compliance with Building Regulations or some other standard of satisfactory completion, to meet the requirements of a finance organisation. This is often the case where the owner has self-built, or has engaged with an unregistered building group to erect his private house. An architect who has not been engaged to visit the works in progress would be unwise to undertake this service.

12.13.1 Inspections of work in progress

Architects are sometimes engaged to inspect works in progress which are not of their own design, perhaps for a client who has entered into some kind of design and build or package deal contract. They should always establish in advance what rights they have under the building contract in question. If these are limited (and they will often be nonexistent) it is important to advise the client of the limits of the architect's powers before accepting the commission. Architects should never attempt in any way to amend the design or any constructional details during visits; they should simply inform the client of any problem and let the client sort it out with the contractor.

12.13.2 Grant-aided work

Architects involved with grant-aided housing improvement work should be thoroughly conversant with all the rules and conditions and not risk disqualifying the client by breaching them. It is also essential to avoid risking any suggestion of collusion with a client by obtaining grant aid to which the client may not strictly be entitled – some clients tend to take a 'relaxed' view of the rules. The real risk to the architect who becomes involved in such dubious practices is that if at some later date the client makes sole claim against the architect, the latter will not be in a position to defend the claim for fear of exposure of any malpractice.

12.13.2 Handling clients' money

Architects sometime handle money belonging to clients. This may be a matter of disbursement such as the clerk of works' salary, or fees connected with statutory approvals. They may be asked to administer separate trades contracts, making payments to the various firms with the client's money. It is a requirement of the ARB Code that these monies are always paid from a separate 'client's account', and it is important to record that the payments are being made for and on behalf of the client. Architects should never pay out any of their own money, or they may find, for example, that they have taken on the responsibilities and liabilities of the builder – and they will not be covered by their professional indemnity insurance. RIBA members are required to conform with the Members' Rules for Clients' Accounts under the RIBA *Code of Professional Conduct*.

References and further reading

A Client's Guide to Engaging an Architect including guidance on fees, London, RIBA (1999).

A Client's Guide to Engaging an Architect (Small Works) including guidance on fees, London, RIBA (1999).

Blackler, T. and Wevill, J. 'Principles: Appointments', RIBA *Journal*, January 2001, p. 86, and subsequent articles in this series.

Blackler, T. and Wevill, J. 'Principles: Copyright', RIBA *Journal*, March 2001, p. 104, and subsequent articles in this series.

Byrom, R. (2001) *Terms of Engagement and Fees*, London, RIBA Publications, Construction Companion series.

Guidance for Clients on Health and Safety – the CDM Regulations 1994, London, RIBA (1995).

Guidance for Clients on Party Wall Procedures: the Party Wall, etc Act 1996, London, RIBA (1997).

Guidance for Clients to Quality Based Selection, London, RIBA (1999).

Lavers, A. and Chappell, D. (2000) *A Legal Guide to the Professional Lability of Architects*, London, RIBA.

Parkyn, N. (2000) *A Guide to Working With Consultants*, London, RIBA Publications, Small Practices series.

13 CLAIMING FEES

13.1 First steps

13.2 Conciliation

13.3 Adjudication

13.4 Arbitration

13.5 Litigation: small claims

3.1   First steps

If a client is failing to pay invoices due this could be because he or she has no funds available and is unable to meet the debt, or because for some reason, perhaps dissatisfaction with the performance of the architect or the project in general, the client has decided that for the time being he or she does not intend to pay.

Obviously the first thing to do is to remind the client in writing of the obligation to pay, and to try and establish the cause of the lack of payment. The client may not have noticed the clauses in the contract of appointment and be fully aware of their obligation to pay, for example the requirements regarding notices introduced to comply with the Housing Grants Construction and Regeneration Act 1996, or the provisions regarding interest on late payment.

Following the reminder three things could happen:

- the client could give reasons for failing to pay the fee;
- the client could make no response at all;
- the client could acknowledge that the fee is due but state that they are unable to pay.

In very broad terms, the next steps could be as follows:

If the client has indicated in writing that he or she intends to pay, and yet repeated reminders have no effect, then the best course of action may be to pursue the matter in court.

If the client has not responded to any request for payment, then adjudication may be an option. The payment provisions in the appointment together with the lack of any notices from the client would mean that there would be little that the client could raise by way of defence. In addition, the adjudication notice requiring payment of the invoices would define the dispute, therefore the other party would not be able to raise any counter-claim regarding negligence. The claim may therefore stand a good change of succeeding.

If the client has raised complex arguments as to why he or she refuses to pay then the best solution may be conciliation, or litigation or arbitration (depending on which has been selected in the agreement).

Whatever the course of action taken, the architect should inform their insurers that the situation has arisen.

13.2   Conciliation

Conciliation is a method of dispute resolution which aims to assist the parties in reaching a mutually acceptable solution to their differences. The outcome is in the form of a recommendation, which could be the basis of a formal written agreement between the parties, but if the recommendation is not acceptable to one of the parties in dispute it cannot be imposed. However, it is helpful where the parties are keen to resolve their differences, for example where an architect is keen to preserve a good working relationship with a client, and may be prepared to meet the client halfway regarding at least some of the issues.

The RIBA standard forms of appointment all state 'in the event of a dispute or difference arising under the Agreement, the client and the architect may attempt to settle such dispute or difference by negotiation or in accordance with the RIBA Conciliation Procedure'.

The RIBA Conciliation Procedure is operated by the RIBA regions, and coordinated centrally at RIBA HQ. The regional offices are free to set their own fees but typically there will be a registration fee of £150 and conciliators will charge £500 per day.

13.3 Adjudication

Any party who entered into a construction contract after 1 May 1998 has a statutory right to have any dispute resolved by adjudication, as set out in the Housing Grants, Construction and Regeneration Act 1996 (the Act). The Act's definition of 'construction contract' extends to architects' appointments, provided that they are in writing, but the Act does not apply to construction contracts where one of the parties is a residential occupier of the property to which the work relates. The right to adjudication exists even if the contract in question contains no clauses referring to adjudication, as the Act will imply terms to provide for adjudication by means of regulations entitled the *Scheme for Construction Contracts*.

The Act gives brief but significant minimum requirements for adjudication which can be summarised briefly as follows:

- notice of a dispute may be given at any time;
- the appointment arrangements should aim for referral to an adjudicator within seven days of the notice;
- the adjudicator must reach a decision within 28 days of referral, or 42 days with the consent of the referring party, or such longer period as is agreed between the parties;
- the adjudicator must act impartially;
- the adjudicator may take the initiative in ascertaining the facts and the law;
- the decision is binding on the parties until the dispute is finally decided by a process of litigation or arbitration, or the parties agree to accept the adjudicator's decision;
- the adjudicator is not liable to the parties for any of his or her actions in the adjudication.

SFA/99 re-states the right to adjudication. It gives the parties the opportunity to name the adjudicator, and to name the nominating body (if not to be the RIBA). Adjudication is to be according to the CIC *Model Adjudication Procedure*, which includes a form of appointment for the adjudicator. The provisions are generally repeated in the other forms, although if the parties wish to name the adjudicator or the nominating body in relation to CE/99 or SW/99, this must be done in the letter of appointment.

The advantage of adjudication is that it is relatively quick and cheap. Without the referring parties agreement, the period for making a decision cannot be extended and the issues raised cannot be added to, so the dispute is contained in both time and subject area.

The decision is binding in the interim, and the courts will normally enforce an adjudicator's decision promptly. However, the decision is not final as the other party may raise the dispute again in arbitration or litigation, or raise a related but different dispute in adjudication (e.g. the architect's negligence), so although it may secure the fees sought reasonably swiftly, the architect may find themselves facing further proceedings.

13.4   Arbitration

Arbitration refers to legal proceedings otherwise than in a public law court in which the arbitrator has power derived from a written agreement between the parties to a contract. The proceedings are subject to the provisions of the Arbitration Act 1996. Arbitration awards are enforceable at law. An arbitrator's award can be subject to appeal on limited grounds.

If parties wish to have disputes resolved by arbitration then they should ensure that their contract contains a clause stating this agreement, termed an arbitration agreement. Where a contract contains an arbitration agreement, if one party initiates court proceedings the other party may, if it still prefers to go to arbitration, apply for a stay, which the court must grant.

In SFA/99 the articles require the parties to select arbitration or litigation as the final method of dispute resolution. If arbitration is selected this article forms the arbitration. The article is repeated in the majority of the other forms, but with CE/99 and SW/99 the agreement to take disputes to arbitration must be clearly stated in the letter of appointment. No standard or model rules are stipulated in the forms, but the parties may wish to consider adopting the Construction Industry Model Arbitration Rules. These include three alternative proceedings: a short form of procedure, a documents only procedure, and a full procedure.

It is important that if arbitration is selected, this must be clearly explained to the client, otherwise the term may fall foul of the Unfair Terms in Consumer Contracts Regulations 1994. These state that any term which has not been individually negotiated, and may create a serious imbalance between the parties, may be deemed unfair and therefore void. It is therefore important to be able to show that the term was considered and agreed individually by the client.

It should also be noted that, under the RIBA standard forms of appointment, even if arbitration is selected, the parties may elect to go to litigation (in other words the arbitration agreement ceases to be binding) where:

- 'the claim is for a pecuniary remedy which does not exceed £5,000 or such other sum as is provided by statute pursuant to section 91 of the Arbitration Act 1996' (SFA/99 cl 9.5.1);

- the dispute relates to the enforcement of the decision of an adjudicator (SFA/99 cl 9.5.2).

Both these exceptions are important with respect to claiming fees. The first is to enable either party to make use of the small claims procedure (something which the party may have the right to do in certain circumstances, even if the agreement did not contain this clause). The second allows for the swift enforcement of the adjudicator's decisions.

Architects must weigh up the options carefully before deciding whether to select arbitration or litigation. Arbitration is often preferred because of its confidentially – nobody likes seeing their practice named in the legal pages of *Building* – and because the parties can arrange a timetable, venue, etc to suit their circumstances. In addition, under the Arbitration Act 1996 arbitrators now have a duty to avoid unnecessary delay and expense and have considerable power to control costs, therefore arbitration of small claims could become quicker and more efficient. On the other hand, there is a higher level of expertise in the courts, and the Woolf Reforms have gone a long way towards improving the efficiency of the process.

13.5 Litigation: small claims

Claims for less that £5,000 can be pursued using the small claims procedure in the County Courts (the 'small claims track'). Information and application forms can be obtained by telephoning the local County Court – the clerks are usually very helpful. Parties generally represent themselves as there is no allowance for either party to recover its costs. The procedures are reasonably informal – instead of being tried in the normal way the cases are referred to an arbitrator who is usually a district judge or recorder, and the meeting is held around a table rather than in a court room.

Claims between £5,000 and £15,000 may also be heard at the County Count, although not using the small claims procedure. Larger claims would normally be heard at the Technology and Construction Court. Information on all the courts can be obtained at www.courtservice.gov.uk

References and further reading

Burkett, J. (2000) *Disputes without Tears: Alternative Methods of Dispute Resolution*, London, RIBA Publications.

Carnell, N. and Yakely, S. (forthcoming) *Getting Paid*, London, RIBA Publications.

Lupton, S. (1997) *Architect's Guide to Arbitration*, London, RIBA Publications.

Lupton, S. (1998) *Architect's Guide to Adjudication*, London, RIBA Publications.

APPENDIX A: ORIGINS OF THE PROFESSION

1.   Early years

In the 18th century, architects could concern themselves primarily with visual matters of form, space and style. They were responsible for broad profiles and could confidently leave much of the detail in the capable hands of master craftsmen. Architects themselves often had a craft background. There was a directness of working which made conscious management almost unnecessary. Architects often enjoyed a personal working relationship with their patrons, many of whom were themselves knowledgeable about architecture.

In the 19th century, professionalism as applied to architecture was formalised and consolidated. Patronage was at an end. The number of architects increased as wealth and education spread, and the market for their services became predominantly commercial in character. No longer tied to patrons, they were free to offer their skills in return for a fee. Wider opportunities became available and a new way of commissioned working developed.

Then the construction industry itself underwent radical change. Master craftsmen were overtaken by firms of building contractors, headed by people whose aims were profit-orientated and sometimes speculative. Architects were criticised. Allegations of deficient or fraudulent practice were often vociferously expressed by the emerging new species of client industrialists, entrepreneurs, corporations and boards of guardians, some of them less than scrupulous.

Faced with such criticism, it was understandable that practitioners with a common professed interest should band together. In part this was for protection and so as to be able to present a unified approach when tackling injustices; in part it was for promotional reasons. Architects claimed to provide a uniquely impartial and independent service. They wished to have the status of professionals, offering a solid assurance of competence, honesty and integrity. They wished not to be confused with builders or surveyors. The image they sought to promote was that of professional people who were educated and responsible. They wished to be identified with, and to cultivate more explicitly a service of quality. They aspired to devise efficient methods and establish standards and, by learning from each other, to become more proficient.

Characteristics to be found in the newly emergent professions could be summarised as follows:

- intellectual basis: principles, theories and concepts capable of testing and implementation;
- independence of practice: integrity and impartiality in services, personal attention, reward by fee;
- consultancy role: advice, skills, resources, defined liabilities;
- established practices: conduct, conditions, procedures, performance standards;
- representative institute: protection of interests for members and clients, corporate voice and lobby, learned society role, advancement of knowledge and expertise.

These quickly became apparent in the practise of architecture, and are to a large extent still present in the profession today.

In the 1920s, Sydney and Beatrice Webb described the nature of professionalism as 'a vocation founded upon specialised educational training, the purpose of which is to supply disinterested counsel and service to others for a direct and definite compensation'. Practising any profession demands a level of commitment which makes vocation an apt description. In architecture today the educational pattern combines intellectual rigour and theory with practical training, and it is recognised that the need for structured learning and development continues after graduation and throughout professional life. The words 'disinterested counsel and service' are a reminder that architects are seen to be persons of professional integrity who supply advice without fear or favour and above self-interest. Working for a direct and definite compensation is still a straightforward and sensible way of doing business, particularly in a competitive world. The need for services to be adequately defined and the fee basis decided before work is started, is now an obligation as well as an efficient business practice. Providing a professional service has to be pursued with vigour and efficiency but also in line with business ethics.

2.   The RIBA

The Royal Institute of British Architects was founded in 1834 under the style of the Institute of British Architects, and during its first fifty years it set up in embryo form many of the activities which characterise the work of the Institute today.

In the course of its first decade of existence, a register of architects seeking work was instituted, the first library catalogue was published, the first competitions committee was set up, and in 1837 the first Royal Charter was granted by William IV.

During the next 30 years there was the establishment of a professional practice committee, the granting of the Royal Gold Medal, and a great deal of activity directed at improving and rationalising architectural qualifications. The first board of examiners was set up in 1862 and the first voluntary architectural examinations were held in 1863. In the 1860s the first *Scale of Charges and Conditions of Builders' Contracts* was published, and in 1866 the first paid secretary was appointed. Also in 1866, the title 'Royal' was conferred upon the Institute by Queen Victoria.

The Supplemental Charter of 1887 made the examination in architecture compulsory for associate membership of the Institute, and made provisions for regulations to govern exclusion or suspension from membership. The first *Code of Professional Conduct* was published in 1900.

There were major initiatives in the early part of the 20th century directed towards unification of the profession and statutory registration, a policy adopted by the RIBA Council in 1905 following an intensive campaign by the Society of Architects. (This was a body formed in 1884 which consisted mainly of members of the RIBA who were dissatisfied with the Institute's inactivity on this matter.) The 1925 Supplemental Charter provided for the amalgamation with the RIBA of the Society of Architects, and the first draft architects' registration bill was published in 1926. Despite massive opposition and several amendments to the bill (including deletion of the provision for the RIBA to maintain the register), the Architects (Registration) Act 1931 came into force.

After World War II, the Institute became increasingly representative and democratic. It adapted to ensure that architects from specialist interest groups and those in the then burgeoning public service sector could feel that they were part of one professional body. A single corporate membership class was introduced following the Supplemental Charter of 1971, but under Byelaw 2.13, members who were elected before that time could continue to use the affix FRIBA or ARIBA as appropriate.

A watershed study, *The Architect and his Office*, was undertaken by the RIBA in 1962, and this brought to light the need for increased awareness of, and skill in, the business side of architectural practice. As a result, the RIBA published the first *Handbook of Practice and Management*, and the *Architect's Job Book*. Other studies were reflected in such significant reports as *The Practical Training of Architects, Guide to Group Practice and Consortia, Competence*, and *Continuing Professional Development*. These were closely followed by other publications aimed at guiding and assisting practice, and in 1969 the RIBA Companies was formed to progress this work commercially.

3.   Registration of title

Registration for architects first occurred with the Architects (Registration) Act of 1931. Registration was a voluntary matter, but by the Architects Registration Act 1938 use of the word 'architect' in any business style or title was restricted to those persons who were registered (with some exceptions, e.g. landscape architect or golf course architect). Much of the 1931 and 1938 legislation was repealed by the provisions of Part III of the Housing Grants, Construction and Regeneration Act 1996, and this was overtaken in turn by the consolidating Architects Act 1997.

In 1993, long-running arguments about the restriction of title and the protective undesirability of registration were revived in parliamentary circles. Consequently John Warne was appointed to enquire into whether statutory registration and protection of the title 'architect' should be retained. Warne concluded that he saw 'no merit in incurring the cost of retaining the Architects Registration Council United Kingdom (ARCUK) established under the 1931 Act, simply to fulfil a minimal role of keeping a register.' He said, 'If registration is to continue, I consider that instead it should be undertaken by the RIBA. My main recommendation is that the protection of the title "architect" should be abolished and ARCUK disbanded.'

The climate of opinion had changed somewhat by the time the Warne Report was published, and Parliament chose not to repeal immediately legislation for the registration of architects. However, reform was inevitable, and the Housing Grants, etc Act 1996 included a Part III which related to the registration of architects. Under it, the former ARCUK was replaced by a new Architects Registration Board (ARB), with powers to maintain a Register and discipline architects for breaches of its Code. The 1996 legislation was in a sense a measure of expediency, and all the provisions concerning architects' registration are now to be found in a logically structured Architects Act 1997. Generally the changes to the Act clarify the different roles of the professional institute, which is to promote professional knowledge, and the registration body, which regulates the use of the title 'architect' in the public interest.

APPENDIX B: MODEL SAFETY POLICY

SECOND EDITION

© RIBA Companies Ltd 2002, compiled by Roland Phillips

with SAFETY CODES

1   Practice organisation and responsibilities

2   Project design and construction

3   Site visits

4   Miscellaneous procedures

- 1 Accident reporting
- 2 Illness
- 3 Occupational health
- 4 Driving
- 5 Hazardous substances
- 6 VDUs
- 7 Manual handling of loads

5   Fire precautions

6   Sources of safety information

Introduction to the Health and Safety Policy

The Health and Safety at Work, etc Act 1974

The Act[1] at Section 3 [1] says: 'It shall be the duty of every employer[2] to conduct his undertaking in such a way as to ensure, so far as is reasonably practicable, that persons in his employment who may be affected thereby are not exposed to risks to their health and safety.' The Management of Health and Safety at Work Regulations 1999 and other Regulations establish the duty of employers to make 'suitable and sufficient' assessment of the risks to their employees.

Section 2[3] of the 1974 Act requires every employer (where 5 or more people are employed) 'to prepare and as often as may be appropriate revise a written statement of his general policy with respect to the health and safety at work of his employees and the organisation and arrangements for the time being in force for carrying out that policy, and to bring the statement and any revision of it to the notice of all his employees'.

The Safety Policy Statement

Each organisation will need to analyse its own activities, identify the hazards that could arise both in normal everyday running of the business and in unusual circumstances (e.g. a power cut). Although offices in general are low risk environments, it must be remembered that construction professionals may spend significant periods out of the office in potentially hazardous locations.

Some organisations may also wish to include references to related issues, such as a no smoking policy[3] or Continuous Professional Development (CPD) programmes.

The law requires that a Safety Policy Statement[4] is developed in consultation with and takes account of the views of employees and is brought to their notice. The draft pro-forma overleaf combines the functions of issue sheet, Document Register and a record of receipt.

The Policy Statement of a parent or holding company should be issued by any subsidiary organisation as part of and be reflected in its own Statement.

Although the Policy Statement must be a stand-alone document, any related procedures might, with benefit, be incorporated into a Quality Assurance or Office Manual. The developed Policy Statement might also form part of the demonstration of competence required under the Construction (Design and Management) Regulations 1994.

The Model Safety Policy and Safety Codes

This model Safety Policy Statement and the accompanying model safety codes have been devised to help professional organisations in the construction industry to meet these legal obligations. The models may be adopted as published or modified if they are at variance with the practice's own procedures. Some practices may find it more appropriate to create their own codes.

The models follow the advice given in Health and Safety Executive introductory guidance[5] and with advantage might be read and implemented in conjunction with other more detailed guidance published by Health and Safety Executive (see 4.6 of this appendix).

Apart from references to the CDM Regulations, which place obligations on designers, the model codes do not cover the design or construction processes. All businesses are subject to Health and Safety Regulations, many of which are specific to particular industries, trades or substances. Designers may need to refer to the relevant Regulations for specific projects.

Where, as part of the professional services provided to a client, staff will be undertaking hazardous operations, for instance inspecting asbestos removal or switching high voltage electrical systems, special safety codes will be required perhaps to operate in conjunction with a client's or contractor's 'permit to work' system.

Advice and information

Local authorities are responsible for health and safety inspections (usually by the environmental health department) of the office environment. They may be prepared to offer advice about specific safety issues but responsibility for the developed Policy Statement rests with the organisation.

Alternatively, specialist consultants might be employed to develop appropriate policies and/or carry out safety audits. The Independent Safety Consultant's Association (01455 894 145) (www.isca.uk.com), the Association of Consulting Engineers (020 7222 6557) (www.acenet.co.uk), the Chartered Institute of Building (01344 630 700) (www.ciob.org.uk), the Institute of Civil Engineers (020 7222 7722) (www.ice.org.uk) and the Royal Institute of Chartered Surveyors (0870 333 1600) (www.rics.org) maintain lists of such consultants.

Health and Safety Executive [HSE] introductory guidance

1 *Health and Safety at Work, etc Act 1974*
   The Act outlined [HSC2]
   Advice to employers [HSC6]
   Advice to employees [HSC5]

2 *Directors' responsibilities for health and safety [INDG343]*

3 *Passive smoking at work [INDG63(L)]*

4 *Writing a safety policy statement – Advice to employers [HSC6]*
   Stating your business [INDG324]

5 *Ibid.*

From: **Safety Manager**   Date: _____

To: **All members of staff**

SAFETY POLICY AND SAFETY CODES

Please receive the [revisions to the] documents listed below, file them with your copy of the Safety Policy Statement and Safety Codes, amend your copy of the Document Register and sign and return this issue sheet to me by:

_____ [date]

Health and Safety document register	Issue date	Revised page nos.	Issued by	Checked by

Safety Policy Statement

Safety Codes **1 Organisation and responsibilities**

2 Project design and construction

3 Site visits or working away from the office

4 Miscellaneous procedures

    1 Accident reporting
    2 Illness
    3 Occupational health
    4 Driving
    5 Hazardous substances
    6 VDUs
    7 Manual handling of loads

5 Fire precautions

including bombs and bomb warnings

6 Sources of safety information

To: **Safety Manager**

I acknowledge receipt of the [revisions to the] documents listed above and confirm these have been filed with my copy of the Safety Policy Statement and Safety Codes and my copy of the Document Register has been amended accordingly.

Signed: _____

Name: _____   Date: _____

SAFETY POLICY STATEMENT OF _____ [the practice]

Each Principal, which term includes any Partner, Director or member of the management board of the practice, undertakes, collectively and individually, to provide health and safety leadership, to review health and safety performance annually (or when conditions change) and to reflect health and safety intentions in management decisions.

General policy matters

- To issue this Safety Policy together with current Safety Codes or practice notes to all staff and to new staff members. For the purposes of this policy, the term 'staff' includes Principals, Partners, Directors or members of a management board, employees, self-employed persons working for the practice and trainees, including non-employed trainees.

- To actively manage the implementation and to monitor and revise this Safety Policy regularly in respect of its professional functions and working conditions at offices of the practice.

- To appoint a Principal, Partner, Director or management board member of the practice as Safety Manager responsible for implementation and review of this Policy.

- To consult staff on health, safety and welfare matters and take account of comments or receive proposals from staff, jointly or individually, for improving the effectiveness of these procedures and policies.[1]

- To appoint and train safety representatives, first aiders, fire wardens and/or safety wardens as required by law or this Policy.[2]

- To require staff of the practice to comply with Section 3 of this Policy and any relevant guidance published by the Practice.

- To display as required by law an official Health and Safety Law Poster and a copy of the Employer's Liability Insurance certificate maintained by the practice.

Policy in relation to individual employees

- To provide and maintain healthy and safe working conditions and welfare provisions for staff of the practice and for the safety of any persons who may visit its premises.[3]

- To operate this Safety Policy in conjunction with the safety policies of the landlord of any property occupied by the practice.

- To discharge the responsibility to ensure the health, safety and welfare of staff of the practice through line managers, who will also encourage all staff to take reasonable care of their own health and safety and that of other persons who may be affected by their acts or omissions at work, and to co-operate with the practice in meeting statutory duties as required by sections 7 and 8 of the Health & Safety at Work, etc Act.

- To give adequate information, instruction, training and supervision to staff (including non-employed trainees[4] on all aspects of their work to ensure, as far as reasonably practicable, their health and safety at work, including such health surveillance as is appropriate.

  The practice will, in entrusting tasks to staff, take into account their capabilities as regards health and safety and provide appropriate health and safety training:

    - on their being appointed and periodically thereafter, or

    - on their being exposed to new or increased risks.

- To provide, where necessary, protective clothing and equipment and hard hats in accordance with the Construction (Head Protection) Regulations 1989.[5]

- To provide appropriate facilities for first-aid and prompt treatment of injuries and illness at work in accordance with the Health & Safety (First Aid) Regulations 1981.[6]

- To report all accidents and injuries in accordance with the Reporting of Injuries Diseases and Dangerous Occurrences Regulations 1995.[7]

Policy in relation to professional functions

- To comply with the requirements of section 6 of the Health and Safety at Work, etc Act and the Construction (Design and Management) Regulations 1994 as amended[8] so that the design and specification of construction, demolition or installation work and the manner of its execution shall be such that safe working conditions are possible for all during the construction phase or after completion.

- To obtain details from a client of health and safety legislation relating to the client's business, and existing hazards or safety policies affecting the design of specific construction or demolition projects.

- To report observed hazards to health and safety to the relevant 'employer' as defined below:

  The 'employer' with responsibility for compliance with sections 2 and 3 of the Act is the organisation in operational control of the building(s) or site. This may be the occupier of the building or site (the 'client' if the CDM Regulations apply).

  The Main or Principal Contractor is responsible for the area(s) of the works which is/are solely in his charge at any period during the building contract.

  Where buildings, engineering or demolition works are carried out in areas which may also be used by people other than those directly connected with the works then the Main or Principal Contractor and the 'employer' client will both have operational responsibility.

  Section 4 of the Health and Safety at Work, etc Act places obligations on 'each person who has, to any extent, control of premises'.

- To require clients or contractors to discharge in full their duty of care under the Act to staff of the practice visiting or out-posted to clients' property or construction sites.

Risk assessment

- To make, in accordance with the Management of Health and Safety at Work Regulations 1999 and using competent persons, suitable and sufficient assessments[9] of relevant hazards or risks affecting:

  - the health and safety of its employees to which they are exposed whilst they are at work; and

  - the health and safety of other persons not in its employment arising out of or in connection with the conduct of its undertaking.

- To record such assessments and review them from time to time or when there is any change to known risks. Where as a result of any such review changes to an assessment are required, the practice will make them and will record:

  - the significant findings of the assessment; and

  - any group of employees identified by it as being especially at risk.

Health and safety register

- To demonstrate its active management of this Safety Policy the practice will maintain a register of health and safety matters giving details including dates of:

  - review and issue of the Policy Statement and Safety Codes;

  - risk assessments undertaken;

  - training programme and attendance; and

  - accidents and work related illnesses.

- To incorporate in the Health and Safety Register:

  - a COSHH register, if applicable (see 4.4 of this appendix)

  - the Fire Precautions Register (see 5 of this appendix).

Signed

_____
                    [Principal]

for or on behalf of

_____
                 [the Practice]

_____
    [date]

HSE Publications (introductory guides)
1 *Consulting employees on health and safety [INDG232]*
2 *Five steps to information, instruction and training [INDG213]*
3 *Health and Safety Regulations: A short guide [HSC1] Workplace health, safety and welfare [INDG244]*
4 *Health and Safety legislation and trainees [HSC23]*
5 *PPE Safety Helmets [CIS50]*
6 *First aid at work – your questions answered [INDG214] Basic advice on first aid at work [INDG21]*
7 *RIDDOR explained [HSE31]*
8 *Construction [Design and Management] Regulations 1994 [SI No 3140 as amended by SI 2000 No 2380] CDM Regulations: How the Regulations affect you PML54*
9 *A guide to risk assessment requirements: Common provisions in health and safety law [INDG218] Five steps to risk assessment [INDG163] Working alone in safety [INDG73]*

1. Practice organisation and responsibilities – Safety Code: 1

1.1 Introduction

The practice Safety Policy Statement defines the roles and responsibilities of the Practice in relation to Health & Safety matters affecting staff of the Practice and the exercise of professional functions. The Safety Manager is responsible, as set out below, for implementation of this Safety Policy.

All staff have responsibilities to co-operate in meeting statutory duties under Sections 7 and 8 of the Health and Safety at Work etc. Act.[1]

Section 7 of the Act reads as follows:

'It shall be the duty of every employee while at work:

1. to take reasonable care for the health and safety of himself and of other persons who may be affected by his acts or omissions at work; and

2. as regards any duty or requirement imposed on his employer or any other person by or under any of the relevant statutory provisions, to co-operate with him so far as is necessary to enable that duty or requirement to be performed or complied with.'

Section 8 places a duty on all persons, whether they be employers, employees or self-employed, and states:

'No person shall intentionally or recklessly interfere with or misuse anything provided in the interests of health, safety or welfare in pursuance of any of the relevant statutory provisions.'

1.2 Duties and responsibilities of the safety manger

The Safety Manager shall:

- set a personal example in all aspects of health and safety;

- take executive responsibility for the issue of, implementation and supervision of the Safety Policy and the Codes, including risk assessments;

- carry out specific risk assessments for young people and new and expectant mothers;

- take executive responsibility for provision of sufficient resources to meet health and safety needs;

- take executive responsibility review and auditing at regular intervals of the Policy and Codes, and maintenance of the Health and Safety Register;

[NB: If particular elements of safety policy, e.g. fire precautions, are delegated to others, the individuals or appointments should be identified – see Organisation for Health and Safety, opposite.]

- take executive responsibility for the appointment and training of sufficient safety representatives, first aiders, fire wardens and/or safety wardens as required by law or this Policy and publication of their names and responsibilities;

- ensure that health and safety induction training is given to staff on joining the practice;

that sufficient information and other training[2] is provided to all staff to enable them to fulfil their duties in accordance with the Policy; and review individual training records as a basis for providing further health and safety training;

- check that staff working away from the office are given health and safety information by the person responsible for health and safety at the location of their work;

- ensure that particular consideration is given to the safety of female staff who are sent out from the office unaccompanied;

- ensure that all staff co-operate in meeting the aims of the Policy; and

- take appropriate disciplinary action in the event of any breach of or refusal to comply with Statutory Safety Regulations or the Safety Policy and Codes of the practice.

1.3   Responsibilities of staff

All staff must:

- set a personal example in all aspects of health and safety;

- take care of themselves and others who may be affected by their acts or omissions at work;

- ensure that staff under their control have received a copy of the Safety Policy and Safety Codes and understand their obligations as members of staff and under the Act; and

- report any accident, however minor, to their manager.

1.4   Safety of premises[3]

The practice, as freeholders, leaseholders or tenants of its offices, will ensure:

- compliance with the Health and Safety at Work, etc Act 1974, the Offices, Shops and Railway Premises Act 1963, the Fire Precautions Act 1971, and with Safety Code 5;

- offices are laid out, cleaned, and kept in good repair to ensure safety of staff and visitors;

- office machinery is safe, properly maintained, fitted with any necessary guards or safety devices; staff required to use such machinery are trained in its use and are not permitted to carry out repairs without authority;

- a health and safety plan is prepared for all construction, maintenance and repair works at the practice offices, where CDM regulations apply;

- passenger lifts are properly maintained and thoroughly examined by a lift/insurance engineer at six monthly intervals and copies of inspection reports are available for reference;

- electrical equipment and systems in the premises are properly maintained and comply with the Electricity at Work Regulations, 1989;

- pressurised plant and water heating systems and boilers are properly maintained;

boilers, air receivers and steam receivers, as defined, have statutory inspections by an insurance engineer and that copies of certificates are available for reference;

- arrangements are made to prevent the growth of micro-organisms in air conditioning or ventilation systems; and

- installations, such as window cleaning cradles, are properly maintained and examined at six monthly intervals by a lift/insurance engineer and that eye bolts for use by window cleaners are examined at intervals in accordance with current British Standards.

1.5 Basic safety rules for the office

All staff must:

- ensure electrical plugs are safely and correctly wired, and place telephone and electricity cables where they cannot trip anyone;

- not overload socket outlets with adaptors and multiple plugs;

- switch off electrical machines after use or at the end of the day unless otherwise instructed;

- report defective or faulty office equipment to the appropriate manager; untrained staff must not attempt repairs;

- keep escape routes clear (in case of fire); stairways, passageways and space between desks must be kept free of all obstructions;

- report potential hazards, such as loose or frayed carpet tiles, to the Safety Manager;

- open one filing cabinet drawer at a time, close filing cabinets and desk drawers after use;

- not run on stairs or read whilst walking in the office or using the stairs;

- not use sharp knives for cutting paper or opening letters;

- not dispose of broken glass or cigarette ash in wastepaper baskets; and

- notify the Safety Manager of any alterations to the general layout of workspaces and furniture which might invalidate the existing fire certificate (means of escape).

HSE publications (introductory guides)

1 *Advice to employees [HSC5]*
2 *Health and Safety training policy statement [INDG106]*
3 *Office wise [INDG173]*
   Ergonomics at work [INDG90]

ORGANISATION FOR HEALTH AND SAFETY

Health and safety legislation accepts that the obligation can be delegated to persons who are competent, who understand the legislation, and who have a detailed knowledge of operations and the ability to recommend appropriate control measures.

Subject	Detail	Responsible person/appointment (complete as appropriate and name any deputies)
Policy	Implementation, resources, appointments compliance, revision/distribution	The Safety Manager
Quality assurance	Hazards to staff and others at work place (including construction sites) Risk assessments, including VDU workstations Safety audits Health and Safety Register Training of safety wardens	
Training	Organisation of training programme for: H+S at work place CDM Regulations	
Fire	Training of fire wardens fire precautions; Equipment (including maintenance); Fire drills; Evacuation; Bomb warnings; Fire Precautions Register; Fire Certification (see Premises)	
First aid	Training of first aider(s) and deputy(s). Maintenance of first aid box(es)	
Accident reporting	All injuries and work-related illnesses including RIDDOR reports	(By relevant staff member to) Safety Manager

Subject	Detail	Responsible person/appointment (complete as appropriate and name any deputies)
Premises	H+S inspections; Fire certification Insurance inspections of lifts etc. Maintenance and repair	
Equipment and supplies	Purchase (including specification) Maintenance and repair	
Personnel	Records, skills, experience, training	
Safety committee	Convenor Training of safety representatives	
Supervision	As necessary for safety especially for young or new employees	Line manager
Remote staff (e.g. site based)	H+S contact point	Line manager

2. Project design and construction – Safety Code: 2

2.1 Introduction

This Safety Code draws attention to two aspects of Health and Safety affecting Project Design and construction. First, managing risks arising from the design affecting users of the completed facilities and secondly, assessing the risks during construction works.

Both aspects are covered by the original Health and Safety at Work, etc Act 1974. Section 6 of the Act places duties on persons (e.g. the practice) who design, manufacture, import or supply articles for use at work to ensure as far as is reasonably practicable that any plant, machinery, equipment or appliance is so designed and constructed as to be safe without risk to health.

They must also carry out any testing or examination necessary to achieve this and ensure that adequate information will be available about the use for which it was designed and about any conditions necessary for its safe use. They must also ensure that there is adequate information available about this and about any conditions necessary to ensure that it will be safe and without risks to health when properly used.

The Construction (Design and Management) Regulations 1994 as amended[1] establish the duty of employers, of self-employed persons and of managers (i.e. those *not employing but controlling persons at work*) to ensure decisions affecting health and safety during construction works are made following assessment of the risks arising. The term 'construction works' includes maintenance, repair and demolition. These Regulations also impose duties on clients, designers and the planning supervisor. 'Designers' (meaning the practice, not individuals) are required to make clients aware of their duties.

2.2 Risk control

Identification and control of risk to health and safety is a continuous activity to be taken into account with other factors when making design decisions. The general principles of hazard identification and assessment involve:

- listing the processes, tasks or work activities;
- identification of potential hazard(s);
- assessment of each risk in terms of likely frequency and seriousness.

If the hazards cannot be eliminated, follow the hierarchy of risk control:

- alter the design to prevent or remove the hazard; if that is not reasonably practicable;
- combat the risk at source, e.g. provide lifting attachments if appropriate; only then
- consider personal protection e.g. harnesses or respirators, or special training, or access limitation.

2.3 Implementation

The practice when appointed as a designer to a project will discharge, as far as is reasonably practicable, its obligations:

a) to ensure design decisions affecting health and safety during construction works are made following assessment of the risks arising under the CDM Regulations,[2] by:

- allocating members of staff with the necessary competence to undertake specific design tasks;

- providing appropriate (CPD) training to members of staff;

- developing and regularly reviewing relevant office systems, including, *inter alia*, design management (e.g. as RIBA Plan of Work); and keeping records of all risk assessments;

- maintaining a library as source of safety information; and

- quality assurance audit procedures.

b) to ensure that a design and specification meets the requirements of Section 6 of the Act by:

- complying with appropriate Acts of Parliament and subordinate legislation,[3] e.g. the Building Act 1984, Building Regulations, Factories Act 1961, Electricity at Work Regulations 1989 (SI No. 635), Construction (General Provisions) Regulations 1961 and Construction (Working Places) Regulations 1966);

- comply with HSE guidance applicable to specific industrial, sector or substances;

- specify installations, plant, equipment and materials which comply with relevant British or European Standards and Codes of Practice;

- where such Codes of Practice do not exist, use authoritative sources of information, e.g. IEE Wiring Regulations, CIBSE Guides, Agreement Certificates, Approved Documents, etc; and

- consult the HSE Inspectorate in cases where guidance is not available or not clear.

c) To advise the client advised if the obligations under the agreement with the client conflict with the obligations of the practice under the CDM Regulations.

HSE publications
1 *Managing construction for health and safety [L54] ACOP*
  Designing for health and safety in construction
  ISBN 0 7176 0807 7
2 *Ibid.*
3 *An Act states what the law requires; a Statutory Instrument states what the Act requires; an Approved Document or Approved Code of Practice gives guidance on how to comply with the law.*

3. Site visits or working away form the office – Safety Code: 3

3.1 Introduction

When you are making an official visit to other premises or working away from the office, for instance, at the offices of a client, or another consultant or on a construction site, your health and safety is the responsibility of the person or firm or contractor controlling that place.

Nevertheless, the practice, as your employer, is not without responsibility but can only discharge its duty of care with your co-operation.

If you work at home for any period of time the practice also has responsibilities for your health and safety – see 3.11 below.

Your compliance with the following guidelines will help with the achievement of the principal aims of ensuring your safety and the safety of others.

3.2 Time and location of vist

If you will be out of the office for any reason you must enter the precise details of time and location into your desk diary. It is in your interest that you telephone someone at the office if your arrangements change, so that your whereabouts are known.

3.3 Female personnel

Female staff should take special care when visiting sites, inspecting properties unaccompanied, leaving offices or attending appointments after dark and should remain on guard when travelling on public transport late at night or in remote places. They should be wary of escorting strangers around empty properties by themselves. Carrying anti-rape alarms should be considered. Read *Positive steps – help and advice for women on personal safety*, by the Metropolitan Police.

3.4 Permission to vist site

Do not enter sites or buildings without permission.

On construction sites, the contractor is responsible for the safety of persons lawfully on the site. Report to him on arrival and when you leave.

If visiting occupied buildings, you should make prior arrangements with the person in charge and report on arrival to the responsible member of staff in the area or department being visited and on leaving.

You should always seek assistance from others on the site when your safety is at risk.

Do not visit a site or an empty building or unfrequented spaces (e.g. ducts) in existing buildings on your own without permission. Make sure someone knows where you are, what you are doing and report back at an agreed time. Establish an action plan in case of non-appearance after an agreed time.

3.5   Planning a site vist

Plan the visit and make sure that you take appropriate equipment and protective clothing. Apart from taking stout shoes and a hard hat, remember that unoccupied buildings can be dirty, damp, cold and dark; so go prepared.

You must familiarise yourself with all safe working rules applicable to the site or place being visited and comply with them. Such rules could cover access and egress, the wearing of safety helmets, safety harnesses, eye protection, ear protection, footwear and clothing, special precautions in areas of particular hazard, reporting your presence on site, etc. When conducting third parties on construction sites, you must ensure that they always wear hard hats and are wearing appropriate protective clothing. Consider the need for wearing high visibility waistcoats.

3.6   Safety rules

The basic safety rule is that when you perform your duties, you must not put yourself or others at risk whatever pressures are exerted on you by a contractor or others and irrespective of the effect your action may have. You should draw attention to hazards or risks that appear to have gone unnoticed.

When you visit any construction site or are surveying or inspecting premises you must:

- wear a hard hat, suitable clothes and stout shoes or boots with toe caps; do not wear thin-soled or slippery shoes; avoid loose clothes which might catch on obstructions;
- familiarise yourself beforehand with the plan of the building, particularly the exit routes, make sure that security devices on exits will allow you to reach safety quickly;
- not walk and look around at the same time; keep one hand free at all times when moving; make sure that you are in a safe and balanced position whenever making notes or taking photographs; do not become distracted while climbing ladders;
- check on protection when approaching stairwells, balustrades, lift shafts, roof perimeters, etc; do not use lifts;
- ensure that if you need to climb a ladder, you are not alone on the site and that the ladder is securely fixed at the top, beware of ladders with rusty or rotten rungs;
- ensure that there are toe boards to each lift of scaffolding, that planks are secure; beware of overhead projections, scaffolding and plant, and proceed with caution;
- keep clear of excavations; walk over the structural members (e.g. joists, beams, etc) whenever possible – do not rely on floorboards alone; look for defects in the floors ahead, e.g. wet areas, holes, materials that might cover holes; do not lean on guard rails or roof lights;
- not touch any plant or equipment; keep clear of machinery and stacked materials; watch out for temporary cables, pumps, hoses and electric fittings;
- assume that services (e.g. cables, sockets, pipes, etc) are not safe or have not been isolated;

- leave the building immediately if you suspect the presence of gas, flammable liquids, dangerous chemicals or free asbestos fibre;

- take particular care in windy, cold, frosty, wet or muddy conditions.

3.7 Unoccupied site or building

If the building or site is unoccupied, you will also need to anticipate hazards. Do not take chances. Do not visit an empty building if you think it unsafe. Do not visit an unoccupied site if you think it dangerous. Ensure that you have notified the office if you intend to visit an unoccupied building.

Common dangers include:

- rotten or insecure floors and stairs;

- unsupported excavations and trenches;

- hidden pits, ducts, openings, etc;

- fragile construction, e.g. asbestos or plastic sheets on roofs;

- space which has not been used or ventilated for some time;

- contamination by chemicals or asbestos;

- intruders who may still be around; and

- contamination by vermin or birds, or poisons put down to control them.

3.8 Stuctural collapse

If you discover a partial or total structural collapse, consider the need:

- to contact the HSE and/or the Local Authority Building Control Officer;

- to contact the police where the public may be affected;

- for the display of appropriate hazard notices.

3.9 Accidents

If you have an accident, or are notified of an accident, on sites or buildings where the practice is carrying out professional functions, proceed in accordance with the guidance in Safety Code 4.

Building operations and works of engineering construction, both on Crown and other sites, are by definition *factories* under the Factories Act 1961, so the HSE Inspectorate has major powers on all sites. (Local authorities are responsible for health and safety in the office environment.)

3.10 Hazardous or unsafe activities

It is not the intention that you should be safety officers for contractors or others but as informed professionals you have a duty and a legal responsibility to prevent, so far as reasonably practicable, a contractor or others from carrying out unsafe practices and placing staff or visitors in jeopardy.

If you observe any apparent or potentially unsafe or hazardous procedure on a construction site, you have a duty to report this to the contract administrator (or employer's agent) or the clerk of works, or, if they are not available, to the site agent or person responsible for that place. All such reports should be noted and, in the case of a construction site, recorded at the next site meeting.

In the case of any dangerous, or potentially dangerous, site activity, the contractor or person responsible must be advised to cease carrying out that particular activity which contravenes the Health and Safety at Work Act and to continue only in manner which does accord with that Act. You should take steps to ensure your action is confirmed by *written notice* (see below) by the contract administrator (or employer's agent) to the contractor (or person responsible) as soon as possible.

It should be emphasised that failure to deal adequately with the danger will be notified to the HSE Inspectorate. If in doubt as to whether a situation is dangerous or not, err on the side of safety and contact the local HSE Inspector for advice.

NOTICE TO CONTRACTOR

To: _____

Project: _____

Health and Safety at Work, etc Act 1974

It appears that the situation described below is, or may become dangerous in contravention of the requirements of the Act.

Unless you take corrective action immediately in order to comply, the matter will be reported to the Health & Safety Executive.

This notice does not constitute a variation to the contract nor justify an extension of time.

Situation:

Signed: _____

Date _____

cc: Contract Administrator
        Clerk of Works
        File

3.11 Working at home[1]

Note the Workplace Regulations 1992 do not apply to 'domestic premises' and exclude home workers.

If you are required to or voluntarily work at home for any period of time you should consider with the Safety Manager the risks that may arise.

However, self-employed staff who offer services based on working at home using their own equipment are responsible for their own health and safety.

Other staff will be given guidance on relevant issues, such as the risks to new and expectant mothers[2] or working with VDUs[3] and the provision of first aid materials appropriate to the work activity.

Any equipment or materials provided for use at home by the practice will be checked for safety and health risks and any hazards or risks arising will be explained to the user

Arrangements will be made for risk assessments to be made and recorded, usually by the home worker.

HSE Publications (introductory guides)
1   *Homeworking [INDG226]*
2   *New and Expectant mothers at work [HSG122]*
3   *Working with VDUs [INDG36]*

4.   Miscellaneous procedures – Safety Code: 4

4.1   Accident reporting

Any incident which results in injury to any person or damage to any equipment or property affecting or involving the practice and its staff and all accidents in the practice premises must be reported to your Principal or line manager who will record the incident. On the spot collection of factual information (location, witnesses, measurement, parties involved, police and fire brigade services, hospital, photographs where possible) will be the responsibility of the Principal or manager concerned.

Any accident on a construction site must be reported immediately to the relevant person in charge and to your Principal on return to the office.

In the event of a serious accident on a public sector site, the public sector manager may be required to report the matter to their authority. The relevant manager should therefore also be advised of the facts.

Some incidents must also be reported to the HSE under the Reporting of Injuries, Diseases and Dangerous Occurrences Regulations 1995.[1]

Reports are made to the incident Control Centre in Caerphilly and may be made on HSE form (F2508 and F2508A) by post or fax or by internet (www.riddor.gov.uk). Records will be retained by the practice for three years form the date of the incident.

These Regulations include guidance on:

- notification[a;b] of fatalities, major injury and dangerous occurrences;
- notification[b] of accidents causing more than three days' incapacity for work;
- notification[c] of certain reportable work related diseases;
- definitions and record keeping.

    [a] without delay by telephone;
    [b] on form 2508 within 10 days;
    [c] on form 2508A

4.1.1 Reportable major injuries are:

- fracture other than to fingers, thumbs or toes;
- amputation;
- dislocation of the shoulder, hip, knee or spine;
- loss of sight (temporary or permanent);
- chemical or hot metal burn to the eye or any penetrating injury to the eye;
- injury resulting from an electrical shock or electrical burn leading to unconsciousness or requiring resuscitation or admittance to hospital for more than 24 hours;
- any other injury leading to hypothermia, heat induced illness or unconsciousness; or requiring resuscitation; or admittance to hospital for more than 24 hours;

- unconsciousness caused by asphyxia or exposure to a harmful substance or biological agent;.

- acute illness requiring medical treatment, or loss of consciousness arising from absorption of any substance by inhalation, ingestion or through the skin; and

- acute illness requiring medical treatment where there is reason to believe that this resulted from exposure to a biological agent or its toxins or infected material.

4.1.2 Reportable dangerous occurrences are:

- collapse, overturning or failure of load-bearing parts of lifts and lifting equipment;

- explosion, collapse or bursting of closed vessel or associated pipework;

- failure of any freight container in any of its load-bearing parts;

- plant or equipment coming into contact with overhead power lines;

- electrical short circuit or over-load causing fire or explosion;

- any unintentional explosion, misfire, failure of demolition to cause the intended collapse, projection of material beyond a site boundary, injury caused by an explosion;

- accidental release of biological agent likely to cause severe human illness;

- failure of industrial radiography or irradiation equipment to de-energise or return to its safe position after the intended exposure period;

- malfunction of breathing equipment while in use or during testing immediately before use;

- failure or endangering of diving equipment, the trapping of a diver, an explosion near a diver, or an uncontrolled ascent;

- collapse or partial collapse of a scaffold more than five metres high; or erected near water where there would be a risk of drowning after a fall;

- unintended collision of a train with any vehicle;

- dangerous occurrence at a well (other than a water well);

- dangerous occurrence at a pipeline;

- failure of any load-bearing fairground equipment, or derailment or unintended collision of cars or trains;

- a road tanker carrying a dangerous substance overturns, suffers damage, catches fire or the substance is released;

- a dangerous substance being conveyed by road is involved in a fire or released;

- unintended collapse of: any building or structure under construction, alteration or demolition where over five tonnes of material falls; a wall or floor in a place of work; any false work;

- explosion of fire causing suspension of normal work for over 24 hours;

- sudden, uncontrolled release in a building of flammable liquid or gas or in open air (in various amounts); and

- accidental release of any substance which may damage health

(Additional dangerous occurrences are reportable where occurring in mines, quarries or on railways.)

4.2   Illness

You should not return to work before the expiry of any Certificate relating to any illness or injury without first consulting your GP.

If you contract an infectious disease you must report the matter to your Principal so that any necessary precautions to protect others can be taken.

You should consult your GP before returning to work after a period of illness involving an infectious disease.

Certain infectious diseases and medical conditions must be reported by the practice to the Health and Safety Executive. These include various types of poisoning, various cancers and other conditions which can be caused through occupational hazards.

You should ascertain whether any drugs or medicine prescribed for you are likely to impair performance and judgement.

If you have been equipped with a heart pacemaker or similar medical equipment you should observe any safety precautions of which you have been advised, in particular connection with electrical distribution equipment or equipment emitting or likely to emit radio waves.

4.3   Occupational Health

You are expected to have regard to the maintenance of your own physical and mental well-being in the conduct of your business and personal lives.

Excessive stress in personal or business life can impair performance and lead to illness. If you consider you are suffering from excessive stress, for whatever reason, you should consult your Principal in the first instance, who will treat the matter confidentially.

The Safety Manager will arrange, as part of the Policy audit process, for the accident and work related illness records to be reviewed to establish whether further measures should be implemented to avoid such occurrences.[2]

4.4   Driving

When using a vehicle supplied by the practice you must conform to all requirements of the Road Traffic Acts, associated legislation and the Highway Code.

If you are driving in the course of your employment or driving vehicles supplied by the firm you must:

- Ensure that the vehicle is serviced, maintained and operated in accordance with the manufacturer's guidelines. If in doubt about the condition of a firm's vehicle, seek advice from your garage.

- Be in possession of a valid UK driving licence. This must be checked by your manager every year and endorsements notified to the insurers (for company vehicles).

- Ask your GP if any prescribed medication will affect your driving ability and if so you must refrain from driving.

- Refrain from using mobile telephones whilst driving.

- Wear glasses or lenses if prescribed for this activity.

You should avoid over-the-counter medications such as anti-depressants, antihistamines for hay fever, nettle rash, asthma, eczema, or travel sickness preparations or cough and cold remedies, which can adversely affect driving.

You must not drink and drive. If entertaining choose non- or very low alcohol content beverages or use public transport.

You must:

- check tyre pressures and visual condition (cuts or obvious damage, especially to the tyre walls);

- check seat belts – working and in good order and worn by all vehicle occupants where provided;

- check operation of brakes, horn, lights, indicators and steering;

- beware of un-metalled roads and soft ground on sites; where possible park off-site (not in an area causing an obstruction to highway or site traffic).

- adjust driving techniques to suit weather and traffic conditions.

A fire extinguisher (dry powder) and a first aid kit will be provided for company vehicles.

When driving on business of the practice in a vehicle not supplied by the practice you must have full comprehensive insurance cover to cover the driver and any passengers in the course of such business.

4.5   Hazardous substances

When any potentially hazardous substances are used at work, the Control of Substances Hazardous to Health Regulations (COSHH)[3] requires a register to be kept listing such risks and warning notices to be posted adjacent to store and equipment using hazardous materials or substances.

[NB: where hazardous substances are in use replace or extend this section with specific guidance.]

All chemicals must be stored in containers bearing the approved safety signage and directions. In the absence of such information, or in case of doubt, arrange for the chemical to be disposed of by an authorised agent.

Do not attempt to top up one bottle from another, since someone may have already stored another chemical in the bottle that might cause a reaction.

If an incident does occur:

- ventilate the area;
- evacuate staff;
- summon emergency services if necessary; and
- ensure a full written report is prepared without delay and submitted to the manager responsible.

The most hazardous materials are likely to be cleaning chemicals. The basic precaution is to avoid mixing any two cleaners that are incompatible, such as powder and acid cleaners, liquid bleaches and powder bleaches. In both cases, toxic gases can be produced. Protective gloves and in some cases goggles must be worn when handling the chemicals.

Chemicals used by staff might include duplicating fluids, glues and solvents and reprographic chemicals. In all such cases, adequate ventilation needs to be available when these materials are used. The warning labels, if any, must be carefully studied and the precautions on them followed. Some of these materials may be flammable and the appropriate precautions, such as prohibition of smoking, should be taken.

4.6   Visual display units (VDUs)

The Health and Safety (Display Screen Equipment) Regulations 1992 require the risks of VDU work to be assessed.[4]

The objectives of the assessment are to meet the following criteria for health and comfort:

- the VDU screen should be positioned to avoid unnecessary reflections on it.
- brightness should be variable, the image should be steady and characters should be clear.
- the chair should be correctly adjusted for height and back support and in good condition.
- the total time an operator works at a VDU should be restricted to six hours per day with pauses of five to ten minutes every two hours in periods of continuous use. Short, frequent intervals are more beneficial than infrequent ones. Work should be arranged so that it is interspersed with other tasks.

VDU operators may request the practice to arrange eyesight tests and provide spectacles if special ones are needed. (Any member of staff who suffers from epilepsy or associated illnesses should see their own medical advisor before operating VDUs).

Discomfort or illness associated with VDUs must be reported to a Principal or Personnel Officer.

4.7   Manual handling of loads

The Manual Handling Operations Regulations 1992 apply.[5]

Do not attempt to lift a load that is beyond your capacity. Do not attempt any lifting if you have a back problem.

The following key points should be taken into account:

- look out for splinters, nails, wire and other protruding sharp surfaces;
- size up the job, remove obstructions;
- make sure there is a clear space where the load has to be set down;
- ensure that there is a clear view over the top of the load when carrying it;
- stand close to the object with feet 200-300mm (8-12") apart, one foot in advance of the other;
- prepare to lift, bend the knees into a crouch position with a straight back – the back can be inclined but should not be bent;
- pull the chin in and avoid dropping head forward;
- a good grip is required, preferably one hand around the front of the load and the other hand underneath to prevent the load slipping forward or down;
- pull the object close to the chest, it is easier to handle and there is less chance of it slipping;
- a smooth easy lift is required to complete the exercise. Avoid a sudden lift or jerk as this could result in a back injury.

Assess the maximum weights which should be lifted manually by reference to the following table:

Load Level		Action
Men	Women	
Less than 16kg (35 lbs)	Less than 11 kg (24 lbs)	No special action
16-34 kg (35-75 lbs)	11-23 kg (24-52 lbs)	Identify individuals able to handle such weights
34-55kg (75-120 lbs)	24-38kg (53-84 lbs)	Effectively supervised, selected and trained individuals or mechanical handling
More than 55kg (120 lbs)	More than 38kg (84 lbs)	Normally mechanical handling or selective recruitment and training. NB: very few people can regularly lift such a weight.

HSE Publications (introductory guides)

1 RIDDOR explained [HSE31]
2 Good health is Good Business – an employer's guide [MISC196]
3 COSHH: A brief guide to the Regulations [INDG136]
4 Working with VDUs [INDG36]
5 Getting to grips with manual handling [INDG143]

5.   Fire precautions – Safety Code: 5

5.1   Legislation

- The Fire Precautions Act 1971
- The Fire Precautions (Factories, Offices, Shops and Railway Premises) Order 1976
- The Fire Precautions (Non-Certificated Factory, Office, Shop and Railway Premises) Regulations 1976
- The Health and Safety at Work Act 1974

5.2   Fire certification

The Safety Manager will obtain and display a copy of the Fire Certificate as to Safe Means of Escape in Case of Fire where required.

In factory and office premises, a certificate is required when:

- more than 20 persons are employed to work at any one time; and
- more than ten persons are employed elsewhere than on the ground floor.

The certificate designates clearways, protected routes, final exits, the location, number and type of fire extinguishers required and some detail on the fire warning system installed.

NB: The Certificate may be issued to the Landlord or Head Lessee.

5.3   Fire precautions register

The Safety Manager will ensure that a Register of Fire Precautions is maintained giving details of checks on escape routes, equipment, systems, fire drills and fire wardens.

5.4   Instructions about means of escape

Staff are required to read and follow the instructions displayed on each floor at the lift areas and by the stairwells. Under no circumstances ignore a fire alarm signal. Obey the directions of a fire warden.

No person will obstruct a means of escape. Fire exit routes must never be obstructed or fire doors wedged open.

Escape routes will be inspected at least twice in each year.

5.5   Fire evacuation procedures and practices

An emergency evacuation/fire drill will be undertaken at least twice in each year.

Certain persons will be designated as fire wardens, who have the following duties:

- to familiarise themselves with the location and operation of fire fighting equipment in their area of responsibility and with the escape routes from that area;
- to advise staff within their area on fire precautions and equipment as necessary;

- to keep alert to any potential fire hazards within their areas, e.g. build up of waste, obstruction of escape routes, and to take necessary action to remove the hazard;

- in the event of an evacuation of their area, to carry out a rapid but thorough check of their area to ensure it is clear of people before they themselves leave, and to report the completion of the search to the designated control outside the building.

Generally, fire fighting operations must be abandoned if:

- the means of escape is threatened;

- the fire is out of control; and

- the extinguisher is exhausted.

5.6   Fire protection systems

System records

Details of all maintenance, testing or alterations to fire protection systems will be recorded in the Fire Precautions Register by or on behalf of the Safety Manager. In the case of fire alarms, details of the causes of all alarms (genuine, practice or test), faults which develop, periods of disconnection, and any further action required will also be recorded in the Register.

Fire alarms

The fire warning system will be checked periodically in accordance with the requirement of the Certificate as to Safe Means of Escape in Case of Fire; additionally, a different call point (following a set sequence) will be activated each week.

Up-to-date drawings and operating instructions are kept adjacent to the control equipment.

Emergency lighting

The installation will be tested every six months, with a full discharge test once per annum. Periodic visual checks of the system will be made by or on behalf of the Safety Manager.

Automatic fire detection

Where installed, this system will be tested every six months.

Automatic fire protection systems

Where installed, these systems, which include wet and dry sprinkler installations (discharging water from tanks or mains) and total flooding (gas) systems, will be tested by suitable contractors at intervals recommended by the supplier.

Where such systems are installed in enclosed areas e.g. computer rooms, or substations, warning notices will be displayed at all entrances and an audible warning system fitted. No one is to enter a room or building fitted with a total flooding system unless the system is locked off or set for manual operation.

Fire fighting equipment

The numbers and type of fire extinguishers is specified in the Certificate as to Safe Means of Escape in Case of Fire. It is also recommended that additional fire extinguishers are held in reserve.

The purpose of portable fire fighting equipment is as follows:

- to extinguish minor fires;
- to protect means of escape as a priority;
- to protect employees and visitors; and
- to protect property.

Fire extinguishers will be serviced at the manufacturer's specified intervals by a specialist company appointed by the Safety Manager and records of such servicing kept in the Fire Precautions Register.

The table below identifies fire fighting appliances.

Colour	Type	Use
Red	Soda/Acid	Wood
Black	Carbon dioxide [CO_2]	Electrical fires
Red box	Glass fire blankets	Oil fires in kitchens, etc
Blue	Dry powder	General
Green	Halon vapourising liquid [BCF]	General

5.7 Bombs and bomb warnings

Suspect letter or package

Do not tamper with it. Place it in a protective container if available, but otherwise leave it alone.

Evacuate the immediate area and adjacent offices/areas, and allow no one in (other than specialist disposal personnel).

Inform switchboard and the Safety Manager immediately. They will summon the police and other assistance.

Bomb warning on the telephone

Notify switchboard and the Safety Manager without delay.

At the same time, attempt to keep the caller talking and note down as much information as possible about both the suspect bomb and the caller, as follows:

- Where is the device?
- How long before the device is due to go off?
- Type of device and size?
- Reason for the device?
- Time the call was received.
- Accent and approximate age of the caller.

On receipt of a bomb warning

Switch of all radios and disconnect batteries.

Switchboard or the Safety Manager will immediately inform fire wardens and nominated contacts throughout the building

Fire wardens will institute and supervise searches within office areas, plan and service areas, common parts, exit routes and the assembly area.

Everyone should stay within their office area and await instructions from their fire warden.

If the building has to be fully or partially evacuated

Instructions, including the exit routes and assembly area to be used, will be passed via fire wardens.

Everyone should then quickly but quietly make their way outside the building, along the exit routes to the assembly area given, to answer the roll call and await instructions.

Keep clear of large areas of glass.

6. Sources of safety information – Safety Code: 6

Principals and staff may also refer, in addition to the HSE introductory guides listed in the Policy and Safety Codes, to the requirements contained in the following Regulations applicable to health, safety and welfare of personnel, and related HSE publications including industry specific and legal guides; Approved Codes of Practice [ACOPs]; etc.

Health and Safety Executive codes referring to books are in italics.

Health and safety in the work place

Management of Health & Safety at Work Regulations 1999	*L21 [ACOP]*
The Workplace (Health, Safety & Welfare) Regulations 1992	*L24 [ACOP]*
Successful health and safety management	*HSG65*
Stress at work – a guide for employers	*HSG116*
Young people at work – a guide for employers	*HSG165*
New and expectant mothers at work	*HSG 122*
Health risk management	*HSG 137*
Manual Handling Operations Regulations 1992	*L23*
Control of Substances Hazardous to Health regulations 1999	*L5 [ACOP]*
Step be step guide to COSHH assessment	*HSG97*
Health & Safety (Display Screen Equipment) Regulations 1992	*L26*
VDUs – An easy guide to Display Screen Equipment Regulations	*HSG90*
Lighting at work	*HSG38*
Reporting of Injuries, Diseases and Dangerous Occurrences Regulations (RIDDOR) 1995	*L73*
Health & Safety (First Aid) Regulations 1981	*L74 [ACOP]*
Personal Protective Equipment at Work Regulations 1992	*L25*
Construction (Head Protection) Regulations 1989	*L102*
Fire Safety – an employer's guide *ISBN 0 11 341229 0*	

Safety policies

Safety representatives and committees	*L87*
Health and Safety (Consultation with Employees) Regulations 1996	*L95*
Guidance to employers whose employees are not members of recognised independent trade unions	*HSC8*
Permit to work systems	*INDG98*
Five steps to risk assessment requirements: Common provisions in health and safety law	*HSG183*

CDM Regulations

Construction (Design and Management) Regulations
1994 [SI No 3140 as amended by SI 2000 No 2380]

Managing construction for health and safety CDM Regulations 1994	*L54 [ACOP]*
CDM Regulations: How the Regulations affect you	*PML54*
Health and safety in construction	*HSG150*
Designing for health and safety in construction *ISBN 0 7176 0807 7*	
Construction. Health and safety check list	*CIS17*
The role of the client	*CIS 39*
The role of the planning supervisor	*CIS 40*
The role of the designer	*CIS 41*
The pre-tender stage health and safety plan	*CIS 42*
The health and safety plan during the construction phase	*CIS 43*
The health and safety file	*CIS 44*
Having construction work done? Duties of clients	*MISC 193*

RIBA Publications

Engaging an Architect: Guidance for Clients on Health and Safety; the CDM Regulations 1994	RIBA
Form of Appointment as Planning Supervisor	RIBA

Other publications

A Guide to the Control of Substances to Health in Construction	CIRIA
Site Safety Handbook	CIRIA